Praise for

BARRED

"For every newspaper photo of an innocent person exiting the prison gates, clutching the hand of their triumphant lawyer, there are uncountable others whom we will never allow to see that day—who will die in prison because our laws make it so difficult to prove their innocence in court. In *Barred*, Daniel S. Medwed gives us an urgent tour of the darkest corners of our judicial system, where persuasive evidence becomes trapped in a labyrinth of legal procedure. Underlying Medwed's sharp legal analysis is a political question: Is this the country we want to be?"
—Maurice Chammah, author of *Let the Lord Sort Them*

"With this insightful book, Medwed exposes the byzantine tangle of legal rules and procedures that keep innocent people in prison. Clear, accessible, and often astounding, *Barred* explains why strong evidence of innocence doesn't matter once a trial is over, and how our criminal system routinely sacrifices accuracy for finality. A leading scholar and expert on innocence, Medwed is also a wonderful educator. This book teaches us all how the wrongfully convicted are trapped by the criminal bureaucracy, by modern appellate rules, and by ancient Latin writs that have been around for hundreds of years."
—Alexandra Natapoff, author of *Punishment Without Crime*

"Most people are by now aware that the criminal justice system, being made up of human beings, makes mistakes. Much has been written about one such mistake: that a scandalously large number of innocent people get convicted and sent to prison. What many people remain largely unaware of is that it is far easier for the government to convict an innocent person than it is for that innocent person to get out of prison. With *Barred*, we finally have a lucid explanation of how exactly this infuriating feature of our system persists. Medwed is one of the nation's leading scholars on wrongful convictions and one of the nation's leading lawyers at helping free innocent inmates. In this groundbreaking book, Medwed brings his expertise as both a scholar and a practitioner to illuminate how something that makes no sense happens routinely. Anyone interested in understanding the magnitude of the chasm between true justice and our actual criminal justice system, and in learning how we as a society might shrink it, should read this book."

—David Dow, author of *The Autobiography of an Execution*

BARRED

WHY THE INNOCENT
CAN'T GET OUT OF PRISON

———————

DANIEL S. MEDWED

BASIC BOOKS
NEW YORK

Basic Books
Hachette Book Group
1290 Avenue of the Americas, New York, NY 10104
www.basicbooks.com

Printed in the United States of America

First Edition: September 2022

Published by Basic Books, an imprint of Perseus Books, LLC, a subsidiary of Hachette Book Group, Inc. The Basic Books name and logo is a trademark of the Hachette Book Group.

The Hachette Speakers Bureau provides a wide range of authors for speaking events. To find out more, go to www.hachettespeakersbureau.com or call (866) 376-6591.

The publisher is not responsible for websites (or their content) that are not owned by the publisher.

Library of Congress Cataloging-in-Publication Data
Names: Medwed, Daniel S., author.
Title: Barred: why the innocent can't get out of prison / Daniel S. Medwed.
Description: New York, NY: Basic Books, 2022. | Includes bibliographical references and index.
Identifiers: LCCN 2022017368 | ISBN 9781541675919 (hardcover) | ISBN 9781541675902 (ebook)
Subjects: LCSH: Judicial error—United States. | False imprisonment—Law and legislation—United States. | Writ of error coram nobis—United States. | Presumption of innocence—United States. | Plea bargaining—United States. | Habeas corpus—United States. | Criminal justice, Administration of—United States—Criminal provisions.
Classification: LCC KF9756 .M43 2022 | DDC 345.73/0122—dc23/eng/20220630
LC record available at https://lccn.loc.gov/2022017368

ISBNs: 9781541675919 (hardcover), 9781541675902 (ebook)

LSC-C

Printing 1, 2022

For my brilliant wife, Sharissa Jones,
whose sacrifices enabled me to pursue my
professional dreams, and for our amazing children,
Clementine and Mili, who will forever remain
actually innocent in my eyes.

CONTENTS

PART III: EXECUTIVE FUNCTION

PART IV: A PATH FORWARD

OPENING STATEMENT

BOBBY FENNELL HAD SPENT SIXTEEN YEARS BEHIND BARS FOR A murder he didn't commit. We were scheduled to meet in person for the first time in the summer of 2001—if I could locate the prison.

I'd never been to Otisville. It's one of many dots on the map of prison towns that stretches from the New York City suburbs all the way to Canada. Otisville lacks the notoriety of other penitentiaries in the state, like Sing Sing (perched along the banks of the Hudson, and genesis of the phrase to be "sent up the river") or Attica (home to the brutal riots of 1971). I considered the facility's low-key reputation a good omen. The corrections officers were less likely to give me grief than at other spots. And I needed a calm interaction with the COs before telling my client the bad news that I felt morally obligated to deliver in person: that we wouldn't be able to prove his innocence in court.

After an accidental detour or two, I found the right place. I parked near the visitors' entrance, rolled down my windows, and reviewed my notes.

———

BOBBY FENNELL'S 1985 MURDER CONVICTION STEMMED FROM the shooting of John Williams outside a "base house" in Manhattan, where people purchased and freebased cocaine.[1] Fennell provided security for the drug operation, which made him a prime suspect. He maintained his innocence from the get-go, insisting he was with his girlfriend at the time of the murder.

The prosecution's case relied on the credibility of a single eyewitness, a man with a lengthy rap sheet and a drug addiction. The witness claimed Williams got into a fight at the base house, which prompted Fennell and another sentry, Joseph Perry, to drag Williams into the street and take turns shooting him. That was all the government had, a shaky witness recounting how two enforcers had gunned down a rowdy customer outside a drug den.

Undeterred by the minimal evidence at its disposal, the state filed murder charges against Fennell and Perry and prosecuted the defendants together in a joint trial. The government lawyer entrusted with litigating the case, an assistant district attorney in Manhattan, asked the eyewitness a series of friendly questions that elicited testimony implicating Fennell and Perry. But the threads holding the story together unraveled on cross-examination by the defense. First, the witness admitted he'd received a sweetheart deal on his pending drug charges in exchange for testifying. Second, his responses at trial differed from his prior statements. There were discrepancies in the number of shots fired and the roles played by the two alleged perpetrators. The jury nevertheless bought his story.

Guilty.

Then an odd thing happened. Right after the verdict, Perry and his attorney met with Fennell's lawyer. Perry said he'd acted alone in the murder. He even indicated that he'd sign an affidavit to that effect. The key question, of course: Why now? Why hadn't Perry come forward *before* trial to help Fennell?

The explanation turned out to be quite simple. Perry didn't want to jeopardize his chance for an acquittal by telling the truth prior to trial. Since the prosecution's case hinged on a weak eyewitness, Perry thought both he and Fennell had decent odds of winning at their joint trial if he just kept his mouth shut. He essentially gambled with his coworker's life, withholding Fennell's trump card until he'd lost his own hand in court.

Perry had still more to lose by coming clean at this late date. He hadn't been sentenced yet, and his admission of guilt could destroy his prospects for a shorter prison bid, let alone any shot on appeal. Although aware he was "sinking himself," Perry executed the affidavit and agreed to testify down the line. Perry had indeed sunk himself. With the affidavit on file, the judge gave Perry the max, twenty-five years to life.

Meanwhile Bobby Fennell's fate hung in the balance. He filed a motion under a New York procedure that permits a defendant to ask the trial judge for a new trial when fresh evidence emerges during the brief interlude between the jury's verdict and the date of sentencing. At the hearing on the motion, Perry reiterated that he alone had shot Williams and that Fennell had not even been on the premises. The defense also tracked down an eyewitness who testified that he'd seen Perry shoot Williams with Fennell nowhere in the vicinity. Another witness recalled that Fennell wasn't scheduled to begin his shift until ninety minutes after the murder occurred.

Despite the compelling new evidence of innocence, the court denied Fennell's motion in June 1985 without any explanation. Judges normally write an opinion after this type of hearing that sets forth the basis for their decision, comments on the evidence, or at least discusses the witness testimony. But the judge didn't even bother to do that in Fennell's case. The judge just rejected his claims and later sentenced him to fifteen years to life in prison. Another court affirmed the conviction on appeal a few years later. That appellate decision effectively served as the last word on the case for more than a decade.

In 2000, Fennell's trial attorney sought assistance from legendary defense lawyer Will Hellerstein. Will was a tenured professor at Brooklyn Law School while I was a young instructor on a short-term contract at the school. We teamed up to form the Second Look Program, a clinic where we worked with our students to investigate and litigate innocence claims by New York inmates.[2]

Prisoners seeking to prove their innocence after conviction often rely on free services provided by entities like Second Look. The most famous is the Innocence Project in New York City, which was founded in 1992 by Barry Scheck and Peter Neufeld and primarily handles cases in which deoxyribonucleic acid (DNA) testing could exonerate a wrongly convicted person. About fifty other groups across the United States can also be classified as "innocence projects," regardless of their official titles. Some are affiliated with law schools, others are freestanding nonprofits, and a few are units within public defenders' offices that receive government funds to represent indigent criminal defendants in their jurisdictions. Some focus exclusively on DNA cases; others don't. Nearly all operate on shoestring budgets, their work contingent on the largesse of donors, law school deans, and the occasional dollop of public support.

In the Fennell case, the timing of his former lawyer's approach to Second Look was perfect. We needed cases to fuel our new venture, Fennell needed help, and his advocate's heartfelt pitch impressed us. We reinvestigated the case, conducting interviews with the defense attorneys involved in the trial and with Fennell's former girlfriend, who verified that she had been with him at the time of the murder. Fennell passed a polygraph test, popularly known as a lie detector. Our efforts to find any of the purported witnesses to the crime didn't pan out, understandably so considering it had been over fifteen years since the murder. Still, our investigation confirmed the thrust of the posttrial hearing: Fennell was flat-out innocent.

Yet we needed a novel legal hook to get back into court—strong, newly discovered evidence that would absolve Fennell. The phrase "newly discovered" doesn't just mean new to us or to our client. It means evidence that *couldn't* have been discovered by Fennell or his lawyer at the time of the trial and the initial posttrial hearing.

No hook existed. The polygraph was of limited value in a courtroom, Perry had already testified, and the girlfriend's statements didn't constitute new evidence because she had been available to testify back then. Many attorneys think jurors distrust alibi testimony that comes from a loved one. Fennell's trial counsel apparently shared this view and thought it unwise to put the girlfriend on the stand, a decision that cast a long shadow over the case.

So, there I was in the visiting room at Otisville Correctional Facility in 2001, going through a mental inventory of the barriers that blocked the path to Bobby Fennell's exoneration. Then he walked in. I dispensed with the pleasantries and cut to the chase. Seconds after shaking his hand for the first time, I told him we wouldn't be taking his case to court. And that I was sorry.

He sat there for a moment, stoic. Uncomfortable with the silence, I redirected the conversation. *How are you doing?* I asked. *Is there anything I can do to make your life inside better?*

I'll never forget his response. *It's not so bad, I have three hots and a cot. Thanks for trying.*

Bobby Fennell was an innocent man trapped in a cage with no clear way out. Yet so accustomed was he to disappointment, so unfazed by my report, that he took pains to put a positive spin on his predicament. To make *me* feel better about failing him.

That meeting in Otisville was not my first, or my last, eye-opening moment while working in criminal justice. I've spent more than twenty years in the field, serving as a public defender who handled appeals on behalf of indigent defendants, as cofounder of a law school clinic that investigated and litigated postconviction innocence claims in New York State, and as a teacher with a passion for justice reform. What I've learned is that my initial ideas about the fairness of the criminal process were wrong. When I was a first-year law student, one of my professors told me, "Give me procedure over substance any day. I'll win with procedure." I scoffed at his assertion back then, believing that substance (truth, justice, merits) would always prevail.

Experience has taught me he was right. It's not just that legal procedure is a crucial tool we can use to fight for the innocent. It's that the rule regime is stacked *against* the innocent, contrary to the popular belief that the postconviction process is full of escape hatches from the prison cell, those imaginary "technicalities" that let people loose.[3] The innocent don't always go free. You can have evidence of innocence—and no one willing to hear it.

THE TERM "PROCEDURE" IN THIS BOOK IS AN UMBRELLA CONcept that covers the wide range of rules that govern the practice of litigation after conviction. How much time do you have to submit a notice that you would like to appeal your case? In which court must you later file your official appeal, and in what form? May you present the legal arguments in your appeal in a written document, through an in-person appearance, or both? May you raise every single alleged error that occurred at trial as part of your arguments, or only some? If you lose your first appeal, are there opportunities to "appeal your appeal" or otherwise seek relief another way? If you find new evidence of innocence after conviction, may you show that evidence to an appellate court? If not, may you put it forward through another postconviction remedy in a different court?

The government has charted the twists and turns of this procedural road through rules enacted by courts or laws passed by legislatures, and it's up to criminal defendants to navigate them. A discussion of procedure may strike some as dry, technical, or arcane; that's what I thought when I was a young pup sitting in my first-year law school class and rolling my eyes at the big-dog professor strutting around the room. The *substance* of whether, say, the police committed misconduct in a particular case—what the cops did and how that behavior measures up against the legal doctrine—felt so much more interesting, so much more important, than the *procedure* surrounding whether and how you could make a misconduct claim in court.

But I learned early on that procedure can't be divorced from substance. If you can't draw on the correct legal procedure to ensure access to the courts or to influential executive branch officials, there's no way to alert anyone in a position of power about a substantive problem in a case. Procedure is the door that allows entry to the corridors of power, where people with the capacity to determine a criminal defendant's fate reside. Without entry there's no chance of justice.

Innocent defendants have passed through that door and earned justice from time to time over the past thirty years. Since 1989, postconviction DNA testing has exonerated 375 innocent prisoners in the United States, and more than 2,000 others have overturned their wrongful convictions without the benefit of that scientific tool.[4] But that's just the tip of the iceberg. Estimates about how many prisoners are actually innocent span from a low of 0.027 percent to a high of 15 percent; most range from 0.5 percent to 2 percent.[5] With an American prison population exceeding one million, even some of the conservative estimates translate to thousands of innocent people.

The reason why so many innocent prisoners remain behind bars is that proving innocence after a conviction is a daunting task. DNA exonerations depend on having access to biological evidence retained from the crime scene that can be subjected to testing. Yet biological evidence is collected in only 10 to 20 percent of cases, not to mention it's often lost or destroyed over time.[6] Even more, procedural barriers to litigating cases after trial all too often stop innocent inmates from prying open the prison gates, with or without DNA. Appeals aren't endless. Every state gives criminal defendants a guaranteed right to appeal their convictions to a higher court once and once only. It's known as the direct appeal, and a defendant may use it to attack the evidence and rulings at trial. The legal issues you may raise on direct appeal are limited; you're restricted to the trial record, to what happened in the lower court. Nothing outside the record is recognized. Also, appellate courts generally only review issues that were "preserved" at trial—those previously identified through a timely objection by the defense lawyer and discussed by the trial participants—and defer to most trial judge rulings. If your conviction is affirmed on appeal, you may solicit a higher court, even the United States Supreme Court, to look at your case. But it's unlikely the court will take it on. That stage of review is discretionary, and scores of cases compete for the courts' attention.

After your direct appeal is exhausted—you've lost in the highest court in your jurisdiction or been denied discretionary review—then you may go back to court and file a habeas corpus petition. This remedy, which we inherited from England, asks government officials to justify why they "have the body" in custody. Historically, it has served to correct jurisdictional or constitutional defects in a case, not to grapple with factual claims of innocence.

The one route that's designed explicitly for innocence claims is to file a postconviction motion for a new trial based on an ancient English remedy known as a writ of error coram nobis ("before us"), which points to new discoveries that cast doubt on the integrity of the verdict. Although coram nobis procedures are geared to address questions of innocence, they are full of obstacles, including narrow definitions of what counts as "new" evidence.

Beyond that, it's catch as catch can. Parole boards don't view innocence claims kindly; they want to see expressions of remorse and acceptance of responsibility before releasing a prisoner to live in the outside world under state supervision. If you're politically connected or have a particularly sympathetic case, you might ask the governor for clemency. But pardons and sentence commutations are rare. Many politicians are plagued by images of a freed inmate on a crime spree, any hope for reelection dashed.

In Bobby Fennell's case, we simply saw no path to prove his innocence in a court of law. The direct appeal had long since been denied, it was too late to file a habeas corpus petition, even if we had a viable claim (which we didn't), and we lacked any newly discovered evidence of innocence for a coram nobis–style remedy. Best-case scenario, we could write a letter to the parole board explaining the situation and begging for mercy.

How is it possible that a prisoner with such a credible innocence claim could have no recourse? In short, the system values finality and efficiency over accuracy, the certainty generated by a fixed end point achieved rapidly over the ambiguity of robust procedures to look at cases anew. Finality and efficiency have their benefits. If cases were never finalized, the system would collapse under the weight of its bursting docket, victims would never have a chance at closure, and guilty defendants might never be forced to take stock and reflect on their misdeeds. And if cases were not finalized in a somewhat efficient fashion, prosecutors, defense lawyers, and judges would be unable to shift their attention to other pressing matters. Viable cases would get dropped; investigations would languish; the wheels of justice would sputter.

Finality and efficiency serve to reinforce one another. Closing cases in short order preserves government resources, which is efficient for the system as a whole. Processing cases efficiently also makes it easier to close them; there are simply fewer ends to tie up. The system runs like a conveyor belt in a factory. A conviction is manufactured at the trial level before it travels up the assembly line. Judges and prosecutors quickly check its components at various workstations before putting a lid on the case for good and dispatching it to the annals of case law.

Finality and efficiency are not the only explanations for the unforgiving nature of American appellate and postconviction procedures, that's for sure. Judges and executive branch officials often defer to decisions made at trial as an expression of respect for their peers in the system and out of a belief that a trial, with its vetting of evidence in open court, is the best forum for resolving the fundamental question of a defendant's guilt or innocence.

Although I explore these other rationales in the pages to come, for now note that finality and efficiency are the main justifications for the procedural regime. They are important considerations, I admit. But not as important as correcting the ultimate injustice: the conviction of an innocent person. Every case where an innocent prisoner is deprived of freedom through the appellate and postconviction process represents an individual injustice and a national disgrace.

This book examines precisely why it's so hard for wrongly convicted people to overcome procedural technicalities and prove their innocence, even when there's good evidence they haven't done the crime. Part I of the book considers how the rules of appellate procedure mask potential innocence cases and make it difficult to identify them. Part II analyzes how other postconviction remedies—including habeas corpus and coram nobis—offer mechanisms to detect (and correct) wrongful convictions in theory but contain a range of obstacles in practice. Part III goes beyond the judiciary to explore the executive branch, where the powers of parole and clemency could be exercised to aid the innocent but often fail to do so. Finally, Part IV delves into potential structural changes that could alleviate some of the harms inflicted by traditional procedures. It's well past time to take a fresh look at these procedures and find ways to ensure that legitimate innocence claims are heard, investigated, and validated through exoneration.

A FEW CRITICAL POINTS BEFORE I BEGIN IN EARNEST.

First, BIPOC (Black, Indigenous, and people of color) communities—especially Black men—are disproportionately represented in the wrongfully convicted population, which is a symptom of a much larger societal illness. Take homicide cases. The exoneration data suggest that innocent Black defendants are *seven times* more likely to be convicted of murder than innocent whites.[7] The stain of racial bias tarnishes every single aspect of the criminal justice system, including the appellate and postconviction process. There's reason to think that judges more readily distrust claims of innocence by BIPOC defendants than by white ones, and that members of BIPOC communities lack meaningful access to the legal resources needed to overturn wrongful convictions.

Race and systemic racism dominate much of the contemporary dialogue about criminal justice, and rightfully so. Sometimes those issues appear explicitly in the pages of this book. More often they're implicit in the subtext of the cases I discuss—cases with victims and defendants from different racial groups, or with jury trials that occur in nearly all-white communities. When racial bias surfaces, I emphasize its presence in the hopes of locating this book within the broader criminal justice debate. Procedure is about so much more than the technical rules of managing a case. It's about power and control. It's about the ways in which those at the top keep those at the bottom from moving up, ways that are all dressed up in legalese.

Second, the murder of unarmed civilians by the police, awareness of the harms wrought by mass incarceration, and the rise of Black Lives Matter have recently inspired calls to eradicate several institutions that keep the criminal justice system afloat. Campaigns to abolish prisons and to reimagine, even defund, the police have moved from the fringe to part of the mainstream conversation about justice reform. While I am sympathetic to many of those revolutionary proposals, this book has a more modest objective: to dig into one rancid slice of the massive criminal justice pie and show how appellate and postconviction procedures betray the innocent.

Finally, this book contains many stories about innocent people like Bobby Fennell. Almost all of them were eventually freed through a variety of legal maneuvers, occasionally decades after their wrongful convictions. The fact that they received freedom in the end does *not* mean the process works. It's often said that justice delayed is justice denied; by that measure all of them were denied justice.

More to the point, keep the iceberg analogy in mind. The groups that litigate postconviction innocence claims in the United States lack resources to accept every case that demands justice and instead engage in triage by pursuing only the strongest.[8] Those cases, compelling as they may be, must steer through the formidable procedural obstacles to exoneration. Documented exonerations therefore reflect just the relatively small number of innocent prisoners we know about. What about all the others who remain locked up, or who died in state custody? Those whose letters never reached an innocence project, whose court filings never led to a hearing, whose stories have not yet been fully told?

This book is for them. For innocent people thwarted by prison—and procedural—bars.

PART I
ON APPEAL

1

SOME BARGAIN

How Plea Deals Evade Scrutiny

IN 2007, GUNMEN BURST INTO A HOME ON RUNYON STREET IN Detroit and killed four people, including a reputed drug kingpin.[1] They nearly murdered a fifth occupant of the home, a woman who was struck with five bullets but somehow fled to a rear bedroom, where she hid under a bed. The woman later mentioned only one assailant to the police—a slim man, about six feet tall, in his early to mid-thirties. Another eyewitness described two perpetrators. He said that one, around six feet tall, carried a rifle; the other, slightly shorter, wielded a handgun. The police canvassed the area, even deploying a dog to track the killers' scent. But they lost the trail about two blocks from the crime scene.

Around the same time, fourteen-year-old Davontae Sanford left his house to check out what was going on. Blind in his left eye, Sanford was only five feet five inches tall and weighed 150 pounds. A sergeant claimed that he tried to talk with Sanford, but the youth's responses were evasive. Suspicious, the sergeant got permission from Sanford's grandmother to take him to the station for questioning. They stopped at the crime scene on the way, where technicians swabbed Sanford in search of gunshot residue. Those tests turned out to be negative.

The police interrogated Sanford outside the presence of his grandmother or any other adult, contrary to Michigan law. That interrogation generated a confession of sorts. Sanford signed a statement divulging that he and four other kids had met at a restaurant to plot the attack. He recalled that they were armed with a .38-caliber gun and other weapons. Sanford insisted that he got cold feet as the plan began to take shape, and that he went home before the shooting began.

Several glaring problems emerged as the police looked into the statement, problems beyond the fact that Sanford didn't match up—in age, height, or build—with the eyewitness accounts. First, the restaurant referenced by Sanford had been closed at the time of the incident. Second, there was no evidence that the murderers had used a .38.

The police brought Sanford to the station later that night. Taking cues from the police, Sanford modified his story. This time around, he cited the correct types of guns implicated in the crime. He also reportedly drew a map of the interior of the home where the shootings had occurred. Once again, the statement contained flaws. His alleged accomplices all had solid alibis, and the police had neglected to give Sanford his *Miranda* warnings—information about his rights to remain silent and to an attorney—until far into the second interrogation. Still, the police arrested Sanford, and he was charged with four counts of first-degree murder.

At age fourteen, he was looking at a lifetime of imprisonment.

The case went to trial the following year. The court gave Sanford a woeful defense attorney who'd chalked up more than a dozen reprimands and admonishments for subpar lawyering.[2] The attorney not only failed to challenge the admission of the confession into evidence (despite the *Miranda* issue) but didn't even cross-examine the police sergeant to undermine the credibility of the witness who'd interrogated Sanford and provided crucial testimony against him. These are basic things that any competent lawyer should and would do in a case of this magnitude.

Sanford's lawyer told him that things were grim—that he should accept a guilty plea if he ever wanted a shot at freedom. Sanford heeded this advice. On the second day of trial, he pled guilty to reduced charges of second-degree murder and illegal use of a weapon. His sentence? Thirty-seven to ninety years in prison for the murders, plus additional time for the gun charge. If he avoided trouble during his incarceration, he might get paroled after reaching middle age. Had he gone to trial and lost, even that sliver of hope would have disappeared.

THE SANFORD CASE MIGHT HAVE GONE UNNOTICED, A NONDE-script chapter in the long-running narrative of blight and violence in Detroit, if not for a stunning development. A month after the guilty plea, the police arrested a suspect in an unrelated homicide. The suspect, Vincent Smothers, admitted he'd been hired to commit that crime. Then the admissions kept coming. He confessed to eleven other contract killings, including the four that Sanford had just pled guilty to. Smothers even led the police to one of the weapons from the Runyon Street murders.

Police and prosecutors did absolutely *nothing* to alert either Sanford or the court about this turn of events.

Sanford's new appellate lawyer didn't learn about Smothers's confession until the following year. When she did learn about it, she filed a motion to withdraw Sanford's guilty plea. What might seem like solid ground for upending a plea—actual innocence—proved to be rickety; the trial court denied the motion.

That denial instigated a journey up and down the Michigan appellate court system. In 2014, six years after Sanford's plea, the Michigan Supreme Court clarified that a claim of actual innocence, even a strong one, was not an adequate legal basis for

withdrawing a guilty plea. Instead, a plea only merited withdrawal "if the trial court determines that there was an error in
the plea proceeding that would entitle the defendant to have the
plea set aside."[3]

The state police ultimately got interested in the case, as did
Kym Worthy, the newly elected chief prosecutor in the county
that encompasses Detroit. Worthy ordered state police to reinvestigate. That investigation produced a scathing 114-page report,
which confirmed that Smothers and a confederate had committed
the Runyon Street murders. It also exposed the fact that a police
detective, not Sanford, had drawn the map of the home's layout.
The state dismissed all charges against Sanford in 2016.[4]

Even assuming there were some slender hooks on which to
hang Sanford's guilt back at the time of his plea in March 2008,
they'd fractured completely a month later given news of Smothers's involvement and his assistance in leading law enforcement
to one of the murder weapons. Why then did it take eight more
years before Sanford's release? A key part of the delay consisted
of the procedural barriers to withdrawing guilty pleas in Michigan. The state Supreme Court ruled that only evidence of an error
in the plea *proceeding* would trigger the withdrawal of a guilty
plea, not a fundamental error in the dispensation of justice.[5]

The Sanford case illustrates some of the hazards of the plea-
bargaining process for innocent criminal defendants. They face
enormous pressure to accept a plea deal or else receive a much
worse outcome if they lose at trial. And if they take the plea and
seek to prove their innocence down the road, they encounter hurdles in the appellate and postconviction process.

How many other innocent people have pled guilty like Davontae Sanford did? The National Registry of Exonerations lists 549
cases where people took guilty pleas and were later proven innocent.[6] We have no idea whether that figure comes close to portraying the scale of the problem. What attorney is going to wage
a postconviction, innocence-based challenge in a routine guilty

plea case—say, a theft where the defendant got a short sentence? It's hard enough to overturn wrongful convictions when the defendant has maintained innocence all along without the added burden of an admission of guilt at a plea hearing. For that reason, innocence projects prefer to take cases from prisoners who went to trial over those who pled guilty.[7]

Innocent defendants know that lawyers seldom fight to exonerate people after they've pled guilty. That's partly why some of them go to trial and put their freedom on the line. But the incentives to avoid that path—to just take the deal and wish for good luck in the appellate process—can be overwhelming. Let's explore those incentives as well as the general features of the plea-bargaining system.

———————

THERE ARE JUST ENOUGH HIGH-PROFILE CRIMINAL TRIALS TO give the impression that heated courtroom battles over guilt or innocence are the norm. That defendants routinely exercise their constitutional right to a trial by jury, allowing the adversary system and regular citizens to decide their future. Think O. J. Simpson. Dzhokhar Tsarnaev. Derek Chauvin. In truth, the criminal trial is a vanishing species, a casualty of the steady rise of plea bargaining.

It's understandable why plea bargaining has displaced the American trial as the main mechanism for resolving criminal charges. Guilty pleas streamline the litigation process and suit the needs of prosecutors obsessed with conviction rates, overworked defense attorneys, risk-averse defendants, and neglectful judges tasked with managing jam-packed dockets. Defense lawyers and prosecutors tend to negotiate pleas quickly, in courthouse vestibules and local watering holes, lives and liberty bartered away by harried attorneys speaking in hushed tones. Prosecutors often demand that to get a plea bargain, defendants must not only forsake their right to trial, but also waive their right to challenge any underlying legal issues in their case later on in an appellate tribunal.

The defendant then appears in court to ratify the deal. At that hearing, the defendant admits guilt, briefly testifies about the facts of the crime, and claims he knows what he's doing in entering the agreement and giving up his rights. A judge accepts the guilty plea and imposes the negotiated sentence, which is typically a fraction of the maximum sentence facing the defendant if the case went to trial.

Justice signed, sealed, and delivered in a matter of minutes.

At first blush, plea bargains seem like a win-win for all key players.[8] A prosecutor can secure a conviction without the time, expense, and risk of a full-blown trial, and spare crime victims the agony of testifying. A defendant can lock in a sentence that's preferable to what he'd likely receive after being found guilty at trial. A defense lawyer can cut her caseload while feeling that she benefitted her client. Judges profit from this arrangement too, as they barely inspect pleas before approving them. This keeps the wheels of "justice" spinning without getting mired in lengthy proceedings, much less risking reversal on appeal.

The upshot of these incentives? Approximately 95 percent of criminal cases are resolved through plea bargaining, a percentage that's gone up since the "tough-on-crime" era of the 1980s.[9] The criminal trial is not just endangered. It's practically extinct.

But the purported advantages of plea bargains wither on closer examination, especially for the innocent. Prosecutors, not judges and juries, dictate the outcomes of cases by crafting plea offers on their own that effectively determine defendants' fates. This creates a terrible quandary for defendants. Take the deal and sacrifice your right to a trial, or roll the dice and potentially receive a much stiffer punishment. What's gained in this process is efficiency and finality. What's lost is a public reckoning and a thorough accounting of the facts in an open forum. And what's unknown is whether the defendant is actually guilty.

Defendants who proceed to trial after shunning a generous plea offer are playing with fire. Indeed, exercising the right to a jury trial is poor consolation to someone later socked with a sentence many multiples of the one contained in the plea offer. This is troublesome enough for any defendant. But what if you're innocent? And what if your innocence claim is hard to prove? Maybe you have a shaky alibi, or the major eyewitness against you is a prominent member of your community and likely to be believed. Do you turn down an offer of a lighter sentence in exchange for just saying you did it? Or do you stick to your guns, head to trial, and run the risk of a much harsher punishment if you lose?

One of my former clients experienced this dilemma.

AT 8:20 P.M. ON FEBRUARY 3, 1999, A LARGE WHITE MAN ENtered El Classico Restaurant in Brentwood, New York, on Long Island.[10] The place was desolate, with only a cook and a waitress inside. The man ordered a shrimp dinner. While the cook prepared it in the kitchen, the man withdrew a knife, put it to the waitress's throat, and demanded she open the cash register. She obeyed. Thirty-two dollars and change. That's all that was in the till. He grabbed the money; she screamed. The cook rushed out, catching a glimpse of the perpetrator as he fled in a white car with a "T" and a "1" in the license plate.

The police arrived. They showed the cook and the witness a "six-pack"—a photo lineup of six men who matched the initial description of the robber. All of them were heavyset, white, and thirtysomething. The two eyewitnesses looked at the lineup and separately identified Stephen Schulz as the perpetrator. He fit the bill in two key respects. First, he was six feet two, 250 pounds, and in his midthirties. Second, he had a criminal record. But nothing in his past indicated a proclivity for violence or the use of a weapon.

The police confronted Schulz. He said that he was home with his roommate watching television at the time of the incident. Unmoved, the police arrested him, and prosecutors later filed robbery charges. As he was too poor to pay for an attorney, the court assigned a lawyer to represent him.

Schulz languished in county jail for several months awaiting trial. During his stint in lockup, he came across an article in the local paper that caught his eye. A man named Anthony Guilfoyle had just pled guilty to six storefront robberies in the Brentwood vicinity that had occurred between January and March 1999, bookending the El Classico theft. Guilfoyle had used his bulk—he was six feet four and weighed more than three hundred pounds— to intimidate employees into handing over money. A mug shot accompanied the story. Puffy cheeks, thick neck, messy hair. He looked a lot like Stephen Schulz.

Schulz's sister called his lawyer. She yelled about Guilfoyle and begged for an investigation. The lawyer didn't comply. Instead, he basically cautioned, *Let's see how the case plays out.*[11]

Well, here's how it played out. The prosecution offered Schulz a deal to plead guilty and get three years in prison. It was an attractive proposal considering the severity of the crime and the length of Schulz's record. He was facing much worse if he lost at trial: a decade or more behind bars. The situation put Schulz in a bind. On the one hand, the case had holes, and proving guilt beyond a reasonable doubt might be tough for the government. That's one explanation for the generosity of the plea offer; prosecutors didn't want to "lose" at trial. On the other hand, there's no sure thing in trial practice. Did Schulz want to wager years of his life by going to trial to prove his innocence?

He did.

AT SCHULZ'S TRIAL, THE PROSECUTION RELIED ON TESTIMONY from the cook and the waitress. The cook insisted the man sitting at the defense table was the person who robbed El Classico. What came out, though, was that the cook had a criminal weapon-possession charge that had gone away during the gap between the robbery and the trial. The defense failed to establish that the cook's testimony was a quid pro quo—a promise to testify against Schulz in return for dismissal of the gun case—but it became clear there was reason to doubt the cook's veracity.

An even more remarkable thing happened when the waitress took the stand. The government asked if the man who had robbed her was present in the courtroom. We've watched this scene countless times on film. In the cinematic version, the victim either points a wobbly finger at the defendant and collapses into tears, or boldly brands the defendant her assailant. But here the witness paused and said no. Now that she saw him in the flesh, as opposed to in a picture, she realized Schulz wasn't the guy. *The robber was taller and heavier.*

Schulz's defense lawyer had a tactical choice to make. He could display Guilfoyle's photo to the waitress on cross-examination. Yet he hadn't interviewed her beforehand and didn't know what she might say.[12] If she identified Guilfoyle, bravo. If she didn't, then that line of questioning would undercut the strength of her astonishing refusal to identify Schulz in court. An old adage of trial work is that you should never ask a question on cross if you don't know the answer. So the lawyer went for a middle-of-the-road strategy, somewhere between showing her the picture and bypassing the topic altogether. He tried to get Guilfoyle's photo admitted into evidence to allow the jury to see on its own how he resembled Schulz. It was a bid to create reasonable doubt, pure and simple. The judge didn't let the photo in, however, because he didn't detect a "sufficient nexus" between Guilfoyle and the El Classico robbery to justify admission.[13]

Without either testimony from the waitress about Guilfoyle or admission of the photo into evidence, the jurors had only an inkling of a possible other culprit. And that inkling didn't do the trick for Schulz. The jury found him guilty of robbery. The judge later sentenced him to eleven years in prison, nearly four times the plea offer.

After Schulz landed at a state correctional facility, he wrote to the Second Look Program at Brooklyn Law School. I was running the day-to-day operations of the clinic at the time and reviewed his letter. Among the first things our new client told me: *I wish I'd taken the plea.*

THE SCHULZ CASE REVEALS THE MAIN DRAWBACKS TO A CASE-processing system that relies so heavily on guilty pleas: the pressure on the innocent to take a deal, and the severe consequences that might flow from a refusal to do so. How did we get to this point?

Some defenders of plea bargaining view the practice as a venerable institution that evolved steadily from seeds sown in colonial America. But the historical record tells a different tale.[14] Although guilty plea rates climbed in the latter part of the nineteenth century, pleas were still rare and their popularity varied from state to state. Even as late as the 1920s, the legal community disapproved of plea bargaining.

Then came a perfect storm that blew apart the trial-centric model. Criminal activity soared, partly due to Prohibition, and legislators responded to an alarmed electorate by expanding the criminal code to encompass a wider range of behavior. Shortly thereafter, the United States Supreme Court revolutionized pretrial criminal practice by vesting defendants with greater protections. The Justices issued opinions that made it easier for defendants to attack police investigative techniques that violated the prohibition against "unreasonable searches and seizures" under the Fourth Amendment. Other cases, like the celebrated *Miranda* decision, put the spotlight on police interrogations that ran afoul of the Fifth Amendment privilege against self-incrimination. Suspects now had certain rights while in police custody, including a right to remain silent and a right to an attorney even if they lacked the resources to pay for one. These Fourth and Fifth Amendment challenges usually took the form of pretrial motions to "suppress" the evidence procured as part of the allegedly illicit search or interrogation. If the defense succeeded with its suppression motion, the evidence couldn't be used by the prosecution at trial. Courts had to devote much of their energy to hearing and ruling on those motions.

An administrative crisis took root. More cases—involving more types of crimes and more extensive pretrial litigation—flooded the courts. Perhaps this crisis could have been averted had politicians funded increases in judicial, prosecutorial, and defender resources. That didn't happen. Passing new criminal statutes was more politically feasible than providing the means to enforce them. And plea bargaining served as the levee to keep the system above water.

By the middle of the twentieth century, plea bargaining had become a vital, maybe even the defining, feature of the criminal justice terrain. It achieved landmark status when the Supreme Court issued five opinions clustered from 1970 to 1971 that gave its blessing to the practice. One of those cases summarized the virtues of plea bargaining:

> Disposition of charges after plea discussions is not only an essential part of the process but a highly desirable part for many reasons. It leads to prompt and largely final disposition of most criminal cases; it avoids much of the corrosive impact of enforced idleness during pre-trial confinement for those who are denied release pending trial; it protects the public from those accused persons who are prone to continue criminal conduct even while on pretrial release; and,

by shortening the time between charge and disposition, it enhances whatever may be the rehabilitative prospects of the guilty when they are ultimately imprisoned.[15]

The Supreme Court correctly labeled plea bargaining "an essential part of the process." But calling it "highly desirable" is a much more dubious proposition.

It's true that plea bargaining became a way to avoid the costs of drawn-out litigation. Judges, prosecutors, and defenders could all manage higher caseloads if they were relieved of the burden of actually trying cases. Yet the interests of individual defendants were not necessarily aligned with those of the institutional players. If a defendant had a chance to suppress evidence seized by the police after a shoddy Fourth Amendment search, then it made sense to litigate the issue. If generating reasonable doubt was a possibility, going to trial looked like a good option.

So incentives had to be calibrated to scare defendants into taking the deals, and prosecutors possessed the discretion to achieve this by choosing what sentence to offer and often what crime to charge. The main incentive for defendants to strike plea bargains lies in the discrepancy between the sentence included in a plea offer and the one they may get if convicted after trial. The greater the discrepancy, the greater the pressure to take a plea. A 2013 report by the nonprofit group Human Rights Watch quantified this phenomenon in the context of federal drug crimes. It found that the "average sentence of federal drug offenders convicted after trial was three times higher (16 years) than that received after a guilty plea (five years and four months)."[16] A similar differential was on display in the Schulz case: a pretrial guarantee of three years in prison versus a posttrial risk of more than a decade. Critics of this practice call the differential a "trial tax," a levy imposed on defendants who exercise their right to a jury trial, as Schulz did. Advocates term it a "plea discount," a deal afforded to defendants who don't glut the docket.

What's more, the nature of the plea offer may fluctuate based on the strength of the case. If the prosecutor has ample evidence against the defendant—and therefore a high chance of getting a conviction at trial—then the differential reflected in the plea might be slight. If the prosecution is unsure about its trial prospects, then the gulf between the offer and the defendant's exposure at trial might be wider.[17] Put another way, weak cases often yield lavish plea offers. This may prove enticing to defendants unaware of the frailty of the evidence—and who may be innocent.

Some jurisdictions recognize variations on the traditional plea, known as no-contest and *Alford* pleas, which contain a further enticement. These types of pleas permit defendants in weak cases to accept the criminal charges against them without formally admitting guilt on the record.[18] While these alternatives have their merits, they generally provide an additional, perverse inducement to get the innocent to throw in the towel by agreeing to a plea, waiving their right to trial, and incurring a conviction and punishment for something they didn't do.

Regardless of whether you take the tax or the discount view of plea bargaining, the whole system might be more justifiable if defendants had access to adequate information about the strength of the case against them. Under a market theory of plea bargaining, each side calculates the risks and benefits of going to trial versus securing a plea, and reacts accordingly. Scholars talk about this in terms of negotiating under the "shadow of trial."[19] A well-informed defendant can measure the likelihood of conviction at trial and determine whether it's prudent to take the plea.

But an information asymmetry exists. Prosecutors have the police reports, the names of potential witnesses, and the physical evidence. They're not obligated to disclose much of this to the defendant prior to trial. In lots of states, prosecutors need not even turn over their witness lists.[20] Based on a 1963 Supreme Court case, *Brady v. Maryland*, prosecutors must disclose certain things to the defense before trial, so-called exculpatory evidence that is favorable to the accused and material to guilt or punishment.[21] Yet even some *Brady* evidence that must be turned over prior to trial may stay hidden before the entry of a guilty plea.[22] Many defendants have attorneys who make their living through a volume business of resolving large quantities of cases swiftly, and who lack investigative resources to dredge up this evidence on their own. Negotiating in such a vacuum may prompt defendants, especially those who are risk averse, to underestimate their odds of success at trial and overestimate the strength of the government's case.

Small wonder so many defendants plead guilty.

Trial judges could stop the plea machine or simply slow it down. But they don't; the formal entry of a defendant's guilty plea is a brief affair. Endorsing a plea without painstaking examination allows trial judges to plow through their own dockets at a rapid clip. Court administrators and outside evaluators often assess judges based on their "dispo" rate, the speed with which they dispose of cases. Those evaluations may affect a judge's ability to earn a promotion or just hang on to her job in states that elect judges or subject them to retention votes.[23] Judges can also rationalize the cursory plea process with classic diffusion-of-responsibility thinking. The prosecutor, defense lawyer, and defendant all have greater knowledge about the case in its early stages than the judge, so it seems appropriate to defer to their arrangement. Trial judges tend to encounter the same prosecutors and defense lawyers each day. They need a smooth working relationship to do their jobs. Gumming up the works by second-guessing plea bargains may not advance any of their professional goals.

Another branch of the judiciary—appellate judges—could scrutinize pleas to protect against miscarriages of justice. These jurists are removed from the trenches and don't interact regularly with the actors who produce the steady stream of guilty pleas on the criminal court assembly line. But despite their distance from the daily grind, appellate judges suffer from some of the same pressures to churn through their dockets as their lower-court colleagues. These pressures deter them from dismantling guilty pleas and reconstructing the available evidence to see whether justice was served.

Even if appellate judges were inclined to be vigilant in reviewing plea cases, there are procedural impediments to doing so. First, there are restrictions on formally withdrawing a guilty plea, as we saw in the Davontae Sanford case from Detroit. Second, as mentioned earlier in this chapter, many defendants are asked to waive their right to appeal any issues in their case as a condition of their plea agreement.[24] These waivers generally weather constitutional challenges on the grounds that they are just one of numerous rights that defendants must forego to get the benefit of a plea. Over the past few decades, appeal waivers have become a key element of the plea-bargaining "game," to the consternation of some observers.[25] A direct consequence of these waivers is that many pleas never reach an appellate tribunal for review.

Appeals courts occasionally dodge the obstacles posed by waivers by deeming them coercive based on the facts in particular cases.[26] Even then, looking under the hood of a run-of-the-mill plea deal reveals little. Often the court file amounts to a thin transcript from the plea proceeding in which the defendant owns up to his misdeeds and admits to the facts. Sometimes the file includes evidence from a suppression hearing that preceded it and that concerned a Fourth or Fifth Amendment issue. There might be vague arrest reports or minutes from a grand jury proceeding. That's about it. Identifying a wrongful conviction under those conditions involves clairvoyance more than deduction.

HOW COULD WE IMPROVE THE CURRENT PLEA-BARGAINING SYStem to reduce wrongful convictions at the front end and increase the chance of detecting (and overturning) them at the back end?

Yes, some guilty defendants get a "good deal." But what's lost is priceless for the guilty and innocent alike. No vetting of the facts, no transparency, no jury verdict. In a sense, no justice.

We could abolish plea bargaining. We really could. Granted, it's a pipe dream—not only because the practice is entrenched, but because abolition is impractical. Without an enormous infusion of resources, the criminal justice system would fall apart if plea bargaining were eliminated, crushed by the avalanche of trials. Prosecutors might react by bringing fewer charges and reducing caseloads. Yet that would antagonize the police, with whom they enjoy a codependent relationship. Police make arrests, prosecutors validate those arrests by filing criminal charges in court, and police help prosecutors by making sure witnesses appear at trial and by testifying themselves.

Eradicating plea bargaining could work, perhaps, if decriminalization truly took off. Fewer crimes on the books, fewer arrests, fewer criminal charges, fewer cases heading to trial. The decriminalization of low-level vice crimes is politically popular at the moment, as is the trend toward electing "progressive prosecutors" who pledge to wield their discretion more fairly.[27] There are limits, though, to how receptive the public might be to the perception of a "soft on crime" movement across the board, especially when it comes to serious, violent offenses.

Also, abolition has been on the table before. Alaska eliminated plea bargaining in 1975.[28] The rationale was grounded in fairness, with the governor at the time proclaiming that the new policy was designed to counter "weakened public confidence in the administration of justice." The conditions seemed ideal. Small population, small(ish) amount of criminal activity, creative attorney general, open-minded governor. The results were initially promising. Although the number of trials in the state rose by 37 percent in the year following the ban, the system appeared capable of absorbing the surge. But the experiment didn't last. A new state attorney general relaxed plea policies in 1980, and bargaining was officially back in the 1990s. By the 2010s, nearly 97 percent of Alaska's criminal cases resulted in pleas. Those who've studied the history of plea bargaining in Alaska attribute the demise of the ban to a change in personnel in the attorney general's office and a decline in state revenues. Trials don't come cheap.

Finally, let's not lose sight of the fact that plea bargaining has its advantages. If done properly, it guarantees that guilty defendants get some form of punishment, and it saves crime victims from having to testify. Maybe the answer lies not in abolition, but in reform. Here are some ideas about how to reduce the chance that innocent defendants will plead guilty to something they didn't do.[29]

Limit the size of the trial tax/plea discount. The most galling aspect of our plea system is the huge differential between a defendant's potential plea and posttrial sentences. It's hard to resist the invitation to plead out when you're offered one year in prison while facing six if convicted after trial. Although there has to be some differential—otherwise it wouldn't be a bargain and no one would take the plea—let's decrease the gap.[30]

Italy has sought to do this.[31] That country restricts its mode of plea bargains to relatively low-level offenses where the stakes aren't too high. It also only permits a negotiated sentence reduction equal to one-third of the defendant's sentencing exposure if the case were to go to trial; a person looking at a six-year sentence in Italy could be offered no less than four in a plea arrangement. Skeptics might view this approach as imposing a "mandatory minimum" sentence on the parties' negotiations that could prolong many prison terms. Even so, similar rules in the United States could ease the pressure on the innocent to take a plea while retaining a motive for the guilty to seriously consider the offer.[32]

Give defendants access to information. A modified plea system, with caps on the trial tax/plea discount, would still contain hazards. Some innocent defendants might succumb to the temptation to take the deal—and a worse one than before—if they think the government has accumulated a mountain of evidence against them.

So let's put defendants in a better position to evaluate the strength of the case by requiring the prosecution to turn over the evidence in its possession before a plea bargain is struck. Scholars often call for "open file" discovery practices in which the government must reveal everything to the defense.[33] Advocates of open file discovery laud its potential to level a playing field currently tilted sharply against defendants. Opponents decry it as unworkable and a recipe for disaster by putting witnesses at risk of intimidation and giving the accused a chance to fabricate a defense to neutralize the evidence. Some on the left fear it might give defendants a false sense that they are receiving every shred of information.

Even without complete disclosure, defendants on the verge of entering a guilty plea should at least get the information from the prosecution they're entitled to receive before trial, scanty as it is. That means *Brady* material. The Supreme Court has never held that this information must be turned over before a guilty plea, only that it must be disclosed prior to the beginning of trial. This must change, either by convincing the Supreme Court to reconsider its position or by enacting laws in each state to mandate disclosure during plea negotiations.[34] Imagine if before any plea, prosecutors turned over all leads about third-party suspects, contradictory statements by government witnesses, evidence of police misconduct, and so on. Defendants armed with this information could see the contours of the case more clearly, make more-informed decisions about their prospects at trial, and weigh plea offers more accurately.

Foster real review. As noted above, trial judges have many reasons to keep their distance from plea negotiations until the bitter end, and then to engage in a perfunctory review. These reasons include efficiency and the opportunity to blame other actors for any flaws in the plea. Another chief reason is that we tell them to stay out of it. The Federal Rules of Criminal Procedure, as well as the rules in several states, formally limit judicial involvement in the criminal plea process. This stands in contrast to civil litigation, where judges are encouraged to play active roles in brokering pretrial settlements.[35] To be fair, there's some justification for keeping criminal court judges at bay. If negotiations were to falter after the judge's intervention, there could be worries about retaliation during the trial or on sentencing day. Also, asking judges to intervene without a full grasp of the facts could be less than helpful and bog down the process.

That said, it's bizarre that we nudge criminal court judges out of the plea process. Judges may not know the minutiae of a case, but they have fewer preexisting views about the matter than prosecutors. This may allow them to be more objective. Plus, judges can give defendants a realistic sense of what sentence they're facing after trial. As for the concern about retribution in the event of failed negotiations, those cases could be reassigned to a different judge.

Some states have encouraged more involvement by judges in plea negotiations. A study of two of those states—Connecticut and Florida—found that "a judge's early input into plea negotiations can render the final disposition more accurate and procedurally just."[36] Reports from another state that permits judicial intervention in the plea process, New York, are less rosy. A 2021 survey of defense lawyers indicated that 72 percent believed that New York state judges pushed defendants to plead guilty by using or threatening enhanced sentences after trial.[37] Despite these mixed results, greater judicial monitoring of pleas could shore up the transparency of the process and its legitimacy.

In tandem with oversight by trial judges, let's also coax appellate courts to monitor pleas more closely. The first step would involve banning appeal waivers as a condition to a plea. It's one thing to ask a defendant to waive his right to a jury trial; it's relatively easy to understand the costs and benefits of doing so. It's something else to ask a defendant to waive his right to appellate review at a time when any issues on appeal might be unknown, potentially unknowable, or at a minimum tough to comprehend. Courts should also be more amenable to withdrawing guilty pleas when there's palpable evidence of innocence, rather than just deficiencies in the plea proceeding. Had this mindset been in place in 2008, Michigan appellate judges might have freed Davontae Sanford years before they actually did.

If we tweaked the plea system in these ways, cases with legitimate innocence claims might go to trial more often, giving defendants a better opportunity to demonstrate they're not guilty of the crimes they've been accused of. But that doesn't mean the truth will prevail at trial—or that the appellate process is set up to course-correct when a trial fails to sort the guilty from the innocent.

2

PRESERVED FOR REVIEW

The Narrow Mandate of Appellate Courts

SAY AN INNOCENT SUSPECT IS CHARGED WITH A CRIME AND withstands the pressure to plead guilty. The defendant wants to put the government's evidence to the test through the crucible of cross-examination and believes that zealous defense advocacy might yield the truth. Assume these hopes are naive. The jury returns a guilty verdict.

Conceivably, the defendant could file a motion for a new trial with the judge in the immediate aftermath of the conviction if he somehow finds fresh evidence to prove his innocence right away. Short of a miracle, he won't find that evidence within the narrow filing window. The statute of limitations for this type of new trial motion in many states is a meager thirty days.[1] Even when a miracle occurs and persuasive new evidence surfaces, most judges are skeptical of motions that challenge the result of a proceeding they just oversaw; they're prone to discount the significance of those filings and stick with the recently rendered jury verdict.[2] We saw this unfold in the Manhattan "base house" murder case, discussed at the start of this book, when Bobby Fennell's codefendant came forward to admit he'd acted alone in the crime. Fennell's lawyer moved for a new trial grounded on the codefendant's statement clearing Fennell of the crime, yet the judge dismissed the motion out of hand. At bottom, new trial motions aren't a genuine option for most innocent defendants convicted after trial.

That leaves the appellate process.

———

IT TAKES A LOT TO REVERSE A CASE AFTER A CRIMINAL DEFENDANT has lost at trial and exercised the right to challenge the conviction in a higher court, a process known as the direct appeal. Although every state grants this right, the direct appeal lacks the stature of the trial within the litigation hierarchy. As the United States Supreme Court observed in a 2017 case, *Davila v. Davis*, "The criminal trial enjoys pride of place in our criminal justice system in a way that an appeal from that trial does not. The Constitution twice guarantees the right to a criminal trial . . . but does not guarantee the right to an appeal at all. The trial 'is the main event at which a defendant's rights are to be determined.' "[3]

The fact that the appeal is viewed as the undercard to the system's main event, the trial, is manifested in the rules and norms that govern the appellate process. For instance, the defendant-appellant is confined to the trial record in raising claims on appeal. That record normally contains a transcript—the verbatim account of the trial produced by the court stenographer—plus any exhibits introduced in the proceeding, pretrial motions and rulings, and grand jury minutes.[4] And that record might be quite voluminous, as I know all too well.

Before running the Second Look Program at Brooklyn Law School, I cut my teeth in the Criminal Appeals Bureau of the Legal Aid Society by handling appeals for criminal defendants who couldn't afford to hire their own lawyers. Many mornings I would enter my office on Church Street in lower Manhattan, located next to the gleaming North Tower of the World Trade Center in the days before 9/11, to find a stack of paper on my desk. This was a clue that my supervisor had assigned a new case. I'd make a beeline for any pictures of the defendant, eager as I was to place a face to the name on the front page of the transcript: *People of the State of New York vs. My New Client.* An oddity of appellate practice is that I seldom met my clients in person; most of them were incarcerated in remote towns upstate that make Otisville look like a metropolis. Legal Aid's budget didn't allow for frequent client visits, nor did my caseload. So, much of my client communication consisted of old-fashioned letters and telephone chats. Once I'd attached face to name, I'd leaf through the pages to piece together the narrative of what had led to the conviction. Grand jury minutes, pretrial motions, and rulings first, then the long slog through jury selection, trial, and sentencing.

The task had a voyeuristic feel. Unlike trial lawyers, who play a vital role in creating the record and ideally have meaningful in-person conversations with their clients, appellate lawyers play a more passive role. Deconstruct what happened at trial, jot down notes about possible legal errors, and formulate a strategy for writing the brief. If a trial attorney is both architect and builder, designing the initial case strategy and helping shape the lower court result, appellate counsel is the critic who evaluates and ultimately pokes holes in the final product. In fact, poking holes is crucial to the job. In the rare event there aren't any holes—your review of the record unearths no viable legal issues to raise on appeal—you must file a brief with the court explaining the absence of contestable claims, an endeavor just as laborious as submitting a brief chock-full of alleged errors.[5]

After you've filed the defendant's brief with the appeals court, it's the government's turn to draft theirs in response to the issues you've raised. There may be another round of submissions known as reply briefs. Then you wait for the court to schedule oral argument, which is the opportunity to present the case to a panel of judges at the courthouse. Some lawyers skip this step and rest on their briefs; others jump at the chance to make their pitch.

States impose a number of restrictions on oral argument. In many busy appellate courts, the clerk may grant you only a few minutes of airtime. Also, the criminal defendants whose appeals are being heard, and who are often imprisoned in far-flung locales, rarely attend in person. Some attorneys who specialize in appeals say that oral argument doesn't make a difference, that cases are won or lost on the briefs alone. I don't quite share that view, despite several disheartening experiences.

I'll never forget my first oral argument as appellate counsel. My client had gotten into a spat with a friend over money. During the dispute, my client sliced her friend across the face and neck with a broken beer bottle, not too far from the jugular vein. The lacerations needed more than thirty stitches to fix—and led to a first-degree assault conviction for causing "serious physical injury." I scoured the transcript on appeal, hunting for issues. Full of zest and naivete, I became convinced the injuries were superficial. That my client had only caused "physical injury," not its serious version, supplying the basis for a reduction to assault in the second degree. I spent weeks fine-tuning the brief, then many more awaiting my moment to argue the case in court.

On the morning of the argument, I put on my best suit and tie, newly purchased, and took the subway to Brooklyn Heights. I strolled a few blocks to the ornate courthouse for the Appellate Division, Second Department, on Monroe Place, an oasis of calm amidst the hustle and bustle of the city. When the clerk called my case, I gathered my notes and strode to the lectern, my knees shaking. Seconds after I uttered my first words—"May it please the court, Daniel Medwed of the Legal Aid Society"—the presiding judge interrupted me. "Some cases shouldn't be argued," he bellowed. "And this is one of them."

In retelling this story to my students, I often say that I paused a beat before declaring "My client feels otherwise, your honor" and proceeding with my argument. Truth be told, that may be embellishment; my real reaction is lost to the haze of time. I suspect I just stood there, stunned into silence, until my supervisor prodded me (and my fancy threads) away from the dais.

It should come as no surprise that I lost the appeal in a unanimous decision.

———

TYPICALLY, THE TRIAL RECORD HAS QUITE A FEW HOLES, SPOTS where you think your client got a raw deal. Those merit research and potential inclusion in your final legal brief to the appeals court as well as vigorous presentation during oral argument. But you can't stray beyond the trial record at all.

Take the Long Island robbery case from Chapter 1. Our team at the Second Look Program entered the matter while the direct appeal of Stephen Schulz's conviction was still pending. We dove right into the case. The holes strewn throughout the case soon became cavernous as our investigation substantiated Schulz's innocence and accumulated evidence against Anthony Guilfoyle, the local serial robber who could pass for a heavier and taller body double of our client.

- We verified Schulz's alibi. He had been home with his roommate watching a particular episode of *Dharma and Greg*, an ABC sitcom that aired between 8:00 and 8:30 on the evening of February 3, 1999. The roommate, a mechanic with a kind disposition, struck us as very credible.
- We found out that Guilfoyle's family member had a white Oldsmobile with a "T" and a "1" in the license plate, which lined up with the description of the perpetrator's getaway car.
- The pièce de résistance came in the form of an interview with the robbery victim, a waitress, who was hard to

locate. We showed her a photograph of Guilfoyle, and she identified him as the man who robbed her. When pressed, she insisted she was 90 percent sure he was the perpetrator.

But this new evidence we discovered pointing to Schulz's innocence could *not* be presented to the court through the direct appeal because it hadn't come up at trial.

You not only are barred from introducing new evidence on direct appeal, but generally may only cite issues that are adequately "preserved" at trial for appellate review. An issue is preserved, and eligible for a close look on appeal, if the defense lawyer raised it with the lower court judge and discussed it thoroughly. Consider the process of canning fruits and vegetables. You put them in a jar while they're fresh with a plan to eat them later, nutrients intact. If the jar isn't sealed, the food becomes inedible. Likewise, if a defense lawyer doesn't object to an issue at trial in timely fashion and state the reasons for her objection on the record, that issue perishes, unlikely ever to be consumed by the appellate court.

There are two main rationales for the preservation requirement. The first is efficiency. We want major legal issues vetted and resolved at trial. The preservation doctrine incentivizes lawyers to lay their cards on the trial table, for judges to see, maximizing the likelihood that justice will be served in that phase of litigation. If you make a sound objection, maybe the judge will sustain it— and there will be no need to appeal it at all. Or she'll reject it, set forth the grounds of her decision, and leave a trail of bread crumbs for the appeals court to follow in evaluating it down the road.

Second, there's the need to deter "sandbagging," the purposeful withholding of a legal argument at trial in order to save it for a potential appeal. Suppose a lawyer is worried about objecting too much and coming across as obstructionist or, well, objectionable to the jury. Without the preservation requirement, she might hold back on an objection, keeping her views secret. If things go sideways and her client is convicted, the defendant could still try to argue the issue for the first time on appeal. That kind of games-manship is simply inconsistent with fair play.

The downside of preservation is that it makes appellate lawyers dependent on the skills and tactical decisions of the defense attorney who handled the case originally. As an abysmal case from Texas shows, preservation also constrains the ability of appeals courts to aid an innocent prisoner.

———————

A MAN RAPED A WOMAN IN DALLAS ON A MONDAY EVENING IN December 1982, and the survivor wasn't sure who'd committed the crime.[6] The case lay dormant for several months until she notified the police that Keith Edward Turner may have been her assailant. The victim and Turner worked in different branches of the same company and didn't know each other well. But something about his appearance and the sound of his voice made her think he was the culprit.

In March 1983, Turner met with officers at the Dallas Police Department, where he denied any involvement in the assault. He returned in April to give a blood sample. In the era before the evolution of DNA technology, forensic analysts relied on serology tests of biological evidence from the crime scene—rudimentary ABO blood typing of semen or other bodily fluids—to winnow the pool of suspects to a subset of the population. A week later the police arrested Turner.

Things looked bleak for Turner. His blood type seemingly matched that of the assailant, the survivor appeared convinced of his guilt, and he'd neglected to give any details of his whereabouts on that Monday night in December during his conversations with the police. But he did have an alibi. Like many Texans in the early 1980s, he had a very specific event on his calendar for that day of the week: watching *Monday Night Football* on television with multiple friends and family members.

Turner decided to go to trial and take the stand in his own defense, which was a risky move. By forsaking his constitutional right to remain silent, a criminal defendant opens himself up to "impeachment" by the prosecutor, who may launch any number of heated questions to undercut the defendant's credibility. Almost anything is permissible. The prosecutor may ask about prior inconsistent statements to suggest the witness is lying now, inquire about the witness's criminal record based on the notion that people who violate the law are more likely to commit perjury, and bring up any past acts that point to dishonesty. For those reasons, among others, it's standard practice for defense lawyers to caution their clients against testifying.

Turner threw caution to the wind. He was twenty-two years old. Testifying seemed like his best bet.

———

THE SURVIVOR IDENTIFIED TURNER AT TRIAL AND SWORE SHE'D never forget his face. The prosecution expert buttressed this testimony by insisting that the serology testing put Turner within the relatively small band of men who could have produced the semen found in the rape kit.[7]

After the DA presented the government's case, it was go time for Turner. On direct examination by his lawyer, Turner offered up his alibi. Then the prosecutor cross-examined him about whether he'd ever told the police about his alibi prior to his arrest. Turner acknowledged he had not. That wasn't too damaging to the defense. A juror could infer that an innocent man would see no need to provide an alibi at such an early stage in the process.

The damage soon followed.

The prosecutor asked whether, after his arrest, Turner had ever told any law enforcement official, "Hey, you got the wrong man."[8] That question was out of bounds. You ordinarily can't impeach a defendant with evidence of *postarrest* silence because it places the witness in an untenable position. One option is that the witness could just refuse to answer the question. Yet doing so would leave the jury to speculate that even when the situation was dire and the defendant had been arrested, he still hadn't mentioned the alibi and had probably contrived it for use at trial. A second option is that the witness could answer the question by explaining that he was asserting his right to remain silent after his arrest. Some jurors might accept that explanation as legitimate; others might view it as an excuse, believing that innocent people don't cower behind the Constitution.

It's bad enough that the assistant district attorney pursued such a problematic line of questioning. What added salt to the wound was that Turner's defense lawyer didn't object properly, even as the prosecutor repeatedly went back to this well, asking in myriad ways whether Turner ever mentioned his alibi after his arrest. The jury found Turner guilty of sexual assault, and he received a twenty-year prison sentence.

Turner appealed his conviction. The case landed in the Texas Court of Criminal Appeals, where Turner cited the assistant DA's egregious inquiry into his postarrest silence as grounds for reversal. In a 1986 opinion, the appeals court agreed that the prosecutor had committed an error, but ruled that it had not been adequately preserved. The court noted that "trial counsel failed to make timely objections each time the appellant was questioned regarding his postarrest silence. At no time did he request a running objection to all questions put to the appellant on this matter." The court went on to observe that "trial counsel also failed to identify exactly what he was objecting to and to specify the grounds for his objections." Absent a specific and timely objection, this legal issue was deemed inappropriate for appellate review, prompting the court to uphold Turner's conviction.

We'll never know whether the questioning about Turner's postarrest silence led to his conviction. It's safe to assume, though, that it may very well have helped the jury see him as guilty.

———

TURNER'S MOTHER DIED SHORTLY AFTER HE WAS SENT TO THE penitentiary, and he spent six miserable years behind bars before his release on parole. In 1999, the authorities ordered Turner to register as a sex offender, which included wearing a monitor and placing a sign in his yard to let neighbors know about his status. One day he was watching television when he came across a program about DNA exonerations. He went to the courtroom of the judge who'd sentenced him and demanded DNA testing of the biological evidence in his case. The judge told him to hire a lawyer; Turner replied that he had four kids and no money. The judge appointed a lawyer and an investigator.

Turner had other hurdles to clear. He had to convince someone—the court, the prosecutor, maybe the governor—to permit DNA testing of the evidence. Then he had to discern whether that evidence existed. (Even today, there's no automatic right to have biological evidence retained in your case, or to have access to it when it is, a topic covered in Chapter 7.)

Turner cleared the first hurdle with ease. After he passed a polygraph, the DA's office agreed to the testing. The next one proved surmountable too. Unlike most cities, Dallas had a custom of preserving biological evidence from criminal cases in a private lab. Retaining evidence allowed the lab to keep its accreditation and gave Dallas prosecutors access to the samples in the event a defendant was granted a new trial and prosecutors wanted to try him again.

The DNA results came back in 2005, nineteen years after the Texas Court of Criminal Appeals had denied Turner relief because his key legal issue had been unpreserved for review. The results proved he wasn't the rapist. Later that year Governor Rick Perry pardoned Turner and declared him actually innocent.

Turner took the DNA report to his mother's grave to deliver an important message: *I told her she didn't need to worry about me.*

WE ALL SHOULD WORRY ABOUT WHAT HAPPENED TO KEITH Turner. Could he have been spared six years in prison and over a decade on parole as a registered sex offender if the appeals court had skirted the preservation rule and granted him a new trial? Like so many questions about the exonerated, the answer is unknown and unknowable.[9] But we do know that a less rigid approach to preservation could have led to a more extensive assessment of his case and a higher chance that the truth would have emerged before DNA rescued him.

A partial solution to the preservation problem in innocence cases is for courts to expand what counts as "plain error."[10] That is, some jurisdictions have an exception to the preservation requirement in situations where the trial error is so patently obvious that a judge could have addressed it on her own even if the defense attorney had failed to object. In those scenarios, appellate courts may recognize and correct a trial misstep when it's unpreserved for review in the traditional sense. A prosecutor's inquiry into a defendant's postarrest silence arguably falls into the plain error bucket, depending on the size of the brim.

Here's a tale from my own appellate practice that shows what plain error looks like. The police stopped my client at a driving checkpoint in Brooklyn and suspected him of being intoxicated. The case went to trial, where prosecutors sought convictions on multiple charges, including something called "aggravated unlicensed operation of a motor vehicle in the first degree" and driving while intoxicated. The aggravated unlicensed operation count had two core elements: (1) driving while intoxicated and (2) having certain previous driving infractions. In legal jargon, DWI was a "lesser included offense" of the aggravated unlicensed operation felony; you couldn't be guilty of the latter without being guilty of the former.

What usually happens with lesser included offenses is that, at the end of the trial, the verdict sheet goes to the jury for deliberations with the charges listed in such a way that the greater charge precedes the lesser. That way if the jury decides to compromise and acquits on the top count, prosecutors could still have a valid conviction on the other charge. This type of compromise or "mercy" verdict is all too common, especially in communities where there's distrust of law enforcement and jurors want to send a message.

In my case, instead of listing the charges in descending order of severity, the clerk put DWI at the top of the verdict sheet followed by the aggravated unlicensed operation count. Guess what? The jury tossed the DWI charge and convicted on aggravated unlicensed operation. That didn't make sense as a matter of law. To find the evidence *insufficient* to prove guilt beyond a reasonable doubt of DWI yet *sufficient* for the aggravated unlicensed operation charge, which had DWI as an element? That's what's known as a legally inconsistent or "repugnant" verdict under New York law.[11] The trial lawyer failed to pick up on it and didn't object. So my client was ultimately sentenced on the felony conviction.

The trial record later landed on my desk, one of those many stacks of papers that greeted me when I arrived at work. I cited the repugnant verdict issue as a point in my appellate brief. Even though the issue was unpreserved for review, I claimed that the error was so blatant the trial court should have noticed it on its own, and, since it didn't, the appellate judges should confront it now in the interests of justice. The appeals court agreed and reversed my client's conviction.

It was my first win as a criminal defense lawyer. And it got me thinking: Could an enhanced plain error doctrine lead to the correction of more wrongful convictions on direct appeal?

It could. Yet that solution—a beefed-up vision of plain error—presupposes that the appellate court can detect the error, as with the inquiry into Keith Turner's postarrest silence and my client's repugnant verdict. Sometimes a conviction looks ironclad on direct appeal, its cracks sealed inside the black-and-white lines of the transcript.

One issue in particular that often eludes appellate review—and contributes to many wrongful convictions—involves the failure of the government to turn over exculpatory evidence. As mentioned in Chapter 1, the 1963 Supreme Court case *Brady v. Maryland* requires the government to disclose all evidence before trial that's "favorable" to the defense and "material" to guilt or innocence. The *Brady* doctrine aims to recalibrate the power imbalance between law enforcement and the defense by tipping off the defendant to gaps in the evidence, even the existence of alternative suspects, prior to trial. The rule applies to information held by both police and prosecutors.

In theory, *Brady* ensures that law enforcement can't hide the ball entirely from the other side. If the evidence reveals possible weaknesses in the government case, it must be shared with the defense. In practice, however, *Brady* has never realized its potential as an equalizer, partly because defendants seldom learn that prosecutors have violated this duty until after trial and lack the chance to present the issue on direct appeal.

A harrowing case from the nation's capital shows the limits of *Brady* in action. On June 22, 1981, a Georgetown University student left her summer job at the Watergate complex in Washington, DC.[12] Her corpse was later discovered on a bank of nearby Rock Creek; she had been raped and shot to death.

An informant, Gerald Smith, told the police that a Black man subsequently identified as Donald Gates had confessed to the crime. According to Smith, Gates bragged that he'd tried to rob "a young, pretty white girl," then raped her after she resisted, and shot her to cover his tracks. Smith received $50 for the tip, $250 for identifying Gates in a photo lineup, and $1,300 in total for his assistance in the case. Forensic evidence appeared to corroborate Smith's account. Gates had supplied a hair sample on an unrelated case. An FBI forensic analyst, Michael Malone, compared that specimen with those retrieved from the crime scene and found consistency between the follicles.

Smith testified under oath about the confession and identification at Gates's 1982 trial. Prosecutors also introduced evidence about a prior incident in which Gates allegedly tried to rob a woman as she walked near Rock Creek during rush hour, pushed her into the grass, and pressed his face against hers before help arrived. Malone, the FBI analyst, provided the icing on the conviction cake. He testified that Gates's hair was "microscopically indistinguishable" from those found on the victim's body. With the one-two punch thrown by Smith and Malone—and the body blow about his prior attempted robbery—Gates went down. He was convicted of rape, murder, and gun offenses, and sentenced to twenty years to life in prison.

The defense knew about the payments to the informant, Smith, before trial. That was *Brady* material properly disclosed by the prosecution because it went to the credibility of a government witness. But here's what remained *un*disclosed: Smith had two felony convictions on his rap sheet, and just before the rape-murder he'd been arrested for another felony. Looking down the barrel at a stiff sentence if convicted of his third strike, Smith helped the police with the rape investigation. In exchange for his assistance, voilà, the government dropped the charges. Prosecutors withheld this information from Gates, despite the light it would have shed on the reliability of the main government witness.

All of this was still unknown to the defense at the time of his direct appeal in 1984, which Gates lost in a unanimous decision. Gates managed to have a DNA test conducted on the leftover evidence in 1988. But the technology was still evolving at that time—the nation had yet to generate its first DNA exoneration—and the test produced inconclusive results.

A SERIES OF PROBLEMS INTERSECTED TO CONVICT DONALD Gates. They included (1) the prosecution's atrocious *Brady* violation in failing to turn over facts about its arrangement with the informant, (2) faulty hair evidence, and (3) the introduction of evidence concerning Gates's previous attempted robbery in Rock Creek Park. What kept him behind bars far longer than necessary was the government's refusal to tell the Gates team about the *Brady* material and the flaws with the hair-comparison science.

Notably, in 1997, an internal FBI review exposed errors within its hair-analysis group. It turned out that Michael Malone and several colleagues had made fraudulent forensic reports in which their lab notes failed to back up their findings and courtroom testimony. *Microscopically indistinguishable*, Malone had claimed in reference to hair samples from Gates and the crime scene. Dubious forensic evidence, such as hair-comparison analysis, has figured in more than 40 percent of documented DNA exonerations.[13] In many of those cases, analysts exaggerated the significance of their findings, sometimes by going so far as to declare a "match" between the hair samples when such certainty is scientifically implausible. In 2009, the National Academy of Sciences condemned the whole field of hair microscopy. Six years later, the FBI found that hair examiners had overstated the probability of a match in 95 percent of the cases it had reviewed.

The US Department of Justice warned local prosecutors in 2002 about the potential forensic issue in the Donald Gates case. The district attorney's office never responded to DOJ. And *no one* alerted the Gates team to this development.

———

GATES RENEWED HIS EFFORT FOR POSTCONVICTION DNA TESTing. In 2007, he succeeded in testing a semen specimen from the rape kit retained by the medical examiner's office. Those tests, much improved since 1988, excluded Gates as the murderer and rapist. He left prison in 2009 after twenty-seven years in custody, a free man with $75 and a bus ticket to Ohio.

The next year, a DC judge awarded Gates a certificate of innocence, and Gates filed a federal civil rights lawsuit. The jury concluded that two DC homicide detectives had withheld evidence about the informant, Gerald Smith, and fabricated aspects of the confession Gates reportedly had made to Smith. This spurred city officials to settle the case for $16.65 million, the largest civil rights settlement in the history of the nation's capital at the time.

Money, of course, couldn't make Gates whole. Nor could the truth bring closure to the victim's family. The DNA profile from the Rock Creek murder was eventually linked to a man who'd worked in the victim's office and followed her after she left the Watergate complex on that fateful June day. This news was bittersweet, to put it mildly. Validating for Gates. Unsettling for the victim's family. Enlightening for the legal community. But ultimately meaningless in holding the assailant accountable. By the time of this revelation, the true perpetrator had died.

Like the Keith Turner case in Dallas, it's impossible to know in hindsight whether any single brick in the wall of the prosecution case against Donald Gates made a difference. If more evidence about the informant had emerged at an earlier juncture, perhaps before the direct appeal, would the whole structure have come crashing down?

Informants play an outsized role in wrongful convictions, appearing in roughly one in five cases where postconviction DNA testing later exonerated an innocent person.[14] When prosecutors ignore their *Brady* duties in the informant context, it hurts the defense in profound ways. The immediate effect occurs at trial. The informant's claimed knowledge about the crime proves difficult for the defense to counteract because the prosecution hasn't disclosed everything about its arrangement with the witness. A secondary effect is that, without knowledge of the nondisclosure, the defense can't preserve the specific issue for appellate review and can't hold prosecutors accountable in a higher court for keeping evidence under wraps.[15]

The *Brady* doctrine seeks to level the playing field by requiring the government to turn over all favorable and material evidence before trial, including evidence the defense could use to challenge an informant's account on the witness stand. But prosecutors often disregard this obligation, whether out of a pure desire to win or due to sheer neglect,[16] and that leaves a steep climb for innocent defendants like Donald Gates.

———

WHEN IT COMES DOWN TO IT, PROCEDURAL RESTRICTIONS UNdermine the much-vaunted promise of appellate review. Defendants are hemmed in by the boundaries of the trial transcript, banned from introducing new evidence or novel issues, and discouraged from raising issues that weren't adequately preserved for appeal.

For better or for worse, many legal issues leap off the pages of the trial record and are suitable for appellate review. That doesn't mean appellate courts give them the type of fresh, searching review the issues call for—and that innocent prisoners deserve.

3

IN DEFERENCE

*How Trial Judges, Defense Attorneys, and
Jurors Get the Benefit of the Doubt on Appeal*

EVEN IF MAJOR LEGAL ISSUES ARE PRESERVED FOR REVIEW, AP-
pellate courts are reluctant to question the decisions made at trial.
The end product of this deferential attitude is to maintain the status quo and keep convictions in place even when there are hints
an injustice has occurred.

This chapter explores how the norm of deference toward trial
judges, defense attorneys, and juries operates to uphold tenuous
verdicts. First, appeals courts defer to trial judges through formal
"standards of review" that set a high bar for reversing a lower
court ruling. Second, appellate judges give defense attorneys a
wide berth at trial by creating a test for "effective" performance
that tolerates a broad range of gaffes. Appeals courts have, time
and time again, treated horrendous defense attorney behavior as
acceptable. Finally, appeals courts prize jury deliberations and
verdicts at trial. In fact, it's virtually impossible to show on direct
appeal that a conviction is based on "legally insufficient evidence"

because of Supreme Court precedent that protects and lauds jurors for their efforts in applying law to fact.

Affording so much deference to choices by trial-level actors undercuts the ability of appeals courts to fix mistakes. In some respects, deference is a fig leaf that appellate courts use to hide their failure to look too closely at guilt or innocence in a particular case—and that occasionally covers the naked truth.

JUDGING FROM A DISTANCE

Appellate courts have strict rules about how to evaluate a lower court decision and must apply a precise "standard of review" when asked to reverse a ruling by a trial judge.[1] The standard of review varies depending on the nature of the ruling. At one end of the spectrum, factual determinations by trial judges receive the most deference. A presumption of correctness attaches to findings of fact, and those fact-based rulings will only be overturned on appeal if they're "clearly erroneous." Findings of fact may include historical facts (like whether it rained on a particular day) or more nuanced interpretations (such as whether a witness came across as credible on the stand).

At the other end of the spectrum, appellate courts may take a fresh look and institute their own judgment without any deference if the trial decision is based on a pure question of law, a standard known as de novo review. A question of law could involve any number of inquiries—for example, whether people are guilty of conspiracy when they agree to engage in criminal activity with someone they don't realize is an undercover officer, or whether a burglar's friend who's merely present at the crime scene can be treated as an accomplice.

Trial court decisions often fall somewhere in the middle, characterized as matters of discretion. Many rulings about whether to admit information into evidence aren't reversible on appeal unless the trial judge "abused" her discretion. This is an extraordinarily deferential standard. A trial judge only needs to nominally consider the competing arguments about admitting an item into evidence to ensure that her ruling survives an appeal—regardless of whether the ruling is wrong on the merits.

One decision at a criminal trial that's normally subject to abuse-of-discretion review on appeal concerns the admissibility of evidence about a person's "prior bad acts." Information that a criminal defendant engaged in similar behavior in the past is often relevant to the case at hand. Imagine that a man is accused of forging checks at a grocery store. The fact that he did the same thing at a pharmacy three years before bears upon his potential guilt in this instance, and is something the jury should perhaps know about. But there's a risk the jury could overvalue that evidence and convict based on the person's history, not the details of the current case. For that reason, trial judges typically balance the relevance of the prior act against the danger of "unfair prejudice" toward the defendant to make a judgment call about whether the evidence should come in. Likewise, a defendant might seek to introduce evidence of *another* person's prior behavior to substantiate his own innocence and suggest that the third party committed the crime, forcing the court to weigh the relative attributes of that item as well.

To see how prior-bad-act evidence can arise at trial, let's return to the Long Island restaurant-robbery case. Our defense team couldn't present new evidence related to Stephen Schulz's innocence on direct appeal because we were only allowed to raise issues already in the trial record. Yet his defense lawyer had preserved at least one crucial issue at trial. He'd sought to introduce a photograph of Anthony Guilfoyle, the man whose features resembled those of Schulz and who'd pled guilty to six other robberies in the region during the relevant time frame. After hearing arguments from both the defense and the prosecution, the trial judge sustained the government's objection and refused to admit the photo into evidence. That decision was upheld at the first layer of direct appellate review, and later in New York's highest court, the Court of Appeals, which wrote, "In the circumstances of this case, the trial court did not abuse its discretion in determining that the photograph of Guilfoyle would have caused undue delay, prejudice and confusion, and properly precluded the evidence."[2]

Put aside the judicial lingo for a moment. A person who could be Schulz's doppelgänger had admitted to *six* robberies in the area. Those robberies were somewhat similar to the one in question at Schulz's trial. The defense attorney had a mug shot of the man—*and* made a compelling argument in favor of its admission into evidence. Shouldn't the jurors have been permitted to see the photo and determine for themselves whether the victim might have mistaken Schulz for Guilfoyle? Yes. But the trial judge felt differently, and the abuse-of-discretion standard barred the appeals court from looking at the issue with clear eyes.

Schulz is a prime example of how the abuse-of-discretion standard can work to reinforce a trial judge's decision to exclude evidence that a defendant wanted to use as a shield to protect himself. More often a different scenario crops up. The abuse-of-discretion standard makes it easy to affirm a trial court decision to admit government evidence the defendant wanted *out* and that operated as a sword to skewer the defendant at trial.

Think back to the Rock Creek case from Chapter 2, in which a Georgetown student was assaulted after leaving her summer job. In deconstructing what went wrong, I focused on the prosecution's *Brady* violation—its failure to disclose damning evidence about the state's star informant, Gerald Smith—and, to a lesser extent, the flawed forensic hair analysis. But I mentioned another piece of the case in passing. It concerned a prior incident close in time, place, and manner to the crime at issue. The defendant, Donald Gates, had apparently tried to rob a different woman along Rock Creek on another day, then acted in a way consistent with an attempted sexual assault before being apprehended.

The prosecution sought to introduce evidence of this attack in the rape-murder trial on the basis that it went to Gates's intent or identity and reflected a common scheme. Although the defense objected, the trial judge nevertheless admitted the evidence. On direct appeal, the higher court upheld that decision, acknowledging, "Though the other crimes issue is a sensitive one which calls for a careful balancing to insure against improper prejudice, our role is limited to affording deference to trial court rulings that appear carefully considered after proper objection by the defense. . . . We fail to perceive any abuse in the exercise of discretion in the trial court's balancing."[3]

Whereas a New York trial court kept a photograph of a man who'd committed prior similar bad acts from going to the jury to prove Stephen Schulz's innocence, a District of Columbia judge found Donald Gates's prior similar bad act relevant enough to help prove his guilt. Could those decisions have tipped the scales at trial against two innocent defendants? The Schulz jury was not privy to a photograph of an alternative suspect subsequently identified by the crime victim (with 90 percent certainty) as the true perpetrator. The Gates jury members learned details about the defendant's past crime, a wretched tale akin to the one being discussed at trial, and that news may have weighed heavily on their consciences in the deliberation room.

The decisions to exclude evidence in Schulz and include it in Gates seem susceptible to attack. They certainly do in hindsight. But those rulings were unassailable when it mattered most—on direct appeal—because both fell within the discretion of trial judges, and appellate judges declined to critically reexamine the wisdom of those outcomes.

———

As the Schulz and Gates cases show, it's tough for a defendant to meet the abuse-of-discretion standard on appeal. Any

trial court that appears to weigh the pros and cons of an evidentiary decision will be deemed to have exercised its discretion, if
not wisely, in a fashion that does not plunge to the status of abuse.
Forget about questions of fact, which receive even greater deference. The annals of appellate law contain few cases where a panel
threw out a trial judge's findings of fact as clearly erroneous.

Why do appeals judges defer so much to their lower court
colleagues?

On the one hand, this custom reflects the different roles played
by each body in the litigation process and their unique spheres of
expertise, or as legal scholars like to say, their "institutional competence."[4] A trial court, composed of a single judge, is concerned
with resolving the particular dispute before it. Supervision of the
trial proceedings allows the judge to assess witness credibility and
make real-time decisions on the ground to reach a resolution.
Preferably, one that's both fair and accurate.

Unlike a trial judge, appeals judges aren't at ground level.
They enjoy a bird's-eye view, one that is removed from the mud
throwing down below: the drudgery of monitoring witnesses,
keeping lawyers in line, and ruling on objections. They normally
serve on panels, too, hearing appeals and making decisions as a
group. That distance from trial and the group dynamic help in
evaluating tricky questions of law, which is one reason they may
look at pure legal questions de novo ("anew") without bowing to
the trial court's take. More heads are better than one, especially
when decisions have far-reaching implications. And appellate
decisions that set legal standards have far-reaching implications
because of the nature of case precedent. An opinion issued by an
appeals court binds not only the actors in the specific case but
also every lower court in the jurisdiction going forward.

If the trial judge is the umpire in a particularized dispute, appellate judges are the league commissioners or governing board of
directors, designing the rules of play for all while generally leaving individual game-time decisions to their trial court associates.

This hierarchy justifies leaving the nitty-gritty to the trial judges out there on the field. An appellate court's detachment from the trial doesn't help much in reconsidering factual findings and judgment calls about the admissibility of evidence.

On the other hand, the justifications for deferential standards of appellate review conceal a troubling reality. Trial judges get it wrong. Those errors can and do harm innocent defendants. The absence of a robust appellate mechanism to correct those errors may prolong the imprisonment of the innocent and perhaps foil any chance at freedom.

There's value in deference, I concede. But that value may be outweighed in certain instances by competing values. Not the least of those values are the pursuit of accurate results and justice for the factually innocent. Instead of reversing evidentiary decisions only when the trial judge "abused" her decision, appellate courts should take a less deferential and more skeptical stance when reviewing these choices. They should take a stance that accounts for the substance of trial decisions, not just the process through which they derived.

INDEFENSIBLE

Appeals judges also give deference to the tactical choices made by criminal defense attorneys at trial, choices that can hurt their clients and contribute to wrongful convictions. The notion that defense lawyers should receive latitude in how they try cases has deep roots. Criminal defendants historically had few rights at all when it came to retaining legal representation, or in protesting how their counsel performed at trial. For nearly two hundred years, courts were not even required to assign attorneys to defendants who lacked the resources to pay for one on their own. Defendants were forced to dip into their bank accounts, regardless of the size of their balances, to pay for legal assistance. That practice began to shift in the 1960s—and Clarence Gideon deserves much of the credit.

Before a judicial opinion made him famous, Gideon cycled in and out of jail for decades, with hardly a penny to his name, drifting from his native Missouri to towns throughout the South.[5] He wound up in Florida, where he was accused of felony theft in 1961. Unable to afford an attorney, he represented himself at trial. The results were disastrous. He was convicted and sent to prison. While there, Gideon studied law and became convinced that the trial judge's refusal to give him an attorney violated his constitutional rights. He handwrote a five-page petition, known as a writ of certiorari, seeking review of his case by the United States Supreme Court.

The Court granted review, a rare outcome for a "cert petition" filed without the aid of a lawyer. The Court then appointed Abe Fortas, a confidant of Lyndon Johnson and a future Supreme Court Justice, to argue the case on Gideon's behalf. How ironic. Gideon was denied a lawyer when his liberty was at stake in a Florida trial, but with an appellate appearance in the nation's preeminent court beckoning, he had access to one of the country's brightest legal minds free of charge. The Court ordered a new trial for Gideon in 1963, holding in a milestone opinion that criminal defendants have a right to an attorney in felony trials and that the state must supply that lawyer if the defendant lacks the funds to hire one on his own. Gideon fared much better the second time around at trial. He was acquitted, in no small measure due to the efforts of the trial attorney assigned to represent him. (No, it wasn't Abe Fortas.)

Our current public defender system has its origins in the *Gideon* decision. Nowadays there's even a right to counsel in certain misdemeanor trials, and on direct appeal of a conviction.[6] That's why my former employer, the Criminal Appeals Bureau of the Legal Aid Society, exists. It receives government funding to meet the constitutional requirement to offer appellate representation to the poor.

In the immediate aftermath of *Gideon*, having a right to an attorney proved to be a pyrrhic victory in many cases. Judges often tapped unskilled and inexperienced lawyers to handle criminal cases for low-income defendants, and states were unwilling to open up the purse strings to pay for higher-caliber representation or to offer worthwhile training programs. The Supreme Court confronted this problem in 1970, ruling in *McMann v. Richardson* that felony defendants deserve more than a warm body with a license to practice law; they "are entitled to *effective* assistance of *competent* counsel."[7]

Those words struck the right notes, yet what did "effective assistance of competent counsel" really look like? Could *any* trial mishap overturn a conviction? Just certain foul-ups? Or must there be multiple blunders? In essence, what do you need to show on appeal to prove that your trial lawyer gave ineffective assistance? Those questions largely remained unanswered for more than a decade.

Once again, a Florida case led to a groundbreaking Supreme Court decision that tried to address them.[8] Together with two confederates, David Washington committed a string of gruesome crimes in 1976. After the police arrested the accomplices, Washington surrendered and confessed to some of the offenses. The state indicted him for kidnapping and murder, and the court enlisted a veteran criminal defense lawyer to handle his case. Facing the death penalty, Washington needed all the help he could get.

Death penalty cases typically have two phases. The "guilt" phase involves a jury trial about whether the defendant committed the underlying crime. If the defendant is found guilty, the case shifts to the "sentencing" stage, the moment when the same jury considers whether the defendant deserves life or death. Although judges conduct sentencing in most criminal cases, the jury usually undertakes that role in capital cases based on the idea that the people, not a single jurist, should decide whether the state may take a person's life. At capital sentencing trials, it's standard practice for the prosecution to present evidence about "aggravating" factors that augur in favor of death (such as the killing of a child).

The defense then puts forth "mitigating" factors aimed at adding context to the defendant's behavior in hopes of spurring the jury to exercise mercy (such as evidence of mental health issues).

Washington pled guilty to murder, bypassing the guilt phase, and chose to battle solely about the appropriate sentence. This often happens in death penalty cases because defendants fear jurors might become so horrified by the grisly facts revealed at the guilt phase of the trial that any mitigation evidence would fall on deaf ears at the sentencing phase. So Washington acknowledged guilt and put all his eggs in the sentencing basket. He didn't even try his luck with a jury. He waived his right to a jury under Florida law, leaving the sentencing decision entirely up to the judge.

The strategy adopted by Washington can succeed *if* defense counsel makes a strong case for mitigation. Washington's lawyer failed in this regard. He neither sought out character witnesses to testify on his client's behalf nor pursued a psychiatric examination to strengthen the argument in favor of life. Instead, the lawyer relied on Washington's claims during his guilty plea hearing where he cited extreme stress as the reason for his crime spree. The attorney emphasized that Washington had owned up to his wrongdoing, displayed remorse, and acted under the influence of an emotional disturbance. It was a "less is more" strategy. By neglecting to dive too deeply into Washington's background, his lawyer wanted to prevent prosecutors from engaging in a vigorous cross-examination that would dwell on Washington's dicey explanation of emotional stress. Still, with little to no mitigation evidence available, the trial judge imposed the death penalty.

After a series of pit stops in the lower courts, Washington's case reached the court of last resort. In 1984, the United States Supreme Court upheld the conviction, ruling that Washington's lawyer met the standard for effective performance. In the process, the Court announced a two-part test for defendants trying to prove ineffective assistance of counsel: (1) that the trial lawyer had engaged in deficient performance, and (2) that such deficiency had prejudiced the defendant by contributing to the negative result in the case. This test, the Court proclaimed, is "highly deferential" to the attorney, and the complaining client must show that his lawyer's behavior fell below an "objective standard of reasonableness."

After the Supreme Court denied relief to Washington, neighboring prisoners on death row overheard him weeping in his cell. Journalist David Von Drehle recalled that Washington "was ashamed and remorseful until the end. . . . As his twelve-year-old daughter sobbed through their final visit, he cupped her trembling hand and said 'I want you to look at me, and I want you to see where I am . . . and I want you to do better.'"

Florida executed Washington by electrocution in July 1984.[9]

STRICKLAND V. WASHINGTON STANDS FOR THE PROPOSITION THAT we shouldn't second-guess the trial tactics of defense lawyers too much. If there was a leg to stand on, any reasonable justification at all for the strategy employed by the defense lawyer at trial, then it won't be characterized as substandard. Even if a particular tactic plummets to the level of a deficiency, the error will not produce a finding of ineffectiveness and the ordering of a new trial so long as it didn't affect the outcome. If an appeals court thinks the defendant would have been convicted anyway, it will downplay the error's impact. To use a sports metaphor, think "no harm, no foul."

The consequence is that on appeal, it's exceptionally difficult to win on a claim of ineffective assistance of counsel. According to one study, judges found trial lawyers effective in 97 percent of the cases in which defendants later challenged their counsel's performance.[10] In the post-*Strickland* world, courts have deferred to the most dubious of tactical choices by defense attorneys. They've even affirmed convictions where lawyers slept during parts of a trial or were under the influence of alcohol.[11]

A despicable case from Texas exemplifies how judges tend to write off trial attorney misadventures. Charged with a crime eligible for the death penalty, the defendant had a lawyer who dozed throughout the trial, supposedly because he found it "boring." Aware of the lawyer's behavior, the trial judge proclaimed that "the constitution says everyone is entitled to the attorney of their choice. The constitution doesn't say the lawyer has to be awake."[12]

Now, it's fair to assume that most defense lawyers manage to stay awake at trial and avoid intoxicants. It's also fair to assume that most want to do right by their clients. But some lack the capacity to fulfill that goal; inexperience, poor training, skimpy funding, cultural incompetence, and crushing workloads hobble even the most well-meaning trial lawyers. Others simply make bad decisions with ripple effects that doom the case.

Consider the calculus about whether to put forth an alibi defense. Alibi evidence can reinforce the defendant's account of events or, if he asserts his right to remain silent, carry much of the weight in advancing an innocence argument. Sometimes there's powerful alibi evidence, like a video recording that places the person in a different location at the time of the crime. More often, the alibi evidence is far less certain. Think about it: Could you tell me where you were exactly eight months ago? Even if you could, the alibi might be vulnerable to cross-exam. Maybe you were home with your mother, partner, or children. Might not those loved ones have an incentive to testify in a way that helps you? A 2014 study even found that family alibi witnesses are "associated with erroneous convictions" and "are among the weakest defense witnesses."[13] At the end of the day, alibi evidence is crucial to an innocence defense yet fraught with peril given that jurors might doubt its legitimacy.

The rules surrounding alibi evidence add to the peril. Defense lawyers enjoy vast discretion about whether to present or omit an alibi defense. If the lawyer believes that the alibi isn't credible or will be snubbed by the jury, then she can choose not to pursue it. Appellate courts ordinarily treat that decision as a valid tactical choice—even when it contributed to a wrongful conviction.

The complexities in deciding whether to rely on an alibi witness surfaced in the Long Island restaurant-robbery case. At the time of the crime, as you may recall, Stephen Schulz was home watching the television sitcom *Dharma and Greg* with his roommate. Schulz's trial lawyer didn't put the roommate on the stand. My students and I later interviewed the roommate, a mechanic without a criminal record, and found him credible. We became convinced the lawyer had botched the case by leaving him off the witness list. Looking back, I admit that our judgment may have been tainted by our faith in Schulz's innocence and our desire to prove it. We believed in our client; we were looking for anything and everything to substantiate that belief, perhaps mistaking pebbles for precious stones. Also, even if the roommate was a potentially strong witness, the alibi wasn't especially compelling: watching a network TV program on a random February night. The lawyer's strategy regarding the alibi made me queasy, but I understood it. A case that I became involved with later in my career also contained alibi evidence—and made me downright sick.

AFTER SEVERAL YEARS OF RUNNING THE SECOND LOOK PROgram, I decided to take my career in a different direction. I applied to become a tenure-track law professor, a position that would allow me to focus on research as opposed to overseeing students in a clinical setting. I thought I could better meet my goal of rectifying wrongful convictions by recommending policy reforms from an ivory tower perch than by toiling in the weeds and litigating cases for individual clients. Frankly, I also yearned for the prestige and job security that only a tenured gig could supply. And I was burned out from losing so many cases—from getting my hopes up, then having them ruined by obstinate prosecutors, imperious judges, and intractable procedural roadblocks.

I accepted a position with the University of Utah. In addition to teaching law students and publishing academic papers, I spent eight years on the board of directors of the Rocky Mountain Innocence Center, a nonprofit that investigates and litigates postconviction innocence claims in Nevada, Utah, and Wyoming. One of our cases has rankled me for years, a case in which the defense lawyer's decision not to present alibi witnesses at trial had dreadful repercussions.

In 2000, someone robbed fifty dollars from an elderly woman at a Salt Lake City convenience store.[14] The woman claimed that the perpetrator was a Black man between eighteen and twenty-one years old. The investigation stagnated for three years until the victim saw Harry Miller on the street, a forty-seven-year-old Black man from Louisiana who was in town to visit his brother. She identified him as her assailant, and a clerk later recognized Miller as a frequent customer of the store in 2000.

That was it. A case built on a delayed "cross-racial" identification by the white victim in a city with a tiny Black population coupled with another ID that suggested Miller had patronized the store during the relevant time frame. Cross-racial misidentifications—where a crime victim of one race misidentifies someone of a different race as the culprit—often appear in documented wrongful convictions.[15] This phenomenon is echoed in social science research that shows people generally do better at identifying a person of their own race than someone from a different group. At the risk of oversimplification, one explanation for these results is that Americans lack familiarity with the physical characteristics of other races because the nation remains extremely segregated. Another revolves around a theory known as ethnocentric homogeneity, which holds that people in different racial groups focus on different facial features when identifying individuals within their groups, and that the characteristics relied on to make those identifications don't always translate well to the interracial context. Yet another explanation suggests that bigotry and intolerance factor into at least some cross-racial misidentifications.

The foundation to the Salt Lake City robbery case, based on a flimsy cross-racial identification, buckled even more after Miller told the police that he had lived in Louisiana in 2000, and had suffered a stroke two weeks before the crime. The stroke had nearly incapacitated him, leaving him housebound and necessitating in-home care. A nurse insisted that she'd visited Miller in Louisiana *the day before* the crime.

Undaunted, Utah prosecutors constructed the following hypothesis to justify charging Miller with armed robbery. Yes, he'd endured a stroke and yes, he may have been in Louisiana as recently as twenty-four hours before the crime, but that didn't mean he was innocent. He must have jumped on a plane, flown to Salt Lake City, robbed the woman of fifty dollars, and returned home that same day. At trial, Miller took the stand to refute that narrative. His defense attorney otherwise failed to mount a vigorous alibi defense, neglecting to call witnesses from Miller's hometown who could verify his account. Miller was convicted and sentenced to a term of five years to life in prison in 2004.

Miller claimed ineffective assistance of counsel on direct appeal, contending that "other alibi witnesses could have, and should have, been obtained" to testify on his behalf. The Utah Court of Appeals determined that it was unable to assess the ineffectiveness claim because there were "insufficient factual findings" in the record, and remanded the case to the trial court to make those findings. As requested, the trial court held a hearing, after which it concluded that (1) defense counsel did not act deficiently and (2) even assuming for purposes of argument that the failure to offer a stout alibi defense was a deficiency, Miller wasn't prejudiced because "there is no reasonable probability of a different outcome at trial even if [these alibi witnesses] had testified."

Hold on. *No reasonable probability of a different outcome* if the defense lawyer had put on a more thorough alibi defense? In a case with ample evidence suggesting Miller was bedridden in a state hundreds of miles away at the time of the robbery?

The case went back to the Utah Court of Appeals. Before the appeals court heard oral argument in the case, however, the prosecution and defense jointly submitted a motion to reverse the conviction due to an unspecified error that had occurred at trial. The appeals court granted the motion, and prosecutors prepared to retry Miller in the summer of 2007. A week before the second trial, the district attorney shifted course again, abruptly dismissing all charges.

Miller was freed from prison more than four years after his arrest. With the aid of the Rocky Mountain Innocence Center, Miller eventually obtained a certificate of factual innocence. As meaningful as that recognition was, a piece of paper couldn't make up for years behind bars. Nor could the paltry sum the State of Utah coughed up to compensate him: $124,763.

Lots of things went wrong in the Harry Miller case. There were cross-racial misidentifications and prosecutors who rushed to craft a strange theory of the case, then steamed full-bore ahead in pursuit of it. But the most significant flaw was the failure of Miller's lawyer to develop an alibi defense, a failure compounded by a Supreme Court doctrine that defers to such strategic choices by defense counsel even when they send an innocent person to prison.

INSIDE THE JURY ROOM

Judges and defense lawyers aren't the only trial participants who receive deference when their performance is challenged on direct appeal. Appellate judges also tend to confirm decisions by juries, even bad ones, because of this deferential attitude. The rationales for viewing jury decisions favorably may appear noble, springing from a desire to reinforce the value of civic participation in our constitutional democracy and to hear what everyday citizens have to say in criminal matters. When you dig deeper, though, you see that affording too much reverence to jury decisions on direct appeal, often under the guise of populism, impinges on another feature of our democracy: protecting the minority, in this case the defendant, from the whims of the majority.

From the dawn of the republic, American leaders, like their British forebears, have treated crimes as violations of the public trust that merit a public reckoning. Prosecutors are government lawyers who officially represent the "people" of their jurisdiction, not the individual crime victims. The logic is that all of us suffer when a crime occurs in our midst, and therefore the entire community should mete out justice. Regular citizens contribute to the process chiefly through jury duty.

Touted as a "magistracy" by Alexis de Tocqueville in the nineteenth century, the jury is a hallmark of American society.[16] It enables citizens to participate directly in the administration of justice and hold defendants accountable for their actions in a public forum if the government can prove guilt beyond a reasonable doubt. The right to a jury trial in criminal cases is guaranteed by the Sixth Amendment of the Constitution. It's framed as a right to a "fair" trial by an "impartial" jury. If given appropriate legal guidance by the judge, the adage goes, those selected for jury service in a criminal case will draw upon their common sense to evaluate the evidence and apply their findings to the law in a manner that yields a just result. This takes place in an open courthouse for the community to see.

Part fairy tale, part populist trope, this glorified vision of the jury rests on several shaky assumptions. For one, that we can find twelve fair and impartial citizens who are truly representative of the community aggrieved by the crime. BIPOC communities are often underrepresented on juries, most notably in cases where the defendant belongs to one of those communities. In the past, this frequently stemmed from overt racism. Consider the poll taxes in the Jim Crow–era South that blocked Black citizens from registering to vote and, without being registered, to serve on juries.

More recently, nondiverse juries tend to result from less obvious, yet equally insidious, forms of racism such as machinations by prosecutors that affect the composition of the jury pool. Prosecutors and defense lawyers have several techniques at their disposal to shape a jury. They may challenge a potential juror "for cause," maybe because that person is related to a witness or has a different conflict of interest or a clear bias. They may also strike a set number of prospective jurors for no stated reason through the use of "peremptory challenges." American case law is full of instances where prosecutors manipulated peremptories to keep Black and Brown people off juries, even after a 1986 Supreme Court case, *Batson v. Kentucky*, warned them not to do so.[17]

One of those instances involved Curtis Flowers, a Black man accused of killing four people in a Mississippi furniture store in 1996.[18] Prosecutors engaged in an epic quest to convict Flowers. They took him to trial *six* times. The first three trials resulted in convictions reversed by the state Supreme Court, the fourth and fifth led to mistrials, and the sixth generated a conviction that Flowers appealed all the way up to the United States Supreme Court. In 2019, the Court reversed Flowers's conviction, and the Mississippi attorney general's office dismissed the case the following year. The record showed that prosecutors had used all their peremptory challenges in the first four trials—thirty-six in total—to disqualify Black jurors. In the sixth trial, the prosecutor struck five of the six eligible Black jurors and exhibited an appalling pattern of questioning during jury selection. The lead state prosecutor asked prospective Black jurors an average of twenty-nine questions each, while the eleven white jurors who were ultimately seated faced an average of a single question apiece.

Another dubious assumption about the jury system is the belief that these twelve "fair and impartial" citizens will collectively reach a sound decision if they're emboldened to speak their minds during jury deliberations. While transparency is treasured in every other facet of an open criminal trial, it has no currency in the deliberation room. The doors are slammed shut. It's a long-held axiom that jurors must deliberate in private, with no threat of interference at the time or subsequent interrogation about what went on, for fear that otherwise there would be a chilling effect. The concern is that without the safeguard of privacy, full and frank exchanges would not occur and justice would not result.

Jurisdictions have baked this principle into their rules of evidence, barring postverdict inquiry into what happened during jury deliberations, absent signs of blatant misconduct like juror intimidation or exposure to prejudicial media accounts of the trial.[19] The Supreme Court has also blessed this approach by treating deliberations as sacrosanct. It even upheld a mail fraud conviction in *Tanner v. United States* after two jurors came forward to report that the "jury was one big party": several jurors drank alcohol at lunch throughout the trial, three smoked marijuana, two used cocaine, and two consummated a drug transaction with one another.[20] Justice Sandra Day O'Connor captured the Court's reasoning in her majority opinion in *Tanner*:

> There is little doubt that postverdict investigation into juror misconduct would, in some instances, lead to the invalidation of verdicts reached after irresponsible or improper juror behavior. It is not at all clear, however, that the jury system could survive such efforts to perfect it. Allegations of juror misconduct, incompetency, or inattentiveness, raised for the first time days, weeks, or months after the verdict, seriously disrupt the finality of the process. . . . Moreover, full and frank discussion in the jury room, jurors' willingness to return an unpopular verdict, and the community's trust in a system that relies on the decisions of laypeople would all be undermined by a barrage of postverdict scrutiny of juror conduct.[21]

I share some of Justice O'Connor's misgivings about the hazards posed if the process invited a "barrage of postverdict scrutiny of juror conduct." Yet I'm skeptical about how the current rules work in practice. My skepticism stems from cases where biased juries have contributed to the conviction of innocent defendants, and the secrecy enveloping their deliberations shielded these miscarriages of justice for many years. Take the trial of Darrell Jones.[22]

Guillermo Rodrigues was murdered in Brockton, Massachusetts, on a rainy night in November 1985. Rodrigues, a Cuban immigrant facing drug charges, allegedly had ties to organized crime. No one got a good look at the killer, although several witnesses said they saw a Black man push Rodrigues out of a bar, then shoot him in a nearby parking lot. The bartender recalled seeing a Black man at his establishment, an event that struck him as noteworthy because he rarely had Black patrons.

The police had nothing else to go on until the next night, when an informant told a police sergeant that a Black man nicknamed Diamond had done the shooting. Another informant mentioned Diamond too, adding that the name referred to eighteen-year-old Darrell Jones. It turned out that Jones was on-site at the time of the murder. He'd taken a bus from Boston to drink at the bar, which had a reputation for being lax about checking the ages of customers who wanted to buy alcohol. Jones even admitted that he'd been in the crowd of people who gathered outside after the shooting. Based on this information, Jones became the target of the investigation. The police could place him at the location. Plus, they had the informants' statements, and soon, according to a police report, they had identifications of Jones by two eyewitnesses.

What the police lacked was any physical evidence or motive to link Jones to the crime. The police arrested him on murder charges anyway, and the case went to trial in 1986. It looked like tough sledding for prosecutors to get a guilty verdict. None of their witnesses could identify Jones in court. It also came out that a detective had erased portions of a videotaped interview of a star prosecution witness.

The feeble performance of Jones's defense attorney, however, made the path to conviction gentler for prosecutors. The lawyer, Keith Elias, didn't like for his clients to sit next to him at the defense table; he preferred to relegate them to the prisoner's dock behind him. As Elias explained to the jury at the Jones trial, "I like to be alone. I don't like to be distracted." Ironically, Elias had a host of other distractions at the time, preoccupied as he was with managing his burgeoning law practice and fending off an ethics complaint. He also had a flagrant conflict of interest. At one point, he or his firm had represented *three* of the police officers who'd investigated the Rodrigues murder in unrelated civil matters. One of those matters was still pending. Elias didn't divulge this conflict to the judge until the third day of trial. After a quick consult, Jones agreed to let Elias continue defending him.

Despite his unorthodox tactics, plentiful distractions, and conflicts of interest, Elias attempted to mount a defense. He put three alibi witnesses on the stand, each of whom testified that Jones was in the bar, not the parking lot, at the time of the shooting. It was all for naught. After three days of deliberations, the all-white jury found Jones guilty of first-degree murder. A judge sentenced him to life in prison without the possibility of parole.

The Darrell Jones case contains many of the classic factors that underlie wrongful convictions. Reliance on informants? Check. Dubious eyewitnesses? Check. Possible police misconduct? Check. Meager performance by the defense attorney? Check. But it also contains something else, a dynamic often suspected but seldom documented in innocence cases: racial bias in the jury box.

Jones's conviction was affirmed on direct appeal without any inkling of juror impropriety. He later filed two postconviction motions that went nowhere. A third attempt in 2015, thirty years after the murder, gained attention when two local media outlets launched a series about the case. That investigation led to an interview with a juror who claimed she was initially a holdout at Jones's trial before becoming the last member of the panel to vote guilty. She insisted that, on the first day of deliberations, two jurors stated that Jones must be guilty because he was Black. A judge proceeded to grant Jones's third motion for a new trial, citing this evidence of racial bias as an element in the decision.

After thirty-two years behind bars, Jones left prison with the specter of a new trial looming large. Prosecutors inexplicably went through the rigmarole of another trial. The jury deliberated for just two hours before acquitting him in 2019.

Later chapters in this book explore the procedures used to introduce newly discovered evidence after conviction. For now, it's important to note how the litigation process failed Darrell Jones because it gave little chance to probe into the racially prejudiced atmosphere of the deliberation room. A 2017 United States Supreme Court case, *Peña-Rodriguez v. Colorado*, has made it easier to delve into allegations of racial bias among jurors right after trial.[23] In that case, a Colorado jury voted to convict a Latino defendant of harassment and unlawful sexual contact. The defense attorney visited the jury room immediately after the verdict and learned that a juror had exhibited anti-Latino bias during deliberations. The defense moved for a new trial based on that discovery. The trial judge rejected the claim, citing a Colorado evidence rule that generally prohibits jurors from disclosing what had transpired behind closed doors. The appellate courts affirmed; the state Supreme Court even relied on *Tanner* to support its reasoning.

The US Supreme Court disagreed and reversed the decision. The Court called racial bias "a familiar and recurring evil that, if left unaddressed, would risk systemic injury to the administration of justice" and held that judges should permit postverdict inquiry when there are credible reasons to think that "racial animus was a significant motivating factor in the juror's vote to convict." *Peña-Rodriguez* bodes well for future efforts to investigate whether racism has infested jury deliberations in certain cases. Still, we have a long way to go toward providing the means to unearth information about juror misconduct and a procedure to air it as early as possible.

———

TREATING JURY DELIBERATIONS AS SACRED IS ONE WAY THAT courts show deference to jurors and sometimes camouflage flawed outcomes. Jurors enjoy similar respect when courts entertain appellate challenges to the "sufficiency of the evidence" in a criminal case.

Although defendants may not bring in new evidence on direct appeal, they may take issue with the quality of the *old* evidence. Specifically, they may claim it didn't prove guilt beyond a reasonable doubt and seek reversal of their conviction on that ground, provided the issue was raised at trial and preserved for appellate review. A 1979 Supreme Court case, *Jackson v. Virginia*, explains how judges are supposed to review challenges to the sufficiency of the evidence after trial.[24] The Court announced in *Jackson* that the prosecution's case is legally sufficient, and the conviction may stand on appeal, if "any rational trier of fact could have found the essential elements of the crime charged beyond a reasonable doubt." Stated another way, as a subsequent Supreme Court opinion clarified, "it is the responsibility of the jury—not the court—to decide what conclusions should be drawn from evidence admitted at trial. A reviewing court may set aside the jury's verdict on the ground of insufficient evidence only if no rational trier of fact could have agreed with the jury."[25]

In addition to evaluating legal-sufficiency claims, appellate courts in some states possess the power to reverse a conviction—regardless of any preservation issues—if they find that the verdict went against the "weight" of the evidence.[26] This is a somewhat more forgiving standard that comes in handy for many defendants, especially if their trial attorney failed to preserve the legal-sufficiency claim.

The legal-sufficiency and weight-of-the-evidence inquiries differ slightly, but they share a fundamental driving principle: deference to jurors. They also show how reluctant appeals courts are to question jury assessments of the evidence.

Here's how one state distinguishes legal-sufficiency from weight-of-the-evidence claims.[27] The Ohio Court of Appeals has observed that a sufficiency analysis "requires us to view the evidence in a light most favorable to the prosecution and determine whether rational minds could have found each material element of an offense was proven beyond a reasonable doubt." In contrast, "review of a challenge to the manifest weight of the evidence is broader." The court cited another Ohio appellate decision to spell out what that entails: "The court, reviewing the entire record, weighs the evidence and all reasonable inferences, considers the credibility of witnesses and determines whether in resolving conflicts in the evidence, the jury clearly lost its way and created such a manifest miscarriage of justice that the conviction must be reversed and a new trial ordered. The discretionary power to grant a new trial should be exercised only in the exceptional case in which the evidence weighs heavily against the conviction."

Under the legal-sufficiency standard in Ohio, the trial evidence must be viewed "in *a light most favorable* to the prosecution," and the test asks whether "*rational minds* could have" reached the verdict (emphasis added throughout this discussion). By highlighting the government's spin on the evidence and looking to whether any rational mind could have found guilt, the pendulum on a legal-sufficiency claim swings initially and inexorably toward affirming the conviction on appeal.

A weight-of-the-evidence claim is "broader," permitting judges to review the entirety of the record, assess witness credibility, and act almost like a "thirteenth juror," as commentators have noted.[28] But this thirteenth juror is hamstrung in ways the original twelve were not. The pendulum swings, if not inexorably then steadily, toward upholding a conviction. An appeals court in Ohio can only overrule the verdict if it determines that "the jury *clearly* lost its way" and produced a "*manifest* miscarriage of justice." As if that language isn't strong enough, the court emphasized that reversing a case on weight-of-the-evidence review "should be exercised only in the *exceptional* case in which the evidence weighs *heavily* against the conviction." In acting as a thirteenth juror, an appeals court needs much more than reasonable doubt about guilt, much more than gaps in the government case. It needs craters. And those craters seldom appear on direct appeal.

The legal-sufficiency and weight-of-the-evidence tests both bend over backward to defer to the jury verdict. It's hard enough for appellate judges to measure the strength of the trial evidence in hindsight after a conviction. Applying such deferential standards to that task makes it nearly impossible for appeals courts to do the digging that could excavate wrongful convictions. A disturbing case from the Hudson River Valley shows this quite plainly.

———

FIFTEEN-YEAR-OLD ANGELA CORREA WAS FOUND DEAD IN A park in Peekskill, New York, on the morning of November 17, 1989.[29] She'd last been seen alive two days before, on November 15, and the medical examiner set the time of death between 3:30 and 4:30 that afternoon. The evidence suggested she'd been beaten, sexually assaulted, and strangled.

Investigators located three different hair specimens next to the body as well as a note from Angela to someone named "Freddy" dated "11/15/89." The police interviewed scores of Angela's high school classmates over the next two months. One of them was Freddy Claxton, the teen believed to be the intended recipient of the note. Claxton had an airtight alibi; he was playing basketball with four friends from the end of school on the fifteenth until well after the time of Angela's murder.

Another classmate didn't have an alibi. Jeff Deskovic wasn't close friends with Angela, or with many other classmates for that matter. But he was absent from school on the fifteenth, and people described him as inconsolable about her death, which seemed odd given how far removed he was from her inner circle. He attended all three of her wakes, teary-eyed and emotional. The police interviewed Deskovic multiple times, and they characterized his behavior during those conversations as bizarre. After one grueling interview in January 1990, Deskovic got into the fetal position under a table. Although the interrogation wasn't recorded, the police maintained that Deskovic said he "sometimes hears voices and they make [him do] things [he] shouldn't,'" and that he "realized" he may have committed the crime. That alleged confession led to his arrest and the filing of rape and murder charges against him.

Law enforcement continued to investigate. In March 1990, DNA test results *excluded* Deskovic as the source of the semen from Angela's rape kit. Other tests showed no connection between Deskovic and the hair follicles retrieved from the scene. Prosecutors nevertheless pushed on against Deskovic.

At trial, Westchester County prosecutors acknowledged the "wrinkles" generated by the forensic tests but advanced several, somewhat conflicting theories to smooth them out. First, the assistant district attorney claimed Deskovic had acted with an unknown male accomplice who'd left the biological evidence at the scene. Second, and paradoxically, the government suggested the sperm had been supplied by a boyfriend of Angela's, most likely Freddy Claxton, and that learning about that relationship had sent a jealous Deskovic on a murderous rampage.

These theories had major problems. The accomplice theory contradicted the core idea that Deskovic was a troubled loner with a crush on Angela; the consensual-partner theory didn't have any basis in fact. The police had traced Angela's movements on the fifteenth, and the timeline left little leeway for a clandestine sexual encounter. The prosecution intimated that she may have had sex *before* the fifteenth, and the semen had remained in her body, a dubious proposition that relied on the teenager's failure to bathe in the interim. Most notably, police interviews with her classmates revealed no evidence whatsoever that she was sexually active at the time or even engaged in a romantic relationship with anyone, much less Freddy Claxton.

The trial judge was wary of the accomplice theory, which prompted the prosecutor to withdraw his request to elaborate on it during closing argument. But that didn't stop him from doubling down on the consensual-partner theory. It became a pillar of his closing, in which he argued that "in all probability" the semen belonged to Freddy, effectively transforming the note into a love letter. Tying the semen to Claxton likely made sense to jurors; that hypothesis gave them a means to reconcile Deskovic's confession with the other evidence in the case. The jury found Deskovic guilty of rape and murder, and he was sentenced to fifteen years to life in prison.

The Appellate Division, Second Department, of New York unanimously affirmed the conviction on direct appeal in 1994. Its opinion rejected Deskovic's allegation that his conviction was based on legally insufficient evidence, observing that "overwhelming evidence of the defendant's guilt" supported the result. The Second Department made no mention of any mishaps by the prosecutor during closing argument. The bluntness of the opinion's final sentence, though, spoke volumes about how the court saw Deskovic's claims overall: "We have examined the defendant's remaining contentions and find them to be either unpreserved for appellate review or without merit."[30]

Twelve years later, science proved that Deskovic's plea of innocence had merit. The Innocence Project in New York City urged the newly elected district attorney in Westchester County to subject the remaining biological evidence to further tests and run those results through DNA databases. She agreed to do so in

2006, and the results produced a match to Steven Cunningham, a man in prison for strangling another woman to death. After the police confronted Cunningham with this information, he admitted that he'd acted alone in raping and killing Angela. By the time of his release from prison, Deskovic had spent more than half his life behind bars for a horrid crime he hadn't committed.

The Deskovic case illustrates how appellate courts sometimes overvalue evidence of guilt when looking back at a trial after a conviction. What the Appellate Division saw as "overwhelming evidence" turned out to be anything but. The inherent difficulty that appeals judges have in gauging the quality and quantity of trial evidence is magnified by the deference with which they treat jury verdicts. Instead of truly scrutinizing the evidence of guilt at trial, picking it apart and piecing it back together, appeals courts presuppose that jurors got it right. Appellate examination of the evidence presented at trial is often fast rather than fastidious—and far too often endorses jury decisions even if a careful assessment would give pause.

———————

APPELLATE COURTS' TREATMENT OF JURY DELIBERATIONS AND verdicts reveals a kind of deference not unlike the other types discussed in this chapter. When a case goes up on direct appeal, jurors, like judges and defense lawyers, receive the benefit of the doubt for their trial work, even if there's more than reasonable doubt about whether a wrongful conviction occurred.

By deferring to most decisions made by judges, defense lawyers, and jurors at trial, appellate courts show restraint. Although they're anointed superintendents of the court system, they serve more like hall monitors. Watch cases go up and down the litigation corridor. Glance at hall passes along the way. But hardly ever inspect those cases too closely to ensure accuracy. Only when a case fundamentally doesn't deserve to stand—the hall pass was illegally issued in contravention of clear policy—will appeals courts take corrective action. If the issuance involved the exercise of judgment, then the appellate body will let the case march on.

There are justifications for this deference. Harkening back to a theme from previous pages, the deference that appellate judges apply to review decisions by their trial counterparts, defense lawyers, and jurors promotes the finality of verdicts and the efficiency of the litigation process, yet with a populist twist. This norm makes trials the pivotal moment in the criminal process, avoids too much uncertainty in their wake, and underscores the value of civic participation in our democracy. That appellate judges so clearly and so often construct rules (or interpret rules foisted on them by the legislature) that acquiesce to trial-level actors suggests that something else is going on, something beyond finality and efficiency, even something beyond the judges' place in the litigation hierarchy and their perception of that place.

I'm convinced that collegiality and shared experience partially explain why deference is the default at the appellate level. Trial judges, appellate judges, prosecutors, and defense lawyers share membership in the state bar. They belong to the same club (and probably dine at the same clubs), which means appellate judges identify with their fellow lawyers. Most appeals judges are straight white men who have traveled a well-worn path to their august posts, serving as respected litigators and trial judges earlier in their careers. Studies show that a large proportion of them are former prosecutors.[31] When they look back on their journeys from their perch on the mountaintop, appeals judges may remember where they came from and feel empathy for their comrades in the trial trenches. They may also view jurors fondly as civic-minded people whose contributions are crucial to the legitimacy of the criminal justice process. They may have even served as jurors in their youth or at least understand how imperative it is for people to make the sacrifice of jury service.

Built over the span of decades, the compassion that appellate jurists may have for trial judges, defense attorneys, and jurors likely translates into deference. They identify with the decision makers more than with the people most affected by those decisions: criminal defendants. The journeys of appeals judges rarely, if ever, involve spending time in the state pen. As a consequence, they may struggle to relate to the defendants whose appeals percolate through their courthouses and for whom empathy is in short supply.[32] That enables them to presume the wisdom of choices made at the trial level while ignoring the impact of those choices on the innocent.

4

FOUL PLAY

The Harms of Harmless Error Analysis

IMAGINE THAT ON DIRECT APPEAL A CRIMINAL DEFENDANT SIDE-steps the potholes of preservation and deferential standards of review to show that an error occurred at trial. Maybe a prosecutor engaged in misconduct during closing argument, or the judge permitted the government to introduce explosive evidence that shouldn't have come in.

That's usually not enough to reverse a conviction on appeal. The defense must prove not only the presence of a significant error at trial, but also that the misstep affected the outcome. That means appellate courts affirm criminal convictions upon mere findings that, despite grievous mistakes at trial, the errors were "harmless" in the context of the whole case. This is known as the harmless error doctrine. It exists in some form in every American jurisdiction. And regardless of its name, the doctrine is far from harmless for wrongfully convicted prisoners.

LET'S BEGIN BY GETTING A HANDLE ON THE ORIGINS AND BASIC requirements of the harmless error test.[1] The concept wasn't part of the law we inherited from England. It emerged later on, in the nineteenth century, because of suspicions that too many defendants were gaining relief based on minor errors or, as we sometimes still hear today, "technicalities." Prior to the growth of the harmless error doctrine, almost any trial mistake created a presumption of prejudice on appeal and automatic reversal of the conviction. This approach may have worked in an age when court dockets were a manageable size; appellate tribunals could afford to incentivize litigants and trial judges to aim for perfection. The presumption-of-prejudice model became unwieldy, however, as criminal prosecutions soared and dockets bulged. In the 1800s, the media also began to sensationalize cases that had been reversed on technical grounds, like those granting new trials to convicted murderers due to misspellings in their indictments.[2]

The precise harmless error rule that an appellate court now employs in a case depends on several factors.[3] If the error violates the US Constitution, the harmless error test is quite defense friendly. That test comes from a 1967 Supreme Court opinion, *Chapman v. California*. In that case, the defendant in a state criminal trial invoked her Fifth Amendment privilege against self-incrimination and didn't take the stand.[4] During closing argument, the prosecutor violated the defendant's rights by referring repeatedly to how she chose to remain silent, insinuating that she had something to hide. On appeal, the California Supreme Court acknowledged that the defense had proven that the government had committed an error, but upheld the conviction because the error hadn't yielded a "miscarriage of justice." The United States Supreme Court reviewed the case and fired a salvo in favor of criminal defendants. It held that when a defendant shows on appeal that a constitutional violation occurred at trial, the state bears the heavy burden of proving the error was harmless beyond a reasonable doubt. *Chapman* indicated that appeals judges should ask whether the error "contributed" to the guilty verdict and only let those convictions stand when the answer is a resounding no. If the trial-level blunder doesn't involve the violation of a federal constitutional right, then jurisdictions may depart from *Chapman* and devise virtually any harmless error rule they see fit. In federal court, the inquiry is whether the nonconstitutional error had a "substantial" effect on the jury's verdict.[5]

There are many justifications for the harmless error doctrine. They go something like this: (1) the trial is the main event in the criminal litigation process; (2) mistakes are inevitable during the maelstrom of trial; and therefore (3) reversing a case solely because of an insignificant error is inefficient, elevates form over substance, fails to appreciate the reality of trial practice, and promotes trickery by defense lawyers who might treat trial, in the words of the Supreme Court, as "a game for sowing reversible error in the record."[6] These rationales resemble the "no harm, no foul" tenet noted in Chapter 3 with respect to claims of ineffective assistance of counsel. Appellate courts are encouraged to call out trial errors in their opinions yet toss a conviction only when they believe those errors affected the verdict. In theory, the harmless error concept advances fair play, substantive justice, and the primacy of the trial in resolving criminal disputes.

These rationales aren't entirely without virtue—and they make intuitive sense. Trials are conducted by humans. Like all things made by humans, errors are inevitable. Find me a pristine trial record and I'll find you a unicorn. Reversing cases due to a minuscule mistake, or even a few, would render the trial meaningless, waste scarce judicial resources, foster gamesmanship, and undermine public confidence in the whole enterprise of criminal justice. As the scholar and judge Roger Traynor wrote a half century ago, "Reversal for error, regardless of its effect on the judgment, encourages litigants to abuse the judicial process and bestirs the public to ridicule it."[7]

The problem is that harmless error analysis nowadays focuses less on whether the trial misstep contributed to the verdict and more on the overall evidence of guilt. That is, appellate judges ask not so much whether the error had a hand in the conviction, but whether the conviction would have nevertheless occurred without the error. If other evidence in the case strongly validates the guilty verdict, then courts will affirm the conviction. The phrase "overwhelming evidence of guilt" pops up in legions of appellate opinions, a surefire indicator that any trial errors will be branded harmless. Scholars have observed that a "guilt based approach to harmless error has taken hold in our courts," and in a large swath of cases guilt represents "the sole criterion by which harmlessness is gauged."[8]

The rise of this guilt-based approach to harmless error analysis is dangerous. It's as if appellate courts have decided to look at the evidence from criminal trials through a magnifying glass. All the evidence supporting guilt lies dead center in the frame, appearing larger than it really is and eclipsing the smattering of trial errors on the fringe. Constitutional errors may seem bigger than other mistakes out there on the edge. Even so, those errors seldom outshine the court's perception of the evidence of guilt in a case that the prosecution brought to trial and that resulted in a conviction. And evidence that registers as overwhelming from the appellate perspective may not be. Why?

As a practical matter, it's hard to pierce through the shell of a trial record and discern what, if anything, went wrong. The case comes to the appellate court in a tidy package of transcripts, reports, and briefs that conveys a simple message: criminal conviction inside. These voluminous documents may obscure gaps in the evidence and conceal the impact of any errors. And while it's difficult to gauge the effect of a sole mistake on the trajectory of a trial just by reading the transcript after conviction, it's easy to ascribe significance to evidence seemingly untouched by the error.

Think about the psychological factors at play when one looks at a case from the vantage point of an appeal. Cognitive psychologists have long studied something they label confirmation bias or expectancy bias.[9] It's more commonly known as tunnel vision. If you expect a particular outcome, then you tend to cherish information that supports that result and discount information that doesn't. You interpret data through the lens of your expectations. Appeals judges looking down at a conviction from their lofty post expect to see evidence supporting that result—proof beyond a reasonable doubt.

A psychological study undertaken at Stanford University stands out among the thousands that demonstrate the confirmation bias.[10] Researchers gathered a group of students with firm opinions about capital punishment. Half were opposed in principle while the others backed it. The subjects were asked to react to two academic studies. One study found that the death penalty deterred criminal activity; the other raised doubts about its effectiveness as a deterrent. Both were fictitious and included equally persuasive statistics. How did the students respond? Those that came into the experiment inclined to favor capital punishment rated the deterrence data as extremely credible and the antideterrence data as not. Death penalty opponents swapped that appraisal, lauding the antideterrence research and spurning the contrary claims. Researchers then asked the students once again about their views of the death penalty. The students were more entrenched in their original positions on the topic than before the experiment began.

The confirmation bias is often amplified when the result has *already* taken place, as in the case of appellate judges looking back at a criminal conviction. This is known in the psychological literature as the status quo bias, a phenomenon that explains the struggle people have in changing a decision once it's been made.[11] Lots of experiments show the status quo bias in action. They include studies that demonstrate how Budweiser drinkers stay loyal to their favored beverage even when blind taste tests prove they actually prefer beer produced by a rival brewery, and how Harvard University employees stick with their initial group health insurance plan although an alternative offering provides better coverage.[12] Appellate judges likewise may cling to a criminal conviction secured at trial even when objective data—glaring errors on the record—point to the need for a move from the status quo.

To be sure, it's easier to contemplate changing *someone else's* decision than one's own, and that's what appellate judges are being asked to do when reviewing a criminal conviction. Yet there are incentives to keep that decision intact too. Academics refer to this as the conformity effect: people are reluctant to alter the decisions of those they deem peers.[13] Judges sitting on an appellate bench have many reasons to view their trial colleagues in such a fashion. As noted in the previous chapter, they likely served as trial judges themselves before climbing up the ladder and may share a personal affinity for those who remain down below, an affinity forged through common experiences and frequent interactions. During my Utah days, I occasionally provided continuing legal education training for state court judges. These seminars took place in various resort hotels in the mountains, and my audience included members of the Utah Supreme Court, the Court of Appeals, and district trial courts in the same conference room. Between sessions, I enjoyed spying on their effortless banter and esprit de corps, knowing full well that some had much more power than others—even the power to overrule them. But that dynamic didn't seem to halt the flow of conversation or diminish the air of camaraderie. It must be tough to reverse a court decision made by a fellow judge with whom you've shared a cruller and an awkward laugh at a law professor's dad jokes.

The combined effect of these practical and psychological pressures is that appeals judges presume that convictions were obtained properly. That's part of their mandate, not to mention human nature. Just as we're all groomed to see things through the lens of our expectations, appeals judges may be primed to overvalue the evidence of guilt already generated in front of a trial-level counterpart and undervalue the impact of an error when reviewing a case on appeal. The harmless error doctrine offers an outlet, an ostensibly objective one at that, for this phenomenon to flourish.

———————

THE MOST DISTRESSING THING ABOUT THE HARMLESS ERROR doctrine is that its guilt-based approach lets wrongful convictions slip through the cracks because appellate courts misjudge the strength of the trial evidence. Data compiled by the Innocence Project in 2010 found sixty-three DNA exonerations where defendants had previously raised claims of prosecutorial misconduct on appeal or in a civil suit.[14] In thirty of those cases, courts found that the government had erred at trial. But judges reversed only thirteen of the cases and upheld the other seventeen on harmless error grounds. Wait a second. In seventeen of those cases, courts found the evidence of guilt at trial overwhelming, or at least weighty enough to classify the proven error as harmless. Yet the defendants in those seventeen cases were all later proven to be *actually innocent* through DNA testing, a postconviction wrecking ball that exposed how fragile these cases truly were and how harmful the harmless error doctrine can be.

I concede that without the DNA evidence these convictions may have looked strong on appeal, and that perhaps it's harsh to scold appellate judges for failing to recognize their weaknesses until science exposed them. But that is what's so scary. A trial transcript can be a costume that projects guilt to the outside world and disguises an actually innocent person, even from appeals courts tasked with taking a close look.

The effect of the harmless error doctrine on innocence cases is especially unnerving when you focus on misconduct during closing argument. Attorneys make their closings after the witnesses have testified and the evidence has been admitted, right before the judge instructs jurors on the law and they go to deliberate. The strict shackles of the trial process come off in this phase, as judges give advocates latitude to comment on the evidence. These final words have sway with jurors, especially those uttered by prosecutors because they carry the imprimatur of government approval. Prosecutors represent the voice of the people, unlike criminal defense attorneys, who may be perceived at best as the voice of a single person accused of crimes and at worst as a ventriloquist angling to stretch the truth to help a client.

Misconduct by prosecutors during closing argument often falls within several categories of "cardinal sins."[15] Prosecutors commit one of these sins when they

1. offer a personal opinion about the guilt of the defendant
2. express a view about the credibility of a witness, known as "vouching"
3. argue facts excluded from evidence or mischaracterize the evidence
4. make inflammatory statements designed to rouse jury passions, such as appeals to patriotism, public safety, or racial bias
5. comment on the defendant's refusal to testify
6. mock the defense attorney

These tactics can skew jury decisions because of their timing (just before jury deliberations) and their authoritative source (government prosecutors).[16] Consider the conduct of the prosecutor in the Jeff Deskovic case, discussed in the last chapter, in which a teenager was wrongfully convicted of a vicious rape-murder in Peekskill, New York. During closing argument, the prosecutor tried to explain away the presence of seminal fluid in the victim that didn't come from Deskovic. He attributed it to a consensual sexual encounter that the victim had engaged in with another boy, Freddy, even though there was no evidence to support that theory. The prosecutor's behavior appeared to violate one of the "cardinal sins," the prohibition against arguing facts not in evidence or misstating those that were.

Similar transgressions have happened at trial in many documented wrongful convictions, even if the judges entertaining the direct appeal seldom recognized the full impact of the errors on the verdict. The Innocence Project's 2010 report cited twenty-two cases at a minimum where, prior to being exonerated with DNA evidence, defendants had raised prosecutorial misconduct during closing argument as a legal issue in challenging their convictions. Courts had found, though, that none of those cases contained errors damaging enough to warrant a new trial. How can it be that the mistakes in those trials were harmless? The following case from Illinois affords a glimpse into how judges sometimes deploy the harmless error doctrine to uphold questionable convictions.

NINE-YEAR-OLD LISA CABASSA AND HER OLDER BROTHER, Ricky, were walking on the South Side of Chicago on the evening of January 14, 1976, when Lisa complained of a headache and went home.[17] Ricky couldn't find his sister after he returned to their house later that night. A frantic search resulted in the recovery of her body early the next morning in an alley several blocks away from the family home. She'd been beaten, raped, and murdered. The medical examiner hypothesized that more than one assailant had participated in the act.

An eyewitness soon came forward. She claimed that while she was going home from work on January 14, she saw two young men struggling with a girl whom she recognized as Lisa Cabassa. She also recognized one of the men, Michael Evans, who lived close to her. She didn't identify the other man right away, but later observed a lineup and picked out Paul Terry. Based on those identifications—by a single eyewitness who placed Evans and Terry with the victim roughly seven hours before she was found dead—prosecutors charged the suspects with murder and other crimes.[18]

Evans and Terry were tried jointly. As expected, prosecutors relied on the eyewitness's testimony at trial. She reiterated her identifications and added that Evans had tried to intimidate her from testifying. The defense undermined her account by showing discrepancies between her trial testimony and her prior statements as well as highlighting the possibility that the abduction occurred well before she left work and thus that she'd concocted her story.

The case then shifted to closing arguments. That's when things got ugly.

First, the prosecutor implied that Evans had a prior criminal record even though there was no evidence he'd ever even been arrested. The prosecutor stated that defense counsel "mentioned the passed [sic] conduct of Michael Evans, we are not able to go into that. It is considered prejudicial, we couldn't do it, it would be a mistrial, we can't do it. But why did he—." Defense counsel made an objection, which the trial court overruled. Second, the prosecutor fired off another barb during his closing, one that stung both Evans and Terry: "I don't ask for any sympathy. They tell you we are trying to poisen [sic] your minds by showing you the heinousness of the offense. You should have seen the evidence we kept out of this offense." The trial judge sustained an objection from the defense, but the prosecutor went on to tell the jury to ban sympathy and prejudice from their deliberations, and that their verdict should emerge after looking at all the evidence.

The jury found Evans and Terry guilty of murder along with other offenses. The judge sentenced them to a whopping two hundred to four hundred years in prison on the murder, with lesser sentences on the other charges.

On direct appeal, Evans and Terry claimed that the prosecutor's comments had deprived them of a fair trial. Comments like those made by the prosecutor at their trial are a matter of "special concern," according to the American Bar Association, because they tap into the belief that the government has vast investigative capacity and knows more about the facts than it lets on (or is allowed to let on).[19] Yet allegations of prosecutorial misconduct during closing argument are subject to a stringent harmless error analysis under Illinois law. Improper remarks usually "do not constitute reversible error unless they result in substantial prejudice to the accused" or represent "a material factor in the conviction." The test is "whether the jury would have reached a contrary verdict had the improper remarks not been made."

As to the statement about Evans's purported criminal record, his appellate lawyer insisted this test was satisfied. Counsel argued that given the closeness of the evidence in the case and the failure of the judge to caution the jury to disregard the comment, it's uncertain whether the jury would have convicted Evans without the error. The Illinois Appellate Court for the First District rejected that argument. It agreed that the prosecutor had engaged in misconduct, but noted that the comment was "isolated" and the prosecution didn't try to "exploit" it. The appeals court instead harped on the trial evidence of Evans's guilt to find the error harmless: "Defendant Evans had been positively identified by a witness who had known him as a neighbor. . . . There was also evidence that the defendant Evans threatened this witness. . . . In view of these circumstances, we are unable to say that the verdict would have been otherwise had the prosecutor's remarks not been made."

The appellate judges also downplayed the significance of the prosecutor's problematic comment about Evans and Terry: that the jury "should have seen all the evidence we kept out of this offense." The court mentioned that "while we find such a comment not based on the evidence to be improper, before it is sufficient to merit reversal it must be of substantial magnitude when viewed in light of the entire record and argument." The court found that the comment lacked "substantial magnitude." For one thing, the court cited that the remark arose after the defense claimed that the prosecution was trying to elicit an emotional response from jurors to compensate for the lack of evidence. For another, the appeals court emphasized that the trial judge sustained the objection to this comment and instructed the jury to ignore it.

The Illinois appellate court's analysis is troubling. The prosecutor's comments implied there was more to the story of Evans and Terry than the government was allowed to put forward, which may have reflected a devious effort to take advantage of the myth that courtroom "technicalities" help the accused. Plus, even if the trial judge ordered the jury to disregard one of the comments, such cautionary instructions can be ineffective. Research indicates that cautionary instructions may actually heighten juror awareness of a miscue and cause them to focus on it even more.[20]

The upshot of this harmless error analysis? Convictions affirmed. Even though the prosecution made several outrageous comments during the climax of Evans and Terry's trial—comments implying the government had damning evidence about Evans's past and about the crime itself that it couldn't present in court—the Illinois appellate court wrote them off as minor indiscretions in a case that, in its view, had substantial evidence of guilt.

That assessment didn't hold up.

Years later, an attorney with the Center on Wrongful Convictions in Chicago obtained DNA testing of the semen recovered from the crime victim. In 2002, those tests excluded Evans and Terry as the source and raised alarm bells about the integrity of the conviction. Evans and Terry were freed the next year after prosecutors dismissed the charges, more than a quarter century after they'd been wrongfully accused of raping and murdering a nine-year-old girl.

Prosecutorial misconduct during closing argument is just one example of trial errors that courts all too often brush off as harmless on direct appeal. Many other errors receive that treatment too. Even when *multiple* mistakes occur in a case and have a cumulative effect on the trial outcome, appellate judges are all too willing to belittle their impact and uphold shady convictions. A case from Ohio provides unique insight into how judges conceptualize harmless error.

———————

ONE EVENING IN DECEMBER 1981, A MAN STRANGLED BARBARA Russell to death in her Toledo home.[21] The man also committed several acts of sexual assault.

The murder victim's three children were in the apartment that night, a six-year-old boy and twin two-year-old girls. The boy, Jeffrey, said he was awakened by a loud noise and saw "Danny" enter the apartment. He then claimed to witness a heated argument between Danny and his mother before running to his room, hiding under his bed, and eventually falling back to sleep. A man named Danny Brown had been dating the victim for a few months. Jeffrey identified him in a photo lineup as the person who broke into the apartment on the night of his mother's murder.

A grand jury indicted Brown on murder charges based largely on Jeffrey's testimony. Brown's lawyers challenged Jeffrey's competency to testify at trial, but the judge found him sufficiently reliable to take the stand. In addition to describing the altercation between Danny and his mother, Jeffrey said that he had seen a second, unidentified man in the apartment before he scooted back to his room. The state did little to confirm the existence of this mysterious person. Jeffrey also recalled how Danny had walked through the apartment after the assault and placed a coat hanger around the neck of one of his sisters. Although the sister never testified at trial, the police officer who interviewed her did. He explained that the sister had corroborated Jeffrey's account of the coat hanger incident and claimed the man who had done it was named "Darnell," "Donnell," or "Daniel."

Brown put on an alibi defense. He even testified about his whereabouts that night, as did numerous other witnesses. In the end, the jury believed Jeffrey and found Brown guilty. He later received a life sentence.

Brown raised fifteen different claims of error on direct appeal of his conviction. They included allegations that the trial court shouldn't have ruled Jeffrey competent; that the court should have given the defense access to Jeffrey's grand jury testimony; that the prosecution improperly inquired about Brown's mental condition; and that the court allowed inadmissible hearsay to come into evidence. The Ohio Court of Appeals for the Sixth District, located in Toledo, determined that the lower court hadn't abused its discretion in finding Jeffrey competent. But it held that the judge and prosecutors erred in other respects: (1) the lower court should have reviewed the grand jury minutes to see whether Jeffrey's prior statements clashed with those at trial and gave the defense fodder to attack his credibility, (2) the prosecution went too far in asking multiple questions about Brown's "nerves," and (3) some of the hearsay let into evidence should have been kept out. Still, the appeals court found all these mistakes harmless, stating in its majority opinion that "no trial is perfect, and we reiterate our previous conclusions that errors did occur here. However, these errors related largely to collateral matters, and we conclude that they are harmless beyond a reasonable doubt."

One judge felt otherwise. Peter Handwork had recently joined the Court of Appeals. He wrote a dissenting opinion in the Brown case that rejected "the majority's operative premise . . . that reversal of a jury's verdict can be avoided by selective (but unspecific) reference to those portions of the record favorable to a 'harmless' or 'nonprejudicial' determination." Handwork wrote further that "an accused is not entitled to 'perfect' justice, whatever that may be, or even to an error-free trial. But he does enjoy the absolute right to be tried fairly—to a fair trial, which means: the proper enforcement of legal rules designed to achieve precisely that result." Handwork continued,

Since fairness is the essential characteristic of the American public trial process, errors infringing upon the fair adjudication of guilt and innocence are, without qualification, reversible errors. Yet, to recite ritualistically that the defendant "was not prejudiced or prevented from having a fair trial" because the record contains "other evidence" probative of guilt is merely to utter a non sequitur. That "other evidence" untainted by error may suggest guilt is irrelevant to determining whether acknowledged errors deprived the defendant of a fair trial. To maintain otherwise, simply does violence to any rational understanding of fairness.

Handwork summed up his views about his colleagues' majority opinion with a particularly astute observation: "an unfair trial is not made 'fair' because the jury found the defendant guilty and an appellate court, retrospectively, can rationalize it."

Handwork's dissent is reminiscent of the Supreme Court's 1967 ruling in *Chapman* that an error is not harmless if it contributed to the verdict. By focusing (often selectively) on other evidence of guilt produced at trial rather than the impact of a proven error on the fairness of the trial, appeals courts have taken the harmless error doctrine in an untenable direction. In the process they've indeed done "violence to any rational understanding of fairness."

From Danny Brown's perspective, the majority holding also did violence to his case. Brown wallowed in prison for years before Centurion Ministries, a New Jersey–based nonprofit, helped get DNA testing of the biological evidence from the crime scene. Those tests not only excluded Brown as the perpetrator, but also implicated a man named Sherman Preston, who was in prison for a similar killing. That other homicide had occurred in 1983, more than a year after the Russell murder and the same year the Ohio Court of Appeals issued its opinion in the Brown case.

The court granted Brown a new trial and ordered his release from prison in 2001. Prosecutors chose not to retry him and dismissed the charges. He filed a civil lawsuit the next year seeking damages for his wrongful conviction. The state fought off that claim, in part by insisting that Brown may have been with Preston in the apartment that night, apparently pegging its argument to Jeffrey's reference to a second man. This reference, conveniently, did not seem significant to police or prosecutors during their attempt to put Brown behind bars. Brown filed another lawsuit, which a judge dismissed in 2018 on the basis that the statute of limitations had passed.

In 2020, the Ohio Court of Appeals for the Sixth District named its renovated training and education room after Judge Handwork. He'd retired from the bench in 2013 after serving thirty years on the court, which was a record for an Ohio state judge at the time.[22] I find this very fitting. The jurist whose tutorial on the harmless error doctrine proved so insightful will forever be associated with education.

THE FLAWED TRIALS OF MICHAEL EVANS, PAUL TERRY, AND Danny Brown were propped up on direct appeal through misguided application of the harmless error doctrine. To echo Judge Handwork, in these cases appellate courts retrospectively rationalized unfair trials because they overvalued the jury verdict and any signs of guilt in the trial transcript. What struck appellate judges as overwhelming evidence of guilt was a mirage. For those three defendants, zealous advocacy and the availability of biological evidence later allowed DNA testing to expose the mirage for what it truly was: an optical illusion that concealed a profound injustice. Not every innocent prisoner thwarted by the harmless error doctrine enjoys such good fortune.

For all its infirmities, the harmless error test is worth saving. Picture a world without it. Appeals judges would have to reverse almost every conviction for one reason or another, and our courts are ill-equipped to handle a deluge of retrials. Defense lawyers would be motivated to plant or invite mistakes into the trial record to capitalize on an automatic-reversal regime. Prosecutors would have further incentives to tempt defendants, even innocent ones, to plead guilty to avoid the prospect of endless litigation. Public confidence in the criminal justice system is precarious enough without making the trial process a charade—or more of a charade than it already is.

Maybe we could salvage the best features of the harmless error test. Appellate judges haven't always used a guilt-based model that measures the trial error against the overall evidence of guilt. The Supreme Court essentially held in 1967 that (1) the violation of a federal constitutional right at trial is harmless only if it didn't *contribute* to the verdict and (2) the government bears the burden of proving that it didn't. Adopting this approach for both constitutional and nonconstitutional errors may be the way to go. It would divert appellate courts from the overall evidence of guilt in the record and reorient them toward the error itself. What impact did the mistake have? Did it contribute in any fashion to the verdict? Could it have unfairly marred the trial? On appeal, if the prosecution fails to prove that the error didn't contribute to the verdict, then the appeals court must grant relief to the defendant.

Let's speculate about how the Brown appeal might have played out with this kind of harmless error test. At trial, the government's case hinged on the credibility of six-year-old Jeffrey. Impeaching his testimony lay at the core of the defense strategy. Depriving Brown of access to previous statements by Jeffrey that could show inconsistencies in his account made it harder for the defense to develop its impeachment angle. To worsen matters, casting aspersions on Brown's mental health enabled the prosecution to demonize the defendant in a case with grim facts as it was. To say these errors didn't contribute to some degree to Brown's conviction is far-fetched. Had the appellate court employed a harmless error test that focused on the impact of the errors on the trial rather than the quantity of unrelated evidence of guilt, Brown might have been vindicated years before DNA did the trick. As might scores of other wrongfully convicted prisoners, including Michael Evans and Paul Terry.

One consequence of altering the harmless error test along the lines I propose is that some guilty prisoners will benefit from it. In fact, I'm not entirely convinced Danny Brown is innocent—that he wasn't the "second" man allegedly present in the apartment on the night of the Russell murder. But I am convinced Brown had an unfair trial. Even if this revised approach to harmless error would topple the convictions of some guilty inmates, prosecutors could retry them. If they are subsequently acquitted after a fair retrial, that's a price we should be willing to pay for an equitable justice system. And one that will inspire prosecutors to follow the rules when they first go to trial.

The harmless error principle has made innocent prisoners collateral damage of the appellate process for far too long. It's time to defuse the doctrine.

———

PART I OF THIS BOOK HAS CATALOGUED THE LITANY OF PROCE-dural barriers that innocent prisoners must circumvent to obtain justice on direct appeal. The presumption of innocence fades away with a criminal conviction, replaced by one of guilt. For many reasons, that newly installed presumption is incredibly hard to budge or, in legalese, to rebut.

When appealing their convictions, defendants are confined to issues from the trial record, to what transpired in the courtroom, and may not bring up anything new or extraneous. Also, not every legal issue that cropped up at trial is deemed proper for appellate review; the higher court will only look at those that were adequately vetted or "preserved" down below. Even then, the product of any issues that were preserved at trial, say, a judge's decision to admit incendiary evidence against the accused, receives tremendous deference by the appellate tribunal—so much deference that decisions made by trial judges, defense lawyers, and jurors are almost irrevocable. Finally, assume a defendant manages to persuade an appellate court that a mistake happened at trial, and that it was both preserved and glaring enough to overcome the deference ordinarily applied to it. Proving the existence of a legal error at trial is insufficient to reverse many wrongful convictions because of the harmless error doctrine, a principle used by appeals judges to discount the impact of trial missteps and maintain the status quo.

Like Sisyphus, defendants strain under the weight of pushing claims of legal error up the appellate hill. The direct appellate process is simply an unforgiving environment for reversing criminal convictions, even those with legitimate questions about innocence. Its terrain is marked by steep ascents and deep valleys that exacerbate the inherent difficulty in reversing the presumption of guilt that forms after conviction—no matter whether a defendant follows the appellate road map by presenting only compelling, preserved issues for review.

Luckily, the direct appeal is not the only landscape that innocent prisoners may travel through in seeking to overturn their convictions. They may pursue what are called postconviction remedies, procedures like the ancient writs of habeas corpus and coram nobis, which are seemingly more hospitable to credible innocence claims. Part II of this book shows, though, that these remedies nevertheless impose nearly insurmountable procedural obstacles in front of those striving to move innocence claims forward.

PART II
POSTCONVICTION MATTERS

5

THE NOT-SO-GREAT WRIT

*Habeas Corpus and the Illusion of
Robust Collateral Review*

IN 1993, LEONEL HERRERA WAS ON THE BRINK OF EXECUTION
for killing two law enforcement officers twelve years before.
Here's what put him on death row.[1]

Late one night in 1981, a passerby came upon the dead body
of Texas Department of Public Safety officer David Rucker along
a highway in the Rio Grande Valley. Around the same time, local
police officer Enrique Carrisalez stopped a speeding car a few
miles away from the corpse's location. The driver exchanged a
few words with the officer, then fired a bullet into his chest. Plenty
of evidence linked Herrera to both crimes:

- Before he died nine days later, from wounds sustained in
  the shooting, Officer Carrisalez identified Herrera as the
  assailant.
- A man riding with Carrisalez also identified Herrera and
  noted that he had been the only occupant of the car.

- A license plate check revealed that the car was registered to Herrera's girlfriend.
- Herrera's Social Security card was found next to the patrol car of Rucker, the public safety officer murdered earlier in the evening.
- Blood splatter on the vehicle, Herrera's blue jeans, and his wallet was of the same type as Rucker's.
- A handwritten letter in Herrera's possession implied he'd killed the public safety officer.

Leonel Herrera was convicted of the murders and sentenced to death in 1982.

Years later, his defense team assembled affidavits stating that Herrera's brother, Raul, who was no longer alive, had perpetrated the murders. Those affidavits included one from Raul's former attorney, describing how his client had confessed to the double homicide, as well as another from Raul's son, in which he claimed to have witnessed his father shoot the officers.

But Leonel Herrera hadn't compiled this new evidence in time to present it to his trial judge within thirty days of his conviction, as required for a motion for a new trial in Texas. Plus, he'd wrapped up his direct appeals in the state court system, with the Texas Court of Criminal Appeals denying relief. A criminal defendant like Herrera is deemed to have "exhausted" his direct appeals after he's lost in the appellate court with jurisdiction over his trial and then the state's highest court has either declined to examine the case further or reviewed and rejected the defendant's claims. Not that the direct appeal would have helped Herrera much anyway since litigants are barred from introducing new evidence through that process.

The main way to get back into court at this late stage, more than a decade after trial, is to pursue collateral or "postconviction" remedies. These litigation options attack the conviction indirectly, often with new arguments or new evidence, rather than launching a targeted challenge to exactly what happened in the trial court, which is the purpose of the direct appeal. One of those collateral remedies is a petition for a writ of habeas corpus. Herrera had already filed habeas petitions in both state and federal court without success. Now he wanted to dip his toes into that federal well one more time to see whether courts would recognize a claim of actual innocence in a habeas action.

Even casual observers of the criminal justice system may be familiar with the writ of habeas corpus, an ancient postconviction remedy borrowed from England. A writ is a formal legal action from a court ordering a person to do or to cease doing something. A habeas corpus filing asks government officials to justify why they "have the body" in custody. If no sound reason surfaces, the court may issue a writ to release that person.[2]

The "Great Writ" of habeas corpus was a fixture of early American law. It's even enshrined in the United States Constitution, which commands that "the Privilege of the Writ of Habeas Corpus shall not be suspended, unless when in Cases of Rebellion or Invasion the public Safety may require it."[3] Congress and many state legislatures have transformed the writ from a "common law" cause of action determined by judges on a case-by-case basis to a statutory remedy that's carefully delineated in the legal procedures of the jurisdiction.

Habeas corpus plays a variety of roles in righting perceived wrongs, including when the government has detained someone unlawfully *prior* to trial. The well-known Guantanamo Bay cases show how it can be used to litigate these claims.[4] A week after hijacked airplanes struck the Twin Towers on September 11, 2001, Congress bestowed President George W. Bush with the power to "use all necessary and appropriate force" against those he thought had aided the attacks. The Bush administration interpreted this as go-ahead to detain suspected terrorists at numerous facilities around the world. A detention center in Guantanamo Bay, off the coast of Cuba, at one point housed more than eight hundred "enemy combatants" from forty-two countries. They were kept under lock and key, were interrogated relentlessly, and suffered human rights abuses. Few were ever charged with crimes. An open question during much of that period was whether the detainees could use habeas corpus to force the government to justify this type of prolonged detention, or if the "War on Terror" gave the federal government carte blanche to suspend the writ. In 2008, the Supreme Court ruled in *Boumediene v. Bush* that detainees could utilize habeas.[5]

Prisoners also draw on habeas corpus to attack a criminal conviction *after* the exhaustion of the direct appeal, as in Herrera's case. Habeas filings in the postconviction setting are treated as new civil proceedings, not criminal ones, and normally go to a trial judge in the region where the defendant is imprisoned. There's no guaranteed right to an attorney in a habeas action, so prisoners without the resources to hire a lawyer often litigate their claims pro se, which is the term used for acting without legal representation. These filings occur not only in many state courts to challenge state convictions but also in federal courts to take on both federal *and* state convictions. Seeking habeas corpus at the federal level is perhaps the most popular and significant postconviction remedy available to criminal defendants.

The very notion of federal habeas corpus review of state convictions is controversial. On the one hand, there's a strong interest in a courteous relationship (or comity, in legal parlance) between federal and state governments, a mutual respect that acknowledges the legitimacy and finality of one another's judicial decisions. Permitting federal review of state convictions can chip away at that relationship. On the other hand, the capacity of federal courts to vet state convictions is a critical feature of our national design. It's a method of ensuring that states don't go below the federal constitutional floor established as the "Supreme Law of the Land" and that there are baseline standards of justice in all fifty states.[6] In its purest form, a federal habeas corpus action values state sovereignty yet protects against injustices. It's a delicate remedy to test the validity of convictions after the direct appeal and to hold state governments accountable.

That may all sound lovely, but in truth habeas corpus is a poor vehicle for overturning wrongful convictions in either federal or state court. Its original purpose in the United States was to correct jurisdictional defects, such as if a case was tried in the wrong court. In the nineteenth century, habeas became a tool to tackle constitutional issues as well.[7] Courts were reluctant to extend its reach beyond those narrow categories. Factual issues were considered the province of trials; it struck many jurists as impertinent (to the trial judge) and inefficient (for all parties) to wrestle with the fundamental question of guilt or innocence during habeas review.

That vision of habeas corpus has endured. The Iowa Supreme Court refused to consider a habeas action grounded in new evidence of innocence back in 1917, proclaiming "we are not yet ready to make so radical a venture."[8] Nearly a half century later, the Oregon Supreme Court was not yet poised to make so radical a venture either. It declared that "*habeas corpus* (or its statutory counterpart in post-conviction proceedings) does not provide relief from a conviction resulting from a mistake of fact, where proof of the jury's mistake must depend on the credibility of newly discovered evidence."[9]

At the time that Leonel Herrera submitted his second federal habeas corpus filing to a trial judge, the United States Supreme Court had not yet fully answered the "radical" question of whether a judge's habeas jurisdiction covered issues based on newly discovered evidence of innocence. That was about to change. After Herrera lost in the lower federal courts, the Supreme Court agreed to hear his case and clarify whether factual claims of innocence standing alone could be reviewed by judges in a habeas corpus petition and supply the basis for relief.

In its 1993 *Herrera* decision, the Supreme Court reiterated the classic formulation of habeas corpus. It declared, "Federal habeas courts do not sit to correct errors of fact, but to ensure that individuals are not imprisoned in violation of the Constitution." The Court noted that an actual innocence claim could be reviewed by a court in a habeas action if it was paired with a constitutional claim. The Court even indicated that an innocence claim could serve as a "gateway" to reopen habeas review of a constitutional claim that was procedurally barred, maybe because it had been filed in untimely fashion, strategically withheld from an earlier petition, or not exhausted in state court.[10] But the Court wasn't willing to go further. It suggested that a freestanding or "bare" actual innocence claim is generally *not* recognizable in a habeas action, and that seeking clemency from the governor is the proper route in those situations.

In other words, Leonel Herrera wouldn't get another day in court.

Four months after the Supreme Court chimed in, Texas executed Herrera by lethal injection. His final statement was "I am an innocent man and something very wrong is taking place tonight."

Whether Herrera was innocent is unknown and probably unknowable. What we do know is that he was denied the chance to go before a federal judge and fully present newfound evidence pointing to his brother's involvement. Was the evidence credible or just a last-ditch effort to pin the crimes on a dead man? Again, we'll never find out. But we should have tried to answer those questions through a robust habeas review back when it mattered in 1993. It was "very wrong" to execute Herrera without a more thorough process.

———

AS THE *HERRERA* CASE MAKES PLAIN, A CLAIM OF ACTUAL INNOcence based on newly discovered evidence alone is typically not enough for federal habeas review. Instead, such a claim must be combined with an assertion of constitutional or jurisdictional defect to get the filing heard by a federal judge. The Supreme Court acknowledged in *Herrera* that under other circumstances, "a truly persuasive demonstration of 'actual innocence' made after trial" could make it unconstitutional to execute the defendant and merit "federal habeas relief if there were no state avenue open to process such a claim." The Court emphasized that the bar for showing such a persuasive demonstration "would necessarily be extraordinarily high." In the nearly thirty years since the issuance of *Herrera*, the Supreme Court has not found a single case compelling enough to pass this threshold. The chances that any death row inmate with a freestanding innocence claim will clear this bar are low, let alone any case outside the capital punishment context.[11]

After *Herrera*, it's fair to say that federal courts had their hands tied if they wanted to grapple with actual innocence claims in a habeas petition. Their hands were tied even more tightly three years later, when Congress implemented the 1996 Antiterrorism and Effective Death Penalty Act (AEDPA) to close what some perceived as loopholes in federal habeas that aided guilty defendants.[12] State prisoners aiming to file a habeas corpus action in federal court must now overcome an array of obstacles that deserve a brief primer:

- *Time limits.* A rigid statute of limitations requires prisoners to submit their habeas petition within one year after the completion of the direct appeal. This deadline may be extended if the inmate wants to litigate a constitutional claim based on new evidence—say, revelations about improprieties in the jury room, or trial attorney misadventures. Yet applicants still have only a year to raise the claim from the moment they learned or should have learned about the new information.
- *Effectively one shot.* The AEDPA also enacted a rule that dissuades inmates from filing multiple or "successive" petitions. If the initial habeas filing is denied, the

prisoner may try to submit another one down the road, as Leonel Herrera did. Inmates often try to file additional federal habeas petitions long after the direct appeal, especially if they've lost a *state* postconviction motion (a topic for the next chapter). Ever since the passage of the AEDPA, petitioners must seek permission from the federal Circuit Court of Appeals in the region before a judge will review a successive habeas petition. That gatekeeping decision—about whether to grant a defendant another bite at the habeas apple—is unreviewable.

- *Exhaustion strictly defined.* To get habeas review, a prisoner must have exhausted his direct appellate remedies not only procedurally (his case has gone through the right stages in state court), but also substantively (those courts had a chance to consider the exact claims in the habeas filing). To be precise, before going to federal court for habeas relief, an inmate must have given the state courts a "fair opportunity" to resolve the specific legal issues the prisoner intends to raise. A fair opportunity means the state's highest court has considered and rejected the claims on the merits, declined to decide the issues on the merits, or otherwise had a full chance to determine those issues before the prisoner may switch to federal court. The same rule in essence applies when filing a successive federal habeas petition to challenge the outcome of state postconviction litigation.

- *Deference to state courts.* A federal court in a habeas corpus action must display exceptional deference to state judges when reviewing their rulings. If the prisoner is raising a question of pure law, for example, the federal court may not grant habeas relief for any claims addressed by the state courts unless those state decisions were contrary to, or involved an unreasonable application of, "clearly established federal law, as determined by the Supreme Court." Very few legal issues are "clearly established." The practical effect of this rule is to ban state prisoners from federal habeas relief even for flawed state court decisions about violations of federal constitutional rights, so long as those violations were not clearly established—that is, explicitly spelled out in Supreme Court case law.

- *Summary dispositions.* The AEDPA made it much harder for federal courts to order evidentiary hearings on a prisoner's habeas petition. Rather, it authorized judges to deny petitions "summarily," on the papers alone, without any scrutiny of the evidence or live witnesses in open court.

- *Obstacles to appeal.* Finally, to contest a federal judge's denial of habeas relief, the prisoner must apply for a Certificate of Appealability, which will be awarded if the applicant can make a "substantial showing of the denial of a constitutional right." Only with a certificate in tow may the prisoner file an appeal.

These procedures exalt finality and efficiency over fairness, and they impede prisoners in litigating issues through federal habeas corpus. A 2007 study of habeas outcomes in the decade after the passage of the AEDPA looked at a random sample of 2,384 petitions in cases that didn't involve the death penalty.[13] Of those filings, only 7 defendants ultimately earned relief, or 1 of every 341 cases. Courts were reticent even to conduct evidentiary hearings, and took that step in just 9 cases from the sample.

In the years since the AEDPA became law, the Supreme Court has built upon *Herrera* to clarify that a claim of actual innocence in a federal habeas action can continue to work as a gateway to bypass some of the amendment's most onerous procedural barriers.[14] Just the same, these procedures hinder many prisoners who are seeking to prove their innocence.

To see how the procedures operate in practice, let's go back to Jeff Deskovic's case from Chapter 3: his journey from arrest for a brutal 1989 rape-murder in Peekskill, New York, to conviction after trial, and eventual exoneration in 2006. Nine years before DNA freed him, he had a chance to challenge his conviction through federal habeas corpus.[15] The filing deadline was April 24, 1997. As the date neared, his attorney contacted the court clerk to verify the correct submission procedure. The clerk assured the lawyer the petition would be considered "filed" as of the date of mailing, as opposed to the date of receipt. So the attorney put the final touches on the document and mailed it in on April 24. It arrived at the court for processing on April 28.

It turned out the clerk screwed up. Prior case law required actual receipt of a habeas application on or before the pertinent deadline, which prompted a federal judge to dismiss Deskovic's habeas petition as untimely without ever reaching the merits of his claims. On appeal, a panel of federal judges from the Second Circuit Court of Appeals—a trio that featured future Supreme Court Justice Sonia Sotomayor—evaluated Deskovic's request for an exemption to the stiff limitations period. He sought this exemption under a doctrine known as "equitable tolling" on the grounds that his counsel relied in good faith on the advice of the clerk and that the statute of limitations should be suspended (or tolled) as a matter of simple equity. The Second Circuit rejected that argument out of hand: "Attorneys' failure to comply with statutes of limitations due to their own neglect is no basis for equitable tolling." Likewise, the court stated that it was "unpersuaded that equitable tolling is appropriate based on Deskovic's contentions that the four-day delay did not prejudice [the government], petitioner himself did not create the delay, his situation is unique, and his petition has substantive merit." Actually, Deskovic's situation *was* unique, his case *had* substantive merit, and the four-day delay here paled in comparison to the yearslong lag in justice being served.

Some innocent prisoners fare better than Jeff Deskovic and, despite not following procedures to a tee, get their constitutional claims heard by a federal court through the gateway established in *Herrera*. On rare occasions, an innocent prisoner navigates these roadblocks and earns habeas relief. But that outcome usually occurs when the court detects a constitutional violation rather than actual innocence.[16] Most innocent inmates aren't so lucky, even if they manage to convince a federal court to review their habeas claims. This happened to a Wisconsin woman convicted of an awful crime.

———————

AUDREY EDMUNDS WAS A STAY-AT-HOME MOTHER WHO OFTEN babysat for other families in her suburban enclave outside Madison.[17] On October 16, 1995, a neighbor handed off her seven-month-old daughter, Natalie, to Edmunds. Natalie was in a fussy mood. Edmunds left the baby with a bottle of milk in the bedroom, but when she returned a half hour later, Natalie seemed to be choking and didn't respond to efforts to revive her. Edmunds called 911. The paramedics arrived, only to find Natalie with dilated pupils and labored breathing. She soon stopped breathing and never regained consciousness.

After an autopsy revealed that Natalie had extensive brain damage, a forensic pathologist concluded that the cause of death was something known as shaken baby syndrome (SBS). A theory first developed in 1971, SBS refers to a phenomenon in which a person shakes an infant with such ferocity that the brain rotates within the skull, generating severe internal damage without any external signs of suffering. A diagnosis of SBS traditionally involved three symptoms—brain swelling, brain hemorrhaging, and retinal hemorrhaging. When these symptoms appeared in a case that otherwise lacked any outward marks of trauma, it was assumed that someone had violently shaken the child. Adherents to SBS theory believed that no other pathology or accident could cause this "triad" of symptoms to emerge simultaneously. They also thought the fatal consequences arose immediately: that the last person who handled the physical care of the infant *must* have produced the injuries.

This didn't augur well for Edmunds. In March 1996, prosecutors charged her with murder.

At trial, the prosecution relied on the testimony of medical experts who called Natalie's death a hallmark SBS case, insisting that the child must have died shortly after the infliction of the injuries. Yet Natalie's medical records included dozens of past trips to the doctor. Just days before her death, Natalie's parents had taken her in because of lethargy, vomiting, and irritability, which could indicate a brain injury. Prosecutors and their experts shrugged off this medical history. Instead, they stuck with their argument that Natalie had died from violent shaking on October 16 rather than from any preexisting condition.

Defense counsel could find only a single expert, a pediatric neurologist, willing to testify that the death could have stemmed from injuries acquired before Edmunds had custody of Natalie. The defense argued that one or both of Natalie's parents, most likely her father, had caused the injuries that led to her death. To substantiate this theory, Edmunds put forth evidence that the father was plagued by migraines, Natalie's grouchiness and health issues added to his stress, and he'd been alone with his daughter for nearly an hour on the evening before she died. A number of Edmunds's friends and neighbors testified about her good character, patience, and caretaking ability. The jury, unconvinced by those endorsements, found Edmunds guilty in November 1996. The judge later sentenced her to a prison term of eighteen years.

Edmunds went through the maze of Wisconsin's direct appellate and postconviction remedies, losing at every turn. She eventually set her sights on federal court. Her habeas corpus petition claimed that the state trial court had deprived Edmunds of her federal constitutional right to present a defense when it barred her from introducing testimony about the demeanor of Natalie's parents on the day their child died. Specifically, the state judge had excluded evidence from the following three witnesses:

1. a helicopter pilot who flew Natalie to the hospital and saw the parents walking in the hospital parking lot, without any apparent distress or emotion, and later talking with an "odd" absence of panic in their voices
2. a police officer who spoke with the parents and thought the father came across as "nervous" and "fidgety"
3. a chaplain who met with the parents twice that day and felt they exhibited "a guarded demeanor, showing very limited expression of grief," and that the father had seemed afraid to enter Natalie's hospital room. He also observed that the father stood a few feet behind his wife in the hospital room with his hands in his pockets, and then left while his wife stayed.

The state trial judge had rejected this evidence on the basis that "absent someone who has the expertise to interpret reactions, I don't think the observations have any probative value." Edmunds had raised this constitutional issue—that the right to present a defense should sometimes take precedence over the rules of evidence—throughout the state litigation. But the state courts hadn't tackled the issue head-on in the appellate and postconviction process, treating it as a matter of evidence law over which trial judges exercise discretion.

The federal judge assigned to Edmunds's habeas petition wasn't inclined to tackle it either and denied relief without even holding an evidentiary hearing. Edmunds sought review of the case in the federal Seventh Circuit Court of Appeals, where a three-judge panel affirmed the lower court decision in 2002.

Richard Posner, a well-known judge once short-listed for the Supreme Court, wrote the appellate opinion. He cited the rule enacted by the AEDPA that allows federal judges to reverse state court decisions only if those rulings contain an "unreasonable application" of "clearly established" federal law. In his characteristically flowery prose, Judge Posner asked whether "it would be an unreasonable curtailment of a criminal defendant's constitutional right to put on a defense for a judge to forbid the defendant's lawyer to draw attention to aspects of demeanor that the lawyer thought undermined the adverse witness's testimony." To translate: Was it unreasonable under clear federal law for the Wisconsin trial judge to cut Edmunds off at the pass by excluding evidence that signaled the parents' guilt? Here's how Posner answered that question:

> We cannot find a case on the point, but perhaps only because the suggestion is too outré to have been litigated. The demeanor evidence at issue in this case . . . presupposes a benchmark consisting of "normal" behavior in the face of a shocking incident. Is it true that a "normal" (and innocent) father in the situation of Natalie's father would have strode unhesitatingly into Natalie's hospital room? Would not have kept his hands in his pocket? Would have walked at an abnormal pace in the parking lot? Would have had panic in his voice yet would have been neither nervous nor fidgety? Maybe so; but these propositions, and the others necessary to show that one or both parents manifested lack of grief and consciousness of guilt, are not so obvious that a judge who like [Edmunds's trial judge] thought them devoid of probative value could be thought unreasonable, though again we cannot find a case on the point, let alone a U.S. Supreme Court case—which cannot however help Edmunds.

That answer reveals a lot about the shortcomings of federal habeas corpus. If there isn't a Supreme Court case directly on point that suggests a state trial judge's decision was unreasonable, the ruling will stand regardless of qualms about its overall wisdom or the integrity of the conviction.

The Wisconsin Innocence Project took over Edmunds's case in 2003, a year after Judge Posner's devastating opinion. Despite the federal habeas setback, her new lawyers saw a sliver of hope. Wisconsin has a state postconviction remedy that, like those discussed in the next chapter, permits defendants to present new evidence that casts doubt on the accuracy of the conviction.[18] Recent medical research questioned the validity of the SBS hypothesis. Some experts found it physically impossible for shaking alone to produce such severe brain injuries without visible damage to the spine or skull. Evidence had also materialized that the triad of symptoms long associated with SBS could have other root causes, among them a fall from a short height or birth trauma. Finally, the latest science disputed the notion that an infant experiencing these symptoms would become unresponsive right away.

This new research provoked the forensic pathologist who'd conducted Natalie's autopsy to have a change of heart. He testified in a state postconviction hearing in 2007 that he no longer thought she'd necessarily died shortly after sustaining her injuries and that she may have incurred them earlier. Five other doctors testified on Edmunds's behalf that the available evidence couldn't pinpoint the cause or timing of the injuries with any accuracy. Even though the trial judge denied Edmunds's motion for a new trial, the Wisconsin Court of Appeals disagreed and ordered a new trial. Edmunds was released on bond in 2008. Later that year the prosecution dismissed all charges.

Audrey Edmunds is in select company as one of very few female exonerees. Women represent only about 9 percent of exonerations since 1989.[19] This tiny number is attributable in part to the fact that women aren't typically convicted of the kinds of crimes (rape and murder) in which the perpetrator leaves biological material at the crime scene that's suitable for DNA testing. As of 2020, only eleven women had been freed through DNA.

The data also show that about 40 percent of the crimes that innocent women are convicted of relate to incidents where children or loved ones in their care are injured. Tragic accidents are misconstrued as intentional or reckless behavior by women who've violated society's gendered (and dated) vision of their fundamental role as caretakers.[20]

In addition to revealing how sexism and misogyny can infiltrate the prosecution of women accused of crimes, the Edmunds case illustrates the failings of federal habeas corpus. A federal judge denied relief without a hearing, a panel of three federal judges affirmed that decision unanimously on appeal, and Audrey Edmunds stayed in prison for nearly six more years before the Wisconsin Innocence Project went back to state court to overturn her case.

———

GETTING AN EVIDENTIARY HEARING IS A CRUCIAL STEP TOWARD federal habeas relief—and one that Audrey Edmunds wasn't allowed to take. But it doesn't guarantee success, as the experience of my former client Fernando Bermudez reveals all too clearly.[21]

Bermudez's case began in 1991 with an altercation between some Latino and Black teenagers at a Manhattan nightclub. One of the Black teens socked a Latino youth named Shorty. Aggrieved by this affront, Shorty approached a man and pointed out his assailant, Raymond Blount. The skirmish spilled onto the street, where Shorty again indicated to the man that Blount had battered him. The man shot and killed Blount before fleeing.

The police soon identified Shorty as Ephraim Lopez, a sixteen-year-old New Yorker of Puerto Rican descent. It was harder to figure out the identity of the shooter. The police let five eyewitnesses work together to sort through photographs of suspects and share notes. After a while, they landed on a picture of Fernando Bermudez, a Dominican man nicknamed Most.

The subsequent police interrogation of Lopez failed to prove Bermudez's involvement whatsoever. Lopez denied knowing anyone called Most. On the contrary, he said that the shooter was an acquaintance from his neighborhood who went by Lou, Luis, or Woolu, a spin on the term "wools" that was widely used at the time to refer to crack cocaine packaged in cigarette form. Yet prosecutors offered Lopez a deal. If he cooperated in the case against Bermudez, he'd be immune from any charges stemming from the murder.

So Lopez changed his tune at trial. He identified Bermudez as the "Woolu" who killed Blount and insisted he didn't know the culprit's real name. The defense was none the wiser because the prosecution hadn't disclosed Lopez's previous statements about "Luis" or "Lou" until the eve of trial. Even then, those references were buried under mounds of other discovery material. Lopez's trial testimony meshed with that of the eyewitnesses to strengthen the prosecution case, leading the jury to find Bermudez guilty of murder.

A series of lawyers championed Bermudez's cause in the years that followed and uncovered some amazing things. They learned that Luis Munoz—a Puerto Rican man who lived near Lopez's grandmother, resembled Bermudez, and went by Woolu—had skipped town shortly after the shooting and wound up in Kentucky. They learned that the police had pressured the eyewitnesses to identify Bermudez, and that those witnesses wanted to recant their testimony under oath. And they learned that Lopez wished to make amends for his lies against Bermudez. The Second Look Program at Brooklyn Law School joined forces with a talented solo practitioner to take the baton from those who'd done the real legwork and run with the case. We took it all the way to the federal courthouse in lower Manhattan, where a magistrate judge granted our request for an evidentiary hearing on our habeas corpus petition.

We were ecstatic. Not only had a federal judge seen fit to hold a habeas hearing more than a decade after trial, but the judge also had the ideal pedigree.[22] He had previously practiced law at the Legal Aid Society. Based on that profile, we thought he might be receptive to our arguments.

Over the course of the multiday hearing, we put our witnesses through their paces, including Shorty Lopez, who repudiated his trial testimony. I became increasingly optimistic. During a break one day, I told our client I had a good feeling about how the case was going. Even today, that memory makes me cringe. The judge denied our petition, stopping our run at federal habeas relief short of the finish line in 2004.

Mercifully, another team of attorneys took over and helped overturn Bermudez's conviction through a state postconviction remedy in 2009, five long years after our habeas defeat.[23] A few months after the exoneration, I was giving a talk at a conference in Atlanta when I noticed a familiar face in the audience. Fernando Bermudez sat near the back. I had mixed emotions; I was elated to see him, yet anxious about how he'd react to seeing me. After the speech, I was chatting with some attendees near the lectern when I felt a hand on my shoulder. "Come on Daniel, let's grab lunch." That warm gesture from Fernando gave rise to a friendship, one that has blossomed ever since, even though my colleagues and I failed to convince a federal judge that he deserved habeas relief.

Sometimes, innocent prisoners win their federal habeas corpus petition at the lower court level and get closer to obtaining freedom than Audrey Edmunds and Fernando Bermudez did—unless the federal appeals court has a different view of the case. A case from Louisiana shows how winning your habeas petition at the outset may just be a temporary victory.

———

ONE DECEMBER EVENING IN 1986, BEVERLY S. HAD SOME drinks at a lounge in New Orleans and then drove to pick up food for her son.[24] As she stepped from her car outside the Omelette

Shoppe, a piece of paper fell to the street. Beverly thought it came from her purse, so she retrieved it and jammed it into her pocket. All of a sudden, she felt an object against her back. A man told her to accompany him to a nearby vehicle. He shoved her into the back seat, where he sexually assaulted her and stole fourteen dollars.

The paper that Beverly had stuffed in her pocket turned out to be a bank deposit slip. The police traced it to an account that belonged to Willie Jackson and his mother. But there was a glitch. Willie Jackson no longer lived in the New Orleans area; eight months before the assault, he'd moved to a town several hours away. The police nevertheless searched the family home and recovered a sweater comparable to the one Beverly said the perpetrator wore. It had "Milton" emblazoned on it, which was the first name of Willie's brother. Beverly identified Willie Jackson as the rapist, from both a photo array and an in-person lineup, and his Chrysler Cordoba as the vehicle where the assault took place. Prosecutors charged Willie Jackson with rape and robbery.

The case went to trial. The authorities hadn't recovered any semen from the rape kit but located some blood that was consistent with Willie Jackson's blood type. Jackson did little to refute this evidence or the identification. His attorney, however, elicited testimony that his client had long hair at the time of the crime rather than the shorter style the victim had credited to the perpetrator.

There was another component to the case. The perpetrator had bitten Beverly during the encounter, and prosecutors put a forensic odontologist on the stand (otherwise known as a bite-mark expert) to claim that the dental impression in the victim's skin came from Willie Jackson's teeth. The expert was emphatic about his findings: "My conclusion is that this bite mark on her back, that Mr. Jackson inflicted this bite mark." Bite-mark evidence is notoriously suspect and has factored into convicting more than twenty-five defendants who were later exonerated through

DNA.[25] When you think about it, the idea that biting a malleable surface like human skin could leave a fixed, distinctive imprint of the teeth is absurd. Even so, jurors often value this testimony, wowed by the expert's mystique and sophisticated terminology.

To cancel out the impact of a government expert, defense attorneys ordinarily call their own witness to create a "battle of the experts." Jackson's defense lawyer didn't go down that road, though. He neglected to hire a bite-mark specialist because the Jackson family wouldn't subsidize the cost and he didn't request funds from the court. The defense case instead revolved around several alibi witnesses who testified that Willie Jackson had been in Mississippi at the time of the assault. The jury didn't believe them; it found Jackson guilty of attempted aggravated rape and first-degree robbery. The judge sentenced him to thirty years' imprisonment at "hard labor" for the attempted rape, and an extra ten years for the robbery charge.

MILTON JACKSON EMERGED SHORTLY AFTER TRIAL TO SAY THAT he, not his brother, had done the crimes. He confessed that he'd borrowed the family car on the night of the incident, met the victim at the lounge, and committed the assault and robbery. A bartender partially corroborated this account by placing Milton with the victim at the lounge before she left for the Omelette Shoppe.

There were reasons to take these developments with a grain of salt. Why hadn't this evidence been presented *beforehand*, at trial, when it could have truly helped Willie? Did Milton wait and see how the case played out, then only after things went south pop up to save his brother? If prosecutors ever elected to charge Milton with the rape, he had a terrific, built-in defense—he could just cite his brother's conviction for the same incident as grounds to doubt his culpability. Cynics could view the timing of these new revelations as a dubious effort to save Willie while minimizing the risk that Milton would take his slot in prison. State judges were indeed dubious. Willie Jackson lost his direct appeal and state postconviction challenges in the Louisiana court system.

Fast forward a few years. Willie Jackson filed a federal habeas corpus petition in the Eastern District of Louisiana. His petition made two chief claims: (1) that his lawyer provided ineffective assistance and (2) that he was innocent. The petition initially went to a federal magistrate judge, who screened the case, found no merit in the claims, and declined to hold an evidentiary hearing. In 1996, a federal trial judge adopted the magistrate's findings. On the ineffectiveness point, the judge held that Jackson's trial representation didn't fall below the constitutional standard for reasonable performance, and even if it did, higher-caliber lawyering wouldn't have affected the outcome because of the powerful identification and bite-mark evidence.[26]

As for Jackson's innocence claim, the judge followed the template forged by the Supreme Court. The failure to state a valid ineffectiveness claim meant Jackson had to satisfy the "truly persuasive demonstration of 'actual innocence'" test alluded to in *Herrera* by introducing new facts that "unquestionably" established innocence. And the judge had many questions about Jackson's new evidence. He concluded with the blunt assessment that "Milton's belated 'admissions' lack credibility." Yes, the judge essentially used air quotes in a habeas opinion.

Willie Jackson persisted. He asked the judge to reconsider his decision only on the issue of ineffective assistance of counsel. This gamble paid dividends: the judge ordered an evidentiary hearing. The defense then achieved a much greater feat. The hearing produced various items of evidence that when melded together looked capable of demolishing the state's case. The defense introduced:

- an affidavit from an odontologist excluding Willie Jackson as the source of the bite marks on Beverly's skin and attributing them to his brother Milton

- a police report stating that at the time of the offense, Milton Jackson had recently been discharged from military service and had very short hair
- an affidavit from Milton admitting that he had participated in the events on the night of the rape, including writing a note on the back of the deposit slip, committing the sex acts in the Chrysler Cordoba, and biting the victim
- a report from a document examiner maintaining that it was not Willie Jackson's handwriting on the deposit slip[27]

After examining the new evidence, the judge saw the case in a whole new light—that it was a grave misstep for Willie Jackson's lawyer to have abandoned his efforts to hire a competing bite-mark expert. The odontology evidence had been a key link in the chain of inferences proving Willie Jackson's involvement. And it was a link a competent defense expert could have severed. The judge's decision wasn't based on innocence per se, although that theme was part of the subtext when reading between the lines of the opinion.

But Willie Jackson's ordeal didn't end there. The judge told the state of Louisiana to either retry him or release him within 120 days pending an appeal. The federal Court of Appeals for the Fifth Circuit, based in New Orleans, granted prosecutors' request to appeal. The appellate court took a less charitable view of Jackson's new evidence than the district judge had and reversed his decision in 1997. Even assuming for the sake of argument that Jackson's attorney performed poorly at trial, the Fifth Circuit suggested that deficiency didn't affect the result. In its eyes, "the evidence against Jackson was overwhelming . . . the failure of counsel to retain a forensic odontologist does not render the verdict fundamentally unfair or unreliable."

That's not all the Fifth Circuit had to say. The court derided Jackson for trying to "renew" his actual innocence claim on appeal after having discarded it in his motion for reconsideration. Then the court reiterated the test set forth in *Herrera*: that a federal court will only entertain an innocence claim on habeas corpus in tandem with an independent constitutional claim. Since it deemed the constitutional argument (ineffective assistance of counsel) meritless, the Fifth Circuit refused to assess the actual innocence contention on its own. It didn't even bother to analyze Jackson's case under *Herrera*'s "truly persuasive demonstration of 'actual innocence'" test for stand-alone claims.

The Fifth Circuit wasn't entirely indifferent to the flaws in Willie Jackson's conviction. It just shrouded that indifference in the cloak of habeas corpus jurisprudence: "We are not blind to the evidence suggesting that the wrong man has been convicted of Beverly's rape, nor are we sanguine about our decision to deny habeas relief under these circumstances. The fact remains, however, that the function of federal habeas is to vindicate the constitutional rights of state prisoners, not to relitigate guilt and innocence."

How puzzling—and discouraging. The court professed not to be blind to the potential injustice. But couldn't it see that interpreting "the function" of habeas corpus in a manner that denies courts the chance to examine a possible wrongful conviction prolongs that injustice and brings the whole judicial system into disrepute?

———

WILLIE JACKSON STAYED HOPEFUL, EVEN AFTER THE FIFTH CIRcuit dealt a near-fatal blow to his prospects. With help from some Louisiana lawyers, he sought DNA testing of the biological evidence still in the rape kit. As fate would have it, seminal fluid remained on the victim's pantyhose. DNA test results on that specimen excluded Willie Jackson as the source, and his conviction was overturned in 2005. Subsequent testing in 2006 exposed a not-so-startling detail. The semen's DNA profile matched that of Milton Jackson.

By the time of Willie Jackson's exoneration, the true culprit—his brother Milton—was already incarcerated. Milton had received a life sentence for an unrelated 1998 rape, which occurred more than a decade after the trauma outside the Omelette Shoppe.

––––––––––––

LONG HERALDED AS A WAY TO HOLD GOVERNMENT OFFICIALS accountable, the Great Writ of habeas corpus doesn't deserve its nickname when it comes to issues of actual innocence. For one thing, its focus on constitutional and jurisdictional defects overlooks the fact-based, not law-based, nature of most innocence claims. For another, its burdensome procedural requirements have softened its edges, making it too blunt an instrument to dissect cases with credible questions of guilt or innocence, even when judges are keen to do so. It's more hammer than scalpel. And it's a hammer with an uneven head; federal habeas corpus case law shows too much deference to state court decisions to create a level surface for litigation across the country.

In the title of an influential article a half century ago, Judge Henry Friendly posed a question about the habeas realm: "Is Innocence Irrelevant?"[28] Innocence should not just suffice for habeas relief, Friendly argued, but should serve as a *necessary* precondition in most cases. Prisoners who prove innocence should prevail; those who can't prove it should have their claims dismissed. A provocative argument. And one the courts have never warmed to. It would jettison centuries of habeas case law, devalue the writ's historic role in addressing constitutional and jurisdictional error, and upset the precarious balance between state and federal courts.

Perhaps a middle position is in order. Let's make freestanding innocence claims recognizable in a federal habeas case even without a complementary constitutional claim.[29] Apply a demanding, yet attainable, test for securing relief on innocence grounds. Forget about *Herrera*'s edict that only a "truly persuasive demonstration" of innocence could violate the Constitution. What about affording postconviction relief to prisoners who prove they are more likely than not innocent? The outcome doesn't have to be a walk-off home run for the prisoner—unfettered freedom. Rather, the state could call them up to the plate one more time for a new trial if it so chose. I bet few prosecutors would seek a retrial in such circumstances, given the evidence of innocence. Allowing a retrial option, though, advances comity and dulls the pain of any perceived federal encroachment on state sovereignty.

Modifying habeas corpus along these lines might nudge it closer to becoming a truly great writ—and lend credence to a title that this remedy has held for ages but never quite earned.

6

THE ANCIENT WRIT
OF CORAM NOBIS

An Old Tool to Tackle New Evidence

POSTCONVICTION REMEDIES LIKE HABEAS CORPUS ALLOW PRIS-
oners to attack their convictions even after they've finished their
direct appeals. Yet habeas corpus is an inferior mechanism for
launching an innocent inmate toward exoneration given its focus
on jurisdictional and constitutional errors, coupled with procedural booby traps. The data bear this out. As noted in the last
chapter, a prominent study found that prisoners won their federal habeas corpus petitions at a rate of less than one-third of 1
percent.[1]

Another postconviction remedy that we inherited from England offers more promise. The writ of error coram nobis has
long permitted defendants after trial to present newly discovered
evidence that casts doubt on the integrity of the conviction. Although this basic description suggests it's the ideal route for freeing the innocent, the procedures for litigating coram nobis actions
in the United States are complex and occasionally unforgiving.

Some defendants find justice within their contours, like Audrey Edmunds and Fernando Bermudez from the previous chapter, who prevailed in the end through state coram nobis–type remedies after losing their federal habeas corpus petitions. Others encounter only frustration.

———————

THE WRIT OF ERROR CORAM NOBIS, WHICH TRANSLATES FROM the Latin to "before us," surfaced in sixteenth-century England as a way for courts to amend their own criminal proceedings.[2] Coram nobis petitions traditionally cited the existence of facts unknown at the time of the trial judgment that would affect the soundness of the conviction. As English legal scholar William Blackstone observed, courts didn't impose stiff time deadlines on coram nobis filings, handling applications "however late discovered and alleged."[3] Cautious by nature, courts at first used coram nobis mainly to fix administrative mistakes like clerical errors in charging documents. Later it took on a more substantive gloss, emerging as a tool to repair miscarriages of justice.

American jurisdictions imported coram nobis into their legal framework early on, with the Supreme Court first recognizing the writ in 1810. Many nineteenth-century judges were hesitant to offer full-throated support. Some feared gamesmanship by prisoners who would manipulate coram nobis to disadvantage the prosecution and maximize the odds of success. Others had abstract concerns that the amorphous nature of coram nobis jeopardized the finality of verdicts.

By the twentieth century, most states had placed the writ in their criminal codes through legislation, which mainly served to restrict its use. Put another way, this movement sought to tame coram nobis, a remedy that a Kentucky judge labeled in 1943 "the wild ass of the law which the courts cannot control."[4] Taming coram nobis meant reining in judges who might otherwise wield its extraordinary power liberally. Since then, the wild ass has left the corral to aid the innocent only sporadically.

The modern incarnation of coram nobis is called many different things. A number of states inserted coram nobis into a comprehensive postconviction remedy packaged alongside habeas corpus.[5] Sometimes it's embedded in a jurisdiction's "motion for new trial" system and resembles procedures available in many states that allow defendants to present new evidence in the aftermath of a jury verdict, albeit with strict time limits.[6]

Whatever its official title, coram nobis is currently a mixed bag for the innocent. On the one hand, coram nobis–like remedies have stayed true to Blackstone's observation and normally lack rigid statutes of limitations, giving defendants a way to introduce new evidence years after trial. Courts in most states may field a coram nobis claim so long as the petitioner simply acted with "diligence" after the discovery of the new information. On the other hand, case law has interpreted the concept of "newly discovered evidence" narrowly. It must be forceful evidence— new information that is material (or "of consequence") to the case, wasn't put forth in an earlier proceeding, and couldn't have been found previously. Those are just the prerequisites to enter the courthouse. To gain relief in the end, applicants must cross another barricade. They must prove that had this new evidence appeared at trial, it would have affected the outcome.

Regardless of a state's specific test, the requirements for coram nobis are hard to meet, especially for convictions that occurred long ago. Think about Bobby Fennell's predicament described at the beginning of this book. Fennell was convicted in 1985 of murdering a man outside a New York City drug house and remained in prison even after his codefendant confessed to committing the crime by himself. By the time my colleagues and I at the Second Look Program delved into the case in 2001, any investigative leads had gone cold. The codefendant had died, and the other witnesses had either met a similar fate or were in the wind. Anything Fennell's girlfriend could say about his alibi was not "new" because she'd been available at trial and Fennell's lawyer had chosen not to put her on the stand. We didn't even try to seek coram nobis relief for Fennell despite our firm belief in his innocence.

Assuming a convicted defendant manages to unearth new evidence, applicants for coram nobis usually must file their claim in the original court of conviction through a motion and affidavits that explain the findings. The judge who oversaw the trial is familiar with the case, which aids efficiency, but the hang-up is that she may hold entrenched views about the defendant's culpability. That judge has the authority to deny the filing summarily—just on the papers—without holding a hearing if she thinks the evidence won't satisfy the high standards for relief. Even if a prisoner runs through this procedural gauntlet unscathed, the effect of a successful coram nobis filing is a new trial, rather than outright dismissal of the conviction. This puts the ball back in the district attorney's hands to decide, yet again, whether to prosecute.

Coaxing a judge to grant a hearing on a coram nobis petition isn't easy. In the Long Island robbery case, we tried our luck with a coram nobis–type remedy in New York state court. We stitched together strands of newly discovered evidence to make a patchwork quilt displaying Stephen Schulz's innocence. As noted in previous chapters, these strands included

- an affidavit from the crime victim expressing 90 percent certainty that Anthony Guilfoyle, who had pled guilty to six similar robberies, was the man who'd put a knife to her neck at El Classico Restaurant in Brentwood
- an affidavit from Schulz's roommate asserting that both of them were home at the time of the robbery watching television
- information showing that Guilfoyle's relative owned a white car with a "T" and "1" in the license plate, details

that were observed by one of the witnesses, a cook, on the perpetrator's getaway car

- evidence implying that the cook received favorable treatment on a pending weapon charge in exchange for testifying against Schulz

Although our attempts to gather more details about the cook's gun charge proved fruitless, we thought we'd amassed enough evidence to go back to court and seek a new trial. We filed our motion with the judge who had presided over Schulz's trial, John Copertino, a jurist with a law-and-order reputation and a salty personality.

On a cold January day in 2003, my law student Roger and I drove to the county courthouse in Riverhead, New York, for an oral argument before Judge Copertino. I had dual objectives. My primary goal was to convince the judge to order a hearing and allow us to present our new evidence in open court. The legal scholar John Henry Wigmore once called cross-examination the "greatest legal engine ever invented for the discovery of truth."[7] We wanted nothing more than to subject our witnesses to that whirring engine. We felt they'd withstand the pressure and come across as truthful. My secondary goal was pedagogical. Roger was one of the best students I'd ever had. Analytically sound, socially adept, brutally honest. I hoped to model grace under pressure and, win or lose, impart an important lesson to one of my favorite mentees.

I failed on both counts. I urged Copertino to follow case law in favor of granting postconviction evidentiary hearings "to promote justice if the issues raised are sufficiently unusual and suggest investigation." Copertino wasn't moved by my oratory. He didn't believe that the victim was being sincere in her affidavit, ascribing her reluctance to identify Schulz at trial to "fear." I got rattled by his obstinacy and fumbled my way through other lines of argument.

A month later, Copertino rejected our motion without holding an evidentiary hearing. He never handed the prosecution the keys to the greatest legal engine ever devised for the discovery of truth because, I suppose, he thought he already knew the truth.

We tried to appeal Copertino's summary disposition of our newly discovered evidence claim. The Appellate Division, Second Department, upheld the decision unanimously. The Second Department found that Copertino "providently exercised his discretion" in denying our motion without a hearing.

Sometimes, litigants do better than I did with Copertino and convince a judge to inspect the new evidence out in the open, for all to see at an evidentiary hearing. But that doesn't mean the hearing will produce an exoneration.

CLINTON CORRECTIONAL FACILITY IN DANNEMORA, LIKE MANY prisons in upstate New York, has a medieval quality to it. It resembles a dilapidated castle, replete with turrets staffed by corrections officers. A decades-old prison yard murder afforded a chance for me and my colleagues at the Second Look Program to glimpse inside that fortress.[8]

As the sun set on a snowy day in March 1986, the Clinton yard teemed with more than six hundred inmates wearing identical green uniforms. A white corrections officer, Richard LaPierre, was standing watch on a turret when he noticed some prisoners huddled together 350 feet away. One member of the group approached a Black man, Tyrone Julius, and struck him in the back. Julius collapsed, dead from a knife wound to the neck.

Everyone fled the crime scene. LaPierre grabbed his binoculars to track the assailant's path during the chaos and radioed to his colleagues on the ground. Based on information provided by LaPierre, COs detained two Asian prisoners—the *only* two Asians incarcerated in the facility at the time. One of them was

Kin-Jin "David" Wong, an undocumented immigrant from China serving a sentence for robbery. Wong had worked in a restaurant in the Chinatown section of New York City. After the restaurant withheld his wages, he drove a coworker to his boss's home. The coworker took money from his employer by force, making Wong an accomplice to armed robbery, perhaps an unwitting one. That's what sent Wong to prison. The Julius homicide kept him there much longer than anticipated.

WONG WAS A PECULIAR PERSON TO TAG FOR JULIUS'S MURDER. Lodging a shank into someone's neck produces lots of blood, none of which was found on Wong even though he was nabbed right after the crime. Even more, LaPierre never mentioned that the culprit wore dark gloves, which Wong had on when apprehended, and he acknowledged that the attacker at first "appeared to be white." Later LaPierre identified Wong in a photo array and characterized the assailant as "Oriental." All the investigators really had at this point was an equivocal cross-racial identification, from a football field away, of one man among hundreds of green-clad inmates circulating at dusk.

Then a white prisoner named Peter Dellfava came forward. He claimed he had been in the yard that day, only fifteen feet away from the stabbing, and saw Wong put a knife in Julius's back. Dellfava was certain Wong had committed the crime because he'd allegedly seen him many times before. What neither LaPierre nor Dellfava could explain was motive. Why would Wong kill a fellow prisoner with whom he had no apparent beef?

Wong's defense team could have capitalized on that glaring hole—and other gaps in the government case—to show reasonable doubt. But his two assigned lawyers didn't do that. Or much at all. Their biggest stumble was ignoring a lead that pointed to another suspect. State investigators compiled a report noting that a prisoner "had advised that an inmate named Gutierrez was the subject who had stabbed the inmate in the yard" before recanting his statement in a second interview. In yet a third interview, the prisoner said Wong couldn't have done the crime. The defense lawyers never bothered to interrogate this potential witness or look into the actions of anyone named Gutierrez.

Compounding his attorneys' neglect, Wong struggled to aid in his own defense or understand the legal proceedings. The interpreter assigned to his case didn't even speak the regional Chinese dialect in which he was fluent; she spoke Mandarin, a language Wong barely grasped. His lawyers never asked for an appropriate translator when pressed to do so multiple times by their client.

An all-white jury found Wong guilty of murder in 1987. He received a sentence of fifteen years to life to be served on top of his robbery bid. A juror later recalled that "the jury put a lot of stock" into what both LaPierre and Dellfava had to say.

WONG LOST HIS DIRECT APPEAL IN 1990. HE PERSEVERED, FIL-ing a slew of state and federal postconviction motions throughout the 1990s. One of them contained *seven* affidavits from prisoners who vowed Wong was innocent. While they stopped short of identifying the true perpetrator by name, the witnesses suggested a Latino man had done the crime. Unfazed, the trial court rejected the motion, and an appeals court affirmed that decision.

Jaykumar Menon, a young lawyer with the Center for Constitutional Rights in New York City, took over the case in 1999. If Menon were to succeed where fourteen other lawyers had failed, including fabled civil rights warrior William Kunstler, he had to go back to square one. He had to reinvestigate the facts, interview the original witnesses, and question every assumption. Most of all, he had to locate Peter Dellfava. That's precisely what Menon did, tracking him down in upstate New York. As Menon later

told me, Dellfava seemed relieved by the chance to come clean—
and what he said revealed some very dirty dealings.

Dellfava admitted he had lied. He'd neither witnessed the
stabbing of Tyrone Julius nor ever seen David Wong before trial.
Rather, he'd been on friendly terms with the Clinton prison guards,
one of whom sidled up to him shortly after the murder and asked,
"It was an Oriental guy, wasn't it?" Dellfava saw an opening to
improve his lot. That opening grew into a tall tale about watching
the hit go down. In exchange, Dellfava got a transfer to a facility
closer to his family and a recommendation for early parole, kick-
backs unknown to the defense at the time of trial.

Dellfava signed an affidavit under penalty of perjury that recanted his trial testimony. It was a major breakthrough, yet not
enough on its own to steer the case in Wong's favor. Recantations
aren't viewed kindly by courts. Their basic premise, that a witness fesses up to lying under oath at trial, raises suspicion about
whether the person is telling the truth now. If the person lied before, why should we believe he's being honest in the affidavit? To
be sure, there's a solid retort to this attack. A recanting witness
exposes himself to perjury charges by admitting the past indiscre-
tion and has little reason to fabricate the change of heart. But that
logic alone doesn't jolt many judges from their cynical stance.[9]

So Menon needed more. He reached out to the Second Look
Program at Brooklyn Law School, and we agreed to join the fight.
We knew that the key to unlocking the case was finding the real
perpetrator. Others had already loosened that lock by finding
people willing to describe the assailant as a Latino inmate. Some
witnesses had even provided a newly uncovered tidbit, that the
man had a limp. Those witnesses wouldn't budge further, though.
Giving up a name would make them "snitches," vulnerable to
retribution under prison code.

We plowed forward. My colleague Will Hellerstein and I
spent a good part of 2001 and 2002 traversing the two-lane roads
of upstate New York to meet with prisoners who had been in the

Clinton yard that gloomy day in 1986 and now lived in facilities scattered across the area. In a stroke of luck, several of them gave the name of the killer after news surfaced that he'd died in the Dominican Republic: Nelson Gutierrez.

The pieces to the puzzle fit. The surname Gutierrez had come up way back when prison investigators interviewed possible witnesses. Gutierrez's friends also knew him as "Chino" because of the perception that he had Asian facial features. LaPierre's misidentification now seemed more plausible. And a good-faith mistake is easier to explain to a judge in a coram nobis petition, and for a judge to accept, than allegations of bias by a corrections officer. Particularly when the judge works in a county where prisons dominate the economy.

What about Gutierrez's motive, that elusive component of the case against Wong?

We spoke with the murder victim's widow and a cross-section of the Clinton prison community circa 1986, and a clearer picture of events took form. Julius and Gutierrez had a history. They'd had a run-in at Rikers Island, the sprawling New York City jail complex where defendants convicted of felonies await transfer to state prisons and those convicted of misdemeanors serve their time.[10] One day in 1984, Julius fought with Gutierrez over the use of a pay phone. That altercation left Gutierrez with a bad leg. Two years later, Gutierrez was housed at Clinton when he noticed that Julius had just arrived at the facility, a newcomer without allies. Gutierrez sent word throughout the leadership within the prison community that he planned to retaliate and that it was a personal vendetta, not racial. According to multiple eyewitnesses, Gutierrez avenged the assault to his leg by killing Julius. He even admitted to a friend shortly after the murder, *I got the guy who broke my leg in Rikers Island, and a Chinese guy paid for it. I didn't pay for it.*

By the time we'd gathered our new evidence, it may have been too late for Gutierrez to pay, but not to release Wong from his unearned debt to society. Our affidavits set forth the theory of the murder in excruciating detail. We chronicled the encounter at Rikers, the reunion at Clinton, the cover-up, and the postconviction revelations. As required by New York's coram nobis remedy, we filed our motion with the court of conviction in Clinton County. Wong's trial judge was no longer on the bench, and two other judges recused themselves from the case. Nearly every sector of the economy in the county seat, Plattsburgh, was tied in some fashion to the facility where the murder had occurred. It felt like no jurist wanted to touch the case—and recusal was an expedient way for judges versed in criminal law to drop this political hot potato. Someone had to catch it, though, and eventually a family court judge did: Timothy Lawliss.

Much to our delight, and surprise, Judge Lawliss granted our request to hold an evidentiary hearing.

———

IT WAS QUITE A CULTURE CLASH IN THE SPRING OF 2003 WHEN our diverse legal team descended on Plattsburgh for the hearing, accompanied by dozens of activists from New York City. Menon suspected that local authorities were monitoring our out-of-court activities. I mocked his suspicions as paranoia—at least until the police stopped us one night after dinner, purportedly because I, the designated driver, hadn't turned on my headlights right away when leaving the restaurant's parking lot. I'll never forget the shame I felt as they put me through a field sobriety test in front of my students and colleagues. Stone-cold sober, hot with humiliation.

We didn't humiliate ourselves in court, that's for sure. We put on ten witnesses, the prosecution none. The highlights were:

- Peter Dellfava, who renounced his trial testimony
- six prisoners who witnessed the stabbing in the prison yard, including three who identified the assailant as

Nelson Gutierrez and two who described the killer as having attributes distinctive to Gutierrez
- the victim's widow, who backed up the characterization of the homicide as retribution for a fight at Rikers

Then we waited for Lawliss to act. As the months passed, some of us remained upbeat. Others, especially the political activists on our team, were less sanguine, their hopes dampened by decades of defeat. Lawliss handed down his opinion in September.

Motion denied.

Lawliss didn't pull any punches in an opinion that dripped with disdain for our witnesses. Terming the prisoner testimony "preposterous," he called Dellfava "particularly unreliable." He saw no credible explanation for Dellfava's delay in coming forward and, in so doing, overlooked some obvious ones: the threat of perjury charges, the pull of inertia, and the triggering effect of Jaykumar Menon showing up at his door. Lawliss also scoffed at the idea that Gutierrez would confess to his crimes, or that knowledge of Wong's innocence was widespread within the prison population.

In "stark contrast" to our witnesses, Lawliss praised Officer LaPierre. Noting the lack of evidence "that Mr. LaPierre was anything other than a disinterested, unbiased and credible witness" at trial, Lawliss rejected the argument that the officer simply slipped up—that from a distance, a Latino inmate with features that had netted him the nickname Chino may have been mistaken for Asian. Lawliss even took pains to bolster LaPierre's credibility: "any individual, particularly any individual who works in the correctional facility, would have to understand the significance and enormous responsibility of identifying another human-being as a murderer."

I understand why a judge might be skeptical. To someone not privy to the backstory of the case, our efforts could look like a calculated effort to stick the crime on a dead guy unable to defend himself. But I think Lawliss took his skepticism too far, refusing to see how the evidence led to Nelson Gutierrez. Consider the reference to "Gutierrez" in the original investigative report in 1986, and the rumors that a Latino prisoner had perpetrated the homicide. Also, left unsaid in Lawliss's opinion were any allusions to motive. Not a word about the victim's widow, the Rikers Island incident, or why an Asian man unaffiliated with a gang would risk inciting a race war by killing a new arrival whom he'd never met, with hundreds of witnesses to boot.

We zeroed in on challenging Lawliss's decision. Once permission to appeal was granted by the Appellate Division, Third Department, in Albany, we focused on drafting our brief. I was pessimistic, although I kept my reservations from my colleagues on the defense team. Lawliss had made findings about the credibility of our witnesses that I knew would receive deference on appeal.[11] I also knew that reading the plain text of the hearing transcript and our witness affidavits lacked the power of in-court testimony, which made those items unlikely to sway the Third Department from the status quo.

We filed our brief. And I moved to Utah.

———————

THE WASATCH MOUNTAINS WERE THE PERFECT ANTIDOTE TO the stresses of my Second Look Program tenure. But their peaks couldn't stop me from reliving the hearing, from revisiting our tactics, from conjuring up the image of David Wong in the courtroom, his arms and legs shackled, his face a mask. We had overcome so many of the hurdles in the coram nobis process. We'd accumulated new evidence of our client's innocence, convinced a judge to order an evidentiary hearing, and unleashed our witnesses to tell their stories in open court. But a crushing opinion from a single judge had put another, seemingly higher hurdle on our path.

What stopped me from dwelling on those memories was the receipt of the Appellate Division's opinion in October 2004.

We won.

The Third Department found Dellfava's recantation credible because it risked instigating perjury charges. The appeals court wrote that the "recantation further acquires an aura of believability" because of the other witness testimony and "the lack of trial evidence connecting [the] defendant with the commission of the crime or establishing a motive for him to commit the crime." Finally, someone outside our circle cared about motive. Unlike Judge Lawliss's decision, the Third Department opinion emphasized the Rikers incident, the incentives it provided, and the partial corroboration of that account from Julius's widow. The appellate judges also seemed to get why fellow prisoners would only identify Gutierrez by name at this late date: because "while he was alive . . . a reputation as a 'snitch' would place them in a position of peril in any prison population."

In the end, the Third Department held that had our newly discovered evidence been available at Wong's original trial, it probably would have affected the outcome. The court ordered a new trial. A few weeks later, with what struck us as a great deal of reluctance, the Clinton County DA announced he wouldn't retry Wong.

Our client was released from New York state prison. But we never got the chance to see him emerge from the prison gate, unshackled and unburdened. Due to his prior robbery conviction, he was deported to China.

He lives in Hong Kong these days, married and gainfully employed. In the ensuing years, I've corresponded with David by email, even celebrated his sixtieth birthday with an impromptu Zoom party during the COVID-19 pandemic in 2020. I haven't seen him in person, though, since that 2003 hearing in Plattsburgh. I fear I never will.

DAVID WONG IS FREE BECAUSE A PRINCIPLED APPEALS COURT
looked beyond the onerous procedural requirements of New
York's coram nobis law to overturn a lower court judge's decision, deference to his factual findings be damned. I recognize how
lucky we were. Prisoners seldom receive evidentiary hearings on
postconviction motions grounded in newly discovered evidence.
Rarer still are cases where a prisoner gets an appellate reversal
after having—and losing—a hearing. Another man convicted of
a vile crime in upstate New York in the 1980s knows all too well
what it's like to lose at each stage of the coram nobis process.[12]

Glenn Sterling was convicted of attempting to rape an elderly
woman, Viola Manville, in the hills outside Rochester in 1985.
Three years later, Sterling was still in prison when Manville was
found dead near the site of the previous crime, her battered body
riddled with pellets from a BB gun.

The Manville murder shocked the community and sparked a vigorous police response. Detectives questioned lots of people in late
1988, including Glenn's brother Frank. Although Frank didn't have
a criminal record or a reputation for violence, the police latched on
to him through a guilt-by-association theory: they assumed that he,
like his incarcerated brother, wished harm upon the woman. Yet
Frank had an alibi. He'd worked as a school bus monitor that morning, returned home, and walked to the grocery store. After confirm-
ing the story, the police cut him loose. And the investigation stalled.

More than two years later, the police visited Frank Sterling
again to renew their interrogation. He was working as a truck
driver and had just come back from a trip. Haggard and disori-
ented, he agreed to take a polygraph. When Sterling denied murdering Manville, his answer apparently registered deceit.

A new police interrogator took over close to midnight, one who
was adept at eliciting confessions. Sterling told the interrogator

that he was angry enough about his brother's conviction to kill Manville but insisted he hadn't followed through. The interrogator held Sterling's hands, claimed to be "here for him," and pursued relaxation exercises with him. Hours later, Sterling admitted he'd done the murder. A videotape, recorded around five in the morning, preserved his account for posterity.

Sterling recanted the confession almost immediately. As discussed in the context of the David Wong case, courts normally look askance at recantations. That skepticism is often magnified when the new statement seeks to unwind a confession by a criminal defendant, and a judge found Sterling's recantation incredible.

The case proceeded to trial, where the prosecution depended on the confession and on conjecture about how the brothers' interests were aligned in hurting Manville. The jury deliberated for two days. They even sought multiple instructions from the judge about how to treat the confession evidence before rendering a guilty verdict on the murder charge in 1992.

Then something happened during the gap between the jury verdict and Sterling's sentencing, something very important. One of the people initially questioned about the homicide, Mark Christie, was bragging all over town about how he'd "gotten away with murder." The police interviewed the nineteen-year-old Christie again after learning about his boasts. Christie chalked them up to horseplay, saying that he was "kidding," and denied any involvement in the killing. He even passed a polygraph. Sterling's trial judge, Douglas Wisner, believed Christie's explanation and sentenced Sterling to twenty-five years to life in prison.

IN 1994—THE SAME YEAR IN WHICH STERLING LOST HIS DIRECT appeal—four-year-old Kali Ann Poulton disappeared near Rochester. The investigative trail ran dry for two years before the police caught a break. During an argument with his wife, Mark Christie blurted out that he'd killed Poulton. His wife called the police, leading Christie to confess to investigators that he'd strangled the girl and dumped her corpse in a water coolant tank at his job site. The police recovered her body, which was small consolation to her family and the community. But it provided an opportunity for Frank Sterling.

Sterling filed a motion with his original trial judge, as compelled by New York's coram nobis–style remedy, which called into question the accuracy of his conviction and cited this newly discovered information about Christie. The motion conveyed the facts of the Poulton slaying, as well as evidence that (1) Christie had told friends and acquaintances he'd committed the Manville murder, (2) he had formerly owned a gun, quite possibly a pellet gun, and (3) his alibi for the time of Manville's killing was flawed. Judge Wisner granted an evidentiary hearing and, over the course of three days in 1997, let the defense put on its case. The defense claimed that had this evidence been available at the time of Sterling's trial, the outcome would have probably differed, and therefore Sterling deserved a new trial.

Judge Wisner disagreed. After he "duly" considered the evidence at the hearing, he denied Sterling's motion. The Appellate Division, Fourth Department, based in Rochester, affirmed Wisner's decision in an opinion notable only for its brevity: "Order unanimously affirmed for reasons stated in decision at Supreme Court, Wisner, J." Sterling then sought permission to appeal the Fourth Department's ruling to the Court of Appeals, the highest tribunal in New York. That court was even more taciturn. Permission "denied."

Foiled in his pursuit of a new trial through coram nobis, Sterling turned to the evolving science of DNA. In 2004, he petitioned for DNA testing of the biological evidence retained from the crime scene. Judge Wisner had ascended to the appellate bench by then, and his successor in the county trial court granted Sterling's request to test a single strand of hair. Those tests showed that the follicle came from the murder victim herself.

Other pieces of evidence remained in the case files, however, and the Innocence Project in New York City convinced prosecutors to subject those items to DNA testing in 2006. Scientists scoured Manville's clothes for "Touch DNA" through a technique able to extract a genetic profile from trace amounts of skin cells. The results excluded Sterling as the assailant and implicated Christie. When confronted with this scientific evidence, Christie confessed.

Frank Sterling was officially exonerated in 2010, a middle-aged man with eighteen years of hard time under his belt. The following year, Mark Christie pled guilty to killing Manville. At sentencing, Kali Ann Poulton's mother reflected on how things might have played out had the police targeted Christie, not Sterling, in the wake of the Manville murder. "Of course it has crossed my mind," she said. "What if? . . . But unfortunately it is what it is. We can't go backward."

She was right. We can't go backward; we can't save Kali Ann Poulton. By looking backward to deconstruct what went wrong, though, we can learn lessons to thrust the criminal justice system forward.

––––––––

HOW MIGHT WE ALTER CORAM NOBIS TO MOTIVATE COURTS TO look at newly discovered evidence more closely and better realize its potential for rectifying injustices? And how can we do this without sacrificing the goals of efficiency and finality? Three possibilities come to mind:[13]

First, eliminate statutes of limitations in the handful of jurisdictions that restrict the time period for filing a newly discovered evidence claim. In Tennessee, the state postconviction law requires applicants to submit petitions within one year after direct appellate review, except for those "based upon new scientific evidence establishing that the petitioner is actually innocent."[14]

While I commend the Tennessee legislature for being flexible regarding scientific findings, why not extend the same generosity to new evidence more generally? David Wong never uncovered any scientific evidence of innocence at all, and it took more than a decade after he exhausted his direct appeal for his defense team to obtain Dellfava's recantation and evidence tying Nelson Gutierrez to the crime. If his conviction had occurred in the Smoky Mountains of Tennessee, not the Adirondacks of upstate New York, he might still be in prison.

Every jurisdiction should endorse a standard that obligates petitioners to proceed only with due diligence in filing newly discovered evidence claims. Having a supple "standard" as opposed to an intractable "rule" still signals that dilatory filing will not be excused, yet acknowledges the fact-specific nature of each situation and the reality that some applicants may not be able to meet a firm deadline.

Second, send all coram nobis petitions to a new judge. The notion that newly discovered evidence claims should go to the original trial judge is a vestige of a bygone era, one when the criminal docket wasn't clogged with cases, when judges had the time and energy to devote attention to each matter. Even more, fresh eyes may be necessary to view the new information with detachment and equanimity. Let's assign coram nobis petitions either randomly to a different judge in the county of conviction or to a judge in the place where the petitioner is incarcerated, as is the norm with habeas corpus. What's lost is some degree of familiarity. It will take longer for the new judge to get up to speed than the jurist who presided over trial, however faint her memory may be. What's gained is objectivity, a real chance to look at the new evidence unencumbered by any vested interest or sentiment. That benefit exceeds the cost of any modest inefficiency, which Frank Sterling can attest to.

Third, encourage evidentiary hearings. In the Long Island robbery case, Stephen Schulz never had his newly discovered evidence claims aired at a hearing in state court. Judge Copertino's decision to summarily reject Schulz's claim received deference on appeal, with the appeals court concluding that he "providently exercised his discretion." Why afford such deference to the dispensation of summary justice? Why couldn't appellate benches abandon the abuse-of-discretion standard on the threshold question of whether to hold an evidentiary hearing and review that decision entirely anew? Adopting de novo review would give appeals courts more leeway to evaluate lower court judges' reasoning and alert those judges that their decisions will not be veiled in secrecy. A higher tribunal should hold judges' feet to the fire when they refuse even to look at the newly discovered evidence in open court.

———————

A CHIEF GOAL OF THIS CHAPTER—AND THE ONE ON HABEAS corpus—is to reveal the faults with our postconviction procedures when litigating innocence cases. States have embraced many features of the ancient British writs of habeas corpus and coram nobis, features that fall short, for different reasons, in correcting wrongful convictions.

It's time now to explore how courts handle innocence claims supported by the silver bullet of science, DNA evidence. All fifty states have special laws that give prisoners the right to access biological evidence in their cases to conduct DNA testing after conviction. Yet those laws, like the ones governing habeas corpus and coram nobis, leave something to be desired.

7

THE SILVER BULLET OF SCIENCE

Flaws with State Postconviction DNA-Testing Laws

So far, I've showcased the failings of direct appellate and postconviction procedures. Their hazards include preservation requirements, deferential standards of review, harmless error doctrines, time bars, limits on the claims that courts may consider in habeas corpus actions, and hurdles to receiving evidentiary hearings on coram nobis petitions. The cases I relied on to make these problems come to life often had a distinctive narrative arc: innocent person convicted (beginning), halted by these procedures (middle), vindicated through DNA evidence (end). I hope this method is somewhat satisfying and not too repetitive. The real risk with this approach is that it might leave the impression that DNA testing is the criminal justice system's fail-safe weapon, ammunition that's stored and ready to be fired when all other remedies have been exhausted.

If that's your impression, mea culpa. Yes, DNA technology is amazing. Roughly 99.9 percent of human DNA is identical from person to person; the other 0.1 percent is what distinguishes each of us, and scientists have long sought to pinpoint those differences.

Advancements in DNA testing allow us to identify the source of a genetic profile with unparalleled accuracy and from ever smaller quantities of biological material like blood, semen, hair, saliva, or skin tissue.[1] As a result, the tool has proved the innocence of 375 convicted criminal defendants and led to their exoneration.[2]

But DNA testing is a relatively new phenomenon. The first exoneration based on that technology didn't occur until 1989. Also, biological evidence suitable for DNA testing is found at the crime scene in only about 10 to 20 percent of cases. When it exists nowadays, this evidence is usually analyzed at the front end of the process to weed out innocent suspects and find the true perpetrator if there's a match to a profile in a database. In older cases, though, biological evidence may not have gone through any DNA testing, or at least not the most recent, most refined technologies available.

In those older cases, innocent prisoners may try to locate biological evidence gathered at the time of the crime, access it, and submit it for DNA analysis. Even though all fifty states and the federal government have laws that govern how to retrieve and test biological specimens after conviction, the evidence sometimes gets degraded, lost, or destroyed over time. Worse yet, those laws contain procedural obstacles that occasionally keep the silver bullet of DNA lodged in its chamber, unable to right a possible wrong.

The tally of documented DNA exonerations since 1989 therefore represents a thin slice of the population of prisoners who are actually innocent, because so few cases contain biological evidence suitable for DNA analysis, and the ones with testable evidence don't always bring relief for the wrongfully convicted. A disturbing case from New Jersey shows this phenomenon in action.

———

THE JERSEY SHORE IS KNOWN FOR ITS SURF, BOARDWALKS, AND reality television stars. In 1988, one of its resort towns, Long Branch, gained fame for a more ignominious reason. One evening that September, a man grabbed a teenager walking home from her job at a restaurant, raped her, and stole her purse.[3] Three days later, the survivor saw a Black man, Dion Harrell, in the parking lot of the same restaurant and thought he resembled her assailant.

Harrell protested when the police picked him up, insisting they had the wrong person. He begged the police to let the victim see him so she could get a closer look and clear up the mistake. Procedures like this, called showups, normally happen right after the commission of a crime when the police canvass the area and catch someone who fits the description of the perpetrator. To do a showup days after a crime is unusual (and worrisome) given the vagaries of human memory and the suggestive nature of the procedure. But the police acquiesced to Harrell's demands. They put him in a room with the victim, and she identified him as her rapist. Authorities in Monmouth County charged Harrell with sexual assault.

The victim repeated her identification of Harrell at trial. DNA testing wasn't widely available in New Jersey at the time. Instead, standard blood-type analysis remained the norm in the forensics world. An analyst with the state police crime lab testified that blood typing put Harrell within a tiny subset of the male population—just 2 percent—that could have provided the semen in the rape kit.

Harrell took the stand in his defense. He testified that he had been playing basketball on the night of the crime, and had later ridden his bicycle over to a friend's house. Several witnesses substantiated key portions of his alibi. It wasn't enough, though, to ward off the combined impact of the victim's identification and the forensic testimony. A jury convicted Harrell of sexual assault in 1993, and a judge imposed an eight-year sentence.

Harrell remained in prison until his release on parole in 1997. As a condition of his release, he had to register as a sex offender under Megan's Law, an act named after seven-year-old Megan Kanka, who was raped and killed by a convicted child molester in 1994 after he had moved into her New Jersey neighborhood without anyone being warned about his history. Versions of this law now operate in every state to force people convicted of sex crimes to register with the government. New Jersey mandates publication of an offender's name, face, and address, as well as information about the crime, on the state's online database. These conditions not only give the public notice about sex offenders' whereabouts but also restrict where they can live and with whom.

The sex offender law disrupted Harrell's reentry into society right off the bat because its ban on living near children prevented him from moving in with his sister and nephews as planned. Harrell failed to consistently comply with the registration requirements after that rough start, in part because he refused to admit guilt and brand himself a sex offender. That led to two prison stints over the years. Unable to keep a job because of his sex offender status, Harrell drifted in and out of homelessness when he wasn't behind bars.

Despite the insecurity of his daily life, Harrell was steadfast in his efforts to prove his innocence. He wrote the Innocence Project in New York City asking for help. With a backlog of ten thousand requests, the Innocence Project didn't prioritize Harrell's case, especially after he got paroled. Rather, it simmered on the back burner until the organization investigated the case in 2013 and learned that the forensic analyst had grossly overstated the significance of the serological evidence at Harrell's trial. Contrary to the analyst's assertion that 98 percent of the male population could be excluded as the source of the seminal fluid—thereby placing Harrell within a narrow band of possible suspects—the blood-typing evidence didn't actually rule out *anyone*.

The Innocence Project set out to locate the biological evidence. Monmouth County prosecutors found the evidence in 2014 but declined to turn it over to the Innocence Project because New Jersey's postconviction DNA-testing law confined eligibility for relief only to people who were currently incarcerated. It didn't matter that Harrell had to register as a sex offender, that his liberty was still impaired by the rape conviction. The plain language of the law only granted access to people in custody, and Harrell was not imprisoned at that particular moment. For prosecutors who wanted to adhere to the letter of the law, if not its spirit, that was it. As they declared in opposition to Harrell's request, "The State believes the conviction is entitled to finality."

Innocence Project attorney Vanessa Potkin disagreed. A tireless advocate for the wrongfully convicted, Potkin filed a motion for access to the evidence and made a compelling argument as to why denying testing to a man who had spent nearly twenty years on a sex offender registry was unfair. Mere weeks before a judge was slated to decide the motion in 2015, prosecutors reversed course and consented to the tests. Those tests later excluded Harrell as the rapist, and a court tossed out his conviction.[4]

———

AFTER LOBBYING FROM THE INNOCENCE PROJECT'S POLICY team, New Jersey changed its postconviction DNA-testing law. Now someone like Dion Harrell, out from prison but constrained by sex offender registration requirements, may petition for DNA testing. But other states are less magnanimous. Taking a deep dive into the sea of state postconviction DNA-testing laws is not for the faint of heart. It's disorienting to swim through its reefs and coves, some of which appear situated just to block the innocent from reaching their destination. Others look innocuous at first glance, their dangers only emerging upon inspection.

One explanation for the lack of uniformity in these laws is that the Supreme Court has never recognized a constitutional right to DNA testing to prove innocence. When confronted with the question head-on in 2009, the Court held that the US Constitution does not require states to provide such an opportunity.[5] That case involved a challenge by William Osborne, a man convicted of kidnapping and assaulting a sex worker in Anchorage in 1994. Years after his conviction, Osborne sought the biological material from the rape kit in the hope that DNA tests could exonerate him. Since Alaska didn't have a postconviction DNA-testing law on the books, these types of requests were handled through informal negotiations with law enforcement. In rejecting Osborne's overture, prosecutors called his request frivolous because he'd confessed to the crime and rudimentary DNA tests had placed him within the group of men who could have committed it. What they ignored in turning him down was that advancements in DNA technology could put any gnawing doubts about Osborne's guilt to rest, if only he could get his hands on the evidence.

Osborne filed a federal civil rights lawsuit maintaining that Alaska's failure to turn over evidence that could potentially exculpate him violated due process. The case wended its way through the judicial system until it reached the US Supreme Court. Writing for the majority, Chief Justice John Roberts penned an opinion that was heavy on states' rights (and light on concern for individual fairness). The Court deemed it the prerogative of each state to decide how to field requests for postconviction DNA testing, and held that "to suddenly constitutionalize this area would short-circuit what looks to be a prompt and considered legislative response."[6]

The Chief Justice got it right in one respect: states have reacted to the growth of DNA technology in a rather "prompt" fashion. Every state in the nation passed a postconviction DNA-testing law between 1994 (New York) and 2017 (Oklahoma). *Osborne* even moved the needle in one of the holdout jurisdictions, Alaska, which enacted its own testing statute shortly after the decision came down. Whether these laws represent a "considered legislative response," however, is debatable.

Most state laws demand that to gain access to biological evidence for DNA testing, applicants must make a preliminary showing as to why they're innocent and why test results could support that theory. Substantive rules like that make sense. They dissuade guilty defendants from taking a flyer on the chance that degraded evidence or flawed tests might spring them from prison. Yet the laws also contain rigid procedures that serve little purpose other than to squash access to postconviction DNA testing. In fact, procedural obstacles prevented William Osborne from obtaining DNA testing under the law that Alaska adopted after his Supreme Court loss.[7] Here are some of the main procedural impediments across the nation:[8]

Currently "incarcerated" or "in custody." Some states hew closely to New Jersey's former course and restrict eligibility under their postconviction DNA-testing laws only to people who are in prison at the time of their application. A handful of states use the term "incarceration" or "incarcerated" to communicate this requirement. Others refer to a person "serving a term of imprisonment" or employ the phrase "in custody." States that use this terminology vary in the extent to which they specify whether it includes those on parole, probation, or sex offender registration. Several states make clear that this language excludes anyone not currently residing in a correctional facility.

Only certain convictions. In some states, eligibility under the postconviction testing scheme depends on whether applicants have been convicted of a particular *type* of crime. They must have been convicted of a capital offense in Alabama, murder or rape in Kansas, and one of twenty-four enumerated crimes in South Carolina. Other states confine access to *classes* of crimes. In Maryland, only those convicted of "a crime of violence" may seek recourse, in Alaska, it must be a "serious felony," and in Nevada only a Class A or B felony suffices (felonies at the high end of the severity range). Many states simply reserve their laws for those convicted of a felony, leaving out a huge swath of people with misdemeanors on their records.[9]

Exclusion for guilty pleas and admissions of guilt. As described in Chapter 1, criminal defendants face pressure to take guilty pleas or else risk a much stiffer sentence if convicted after trial. Some unknown number of innocent people succumb to this enticement and plead guilty to something they didn't do. Most states acknowledge this dilemma by allowing people convicted through guilty pleas to utilize postconviction DNA-testing laws. But not all states demonstrate that level of awareness. A person may not request postconviction DNA testing in Ohio for "any offense to which the offender pleaded guilty or no contest." In a few other states, including Kentucky, people convicted through a guilty plea may petition for DNA testing subject to more stringent rules than for prisoners found guilty after trial.[10]

Time bars. Most states allow defendants to apply for postconviction DNA testing at any time. A sizable minority of states, though, impose time bars. Laws in Alaska, Arkansas, Delaware, and Mississippi contain some variation on a three-year statute of limitations after the date of conviction or completion of the direct appeal; Maine, Minnesota, and Oregon offer only a two-year window to file requests; Alabama has a one-year rule. Some state laws, especially early iterations passed in the 1990s and 2000s, implemented what are known as "sunset provisions" that obligate applicants for DNA testing to submit their motions by a certain date, or else the day passes to pursue relief.[11]

Costs. The cost of a DNA test is declining, from thousands of dollars to hundreds. Regardless of the exact price, it's still beyond the financial reach of many prisoners. Most states accept this reality by having the government pay for postconviction DNA tests when the applicant is indigent. Other states fail to clarify who bears the up-front cost, which can generate confusion.[12]

No right to appeal. Petitions for postconviction DNA testing are usually directed to the trial judge who oversaw the original conviction, and that jurist has discretion to choose whether to grant the motion.[13] That ruling, in turn, is appealable in many states, either automatically or by requesting permission. But a few states don't allow for a direct appeal, most notably Virginia, which has no mechanism to challenge the ruling at all. California, West Virginia, and Wyoming forbid an appeal but allow inmates to file a separate action—under a writ of some sort—to protest a denial of access to biological evidence for DNA testing.

Evidence retention and preservation. Perhaps the most galling defect in state postconviction DNA-testing laws revolves around evidence retention and preservation.[14] Many states fall short concerning (1) how long the government must keep evidence after a conviction, (2) the kinds of crimes that trigger a retention duty, and (3) any penalties that flow from the failure to abide by that requirement. For example:

- Iowa expects the government to hold on to evidence for three years beyond the statute of limitations period for charging the crime, and Montana for just three years after the conviction becomes final.
- Some states, like Missouri, allow only specific felony offenses to activate the obligation to preserve evidence.
- Few jurisdictions have stern sanctions for government violations of the duty to preserve evidence. In South Carolina, "a person who wilfully and maliciously destroys, alters, conceals, or tampers with physical evidence or biological material that is required to be preserved" is guilty only of a misdemeanor and subject to a fine of no more than $1,000 for a first offense. That's right. South Carolina imposes a modest fine for malicious tampering with evidence that could exonerate an innocent prisoner.

Also, while most states call for mandatory preservation of evidence in qualifying cases, others make preservation in certain cases contingent on requests from the defendant.[15]

What a tragedy. The promise of DNA testing rings hollow if biological evidence isn't adequately retrieved from the crime scene, stored properly, and preserved over time; there will be nothing available to test even if a court grants access. And with nothing to test, the innocent may remain incarcerated far longer than necessary. Felipe Rodriguez is one of those innocent people who stayed in prison for decades because the biological evidence that could have freed him was nowhere to be found.

On Thanksgiving morning 1987, the lifeless body of Maureen McNeill Fernandez was discovered in a Queens, New York, rail yard known as a "lover's lane."[16] Thirty-seven stab wounds crisscrossed her partially clothed body, and evidence suggested she'd been sexually assaulted. The rail yard was full of forensic evidence, including blood, hair, and tire tracks.

The police began reconstructing the events of the previous night. Fernandez had visited one of her children at Wyckoff Hospital in Brooklyn and left sometime after midnight. She later surfaced at a social club accompanied by a man. The couple left around 3:30 a.m., an hour before the estimated time of her death. A bar patron described Fernandez's companion as having reddish-brown hair. The bartender characterized the man as "stocky," roughly five feet eight inches tall, and between 175 and 200 pounds.

After investigating a few errant leads, the police looked into a tip about a white Cadillac-like car seen leaving the rail yard. It turned out that a security guard back at the hospital, Javier Ramos, owned a vehicle that fit that description. When questioned by a Queens homicide detective, Ramos told a tale about how he had loaned his car to a friend, Richie, who burst into his apartment on Thanksgiving morning and confessed to having killed a woman after an argument. Ramos claimed he had then cleaned up his blood-soaked car without notifying the police. After Richie produced an alibi, Ramos switched his story and insisted he'd farmed out his vehicle to a different friend, Felipe Rodriguez, who was the one who'd rushed into his room and uttered a damning confession: "I had to stab her to prove to her that I was a man."

The story didn't add up. Ramos's shifting narrative—the move from Richie to Rodriguez—was fishy. In addition, Rodriguez didn't match the accounts of the man observed at the bar. He had jet-black hair and was tall and slender. Finally, Rodriguez seemed an unlikely killer. A devoted father, Rodriguez had no arrests, convictions, or history of violence. He harbored dreams of one day joining the New York Police Department.

The police nevertheless targeted Rodriguez. That choice gained momentum after they interrogated him. The police claimed that although Rodriguez denied committing the crime, he said he was fascinated by the Wyckoff Hospital morgue and by dead bodies generally. What's more, over a year after the murder occurred, the patron of the social club and the bartender identified Rodriguez as the man they'd seen with the victim.

So the case rested on the slimmest of reeds when it went to trial in 1990. It consisted of a sketchy account by an obfuscating witness, Ramos, who himself was a suspect, some tardy identifications that didn't jibe with the original description of the homicide victim's escort, and prejudicial statements allegedly made by the defendant that he fantasized about corpses. A good defense lawyer could have snapped those reeds with ease. But Rodriguez didn't have a good lawyer. His attorney had been recently widowed and had started stealing money from clients to mollify loan sharks clamoring for repayment of a family member's gambling debts. Distracted and distraught, the lawyer put on a meager defense. And Rodriguez paid the price. He was convicted of murder and sentenced to twenty-five years to life in prison.

RODRIGUEZ LOST HIS DIRECT APPEAL AS WELL AS HIS ATTEMPTS at postconviction relief. His application for assistance from the Innocence Project in New York City eventually got to the top of the group's seemingly endless wait list, where my longtime friend, the brilliant and tenacious Nina Morrison, took it on in the mid-2000s. With the help of some law students, she tried to locate the forensic evidence retrieved from the crime scene that could be subjected to DNA testing. The blood. The tire tracks. The hair. Morrison even enlisted the help of the Queens County district attorney's office, which, troubled by the case, pledged to reinvestigate. This was a significant development because it meant Morrison wouldn't have to run through the procedural labyrinth of the state's postconviction DNA-testing law to obtain access to the evidence. Access was a given—if only she could find the biological material.

She found nothing.

Much of the evidence that had been collected back in 1987 had long since been destroyed under protocols for both the medical examiner's office and the police department that existed at the time. Whatever other evidence the police had seen fit to retain had disappeared, lost in the chaos of New York City's storage facilities. The arrival of Hurricane Sandy in 2012 wrought further havoc on those facilities. Morrison and her allies spent several more years searching for any scrap of evidence. They managed to find some hair and other items at a warehouse, but DNA testing didn't yield any results for a male profile.

Morrison continued to investigate and mull over her legal options before she petitioned the governor for clemency, an executive branch remedy that is the subject of Chapter 10.[17] Stirred by Morrison's account, New York governor Andrew Cuomo freed Rodriguez in January 2017 through a commutation order that reduced his sentence. Yet the order didn't declare him innocent— and the murder conviction stayed on his rap sheet.

Morrison doesn't give up easily or, in my experience, ever. True to character, she carried on. First, she and her co-counsel confronted Ramos, who admitted he'd lied at trial. Second, she kept pushing the DA's office to hunt down police files that had gone missing—and that were finally unearthed in a warehouse eight years after the Innocence Project got the case. Those files contained documents supporting the misidentification defense and further eroding what was left of Ramos's dwindling credibility. These papers were *Brady* material,[18] evidence that was favorable to Rodriguez and that likely would have made a difference at trial had it been disclosed. Citing the new discoveries, the defense team filed a postconviction motion under New York's coram nobis remedy that resulted in a dismissal of Rodriguez's conviction in December 2019.

Rodriguez spent twenty-seven years in prison for a murder he didn't commit, and another two years trying to clear his name. His agony was presumably prolonged—by a good thirteen years—because New York State had antiquated evidence retention and preservation practices that allowed for the destruction of evidence, even in murder cases, and lackluster storage systems for anything the authorities opted to keep.

———

NO ONE SHOULD HAVE TO GO THROUGH WHAT FELIPE RODRIguez did. If biological evidence is available in a criminal case, it should be retrieved and stored so that innocent criminal defendants can test it without jumping through arduous procedural hoops. Anyone with a potentially valid innocence claim should be eligible for access to biological evidence under state postconviction DNA-testing laws regardless of (1) whether they remain incarcerated, (2) what type of crime they were convicted of, (3) whether they pled guilty or went to trial, (4) their financial resources, or (5) when they submit their application for access. Given that the trial judge who handled the case initially might be inclined to reject an applicant's overture for postconviction DNA testing, let's also create a robust right to appeal those decisions to a higher court. Police and prosecutors who violate the preservation requirement, especially those who act in bad faith, should face a stiff punishment.

Improving and broadening access to postconviction DNA testing would undercut prosecutors' oft-stated interest in the finality of convictions and the criminal justice system's emphasis on efficiency. More defendants would seek testing in more types of cases over longer periods of time. Those requests would be granted more frequently, sometimes on appellate review, and lead to the testing of biological material more often. As I've argued throughout this book, the benefit of achieving justice for the innocent justifies the cost. Finality is a fallacy when it's weaponized to rationalize preventing viable innocence cases from seeing the light of day—and decreased efficiency is well worth the reward of increased justice.

8

THE SUPREMES

Stop in the Name of Innocence

It should be clear by now that procedural obstacles block many innocent prisoners from attaining exoneration through the courts. The Supreme Court of the United States lies atop the judicial food chain in Washington, DC, where nine jurists with lifetime appointments shape the law of the land. Our nation's court of last resort has the power to tackle the pressing social issues of the day—capital punishment, reproductive rights, same-sex marriage, and the like—as well as cases where a criminal defendant pleading innocence has been denied relief in the lower courts. Yet the Supreme Court seldom exercises its power to review credible innocence claims. When it does, the Court's decisions don't normally fall on the side of the angels.

How do claims of innocence make it to the United States Supreme Court? As with all cases, litigants must follow specific procedures to hoist them up the ladder.

Before seeking Supreme Court review, defendants must ex-
haust their remedies in the lower courts. Defendants usually ask
the Supreme Court to take their case at the end of the direct appeal,
but they might also pursue review after they've completed their
postconviction remedies. The process entails filing a petition for a
writ of certiorari from the Supreme Court.[1] The issuance of a writ
of certiorari, which is Latin for "to be more fully informed," orders the lower court to deliver the record in the case (transcripts,
briefs, and exhibits) and signals that the Supreme Court wants to
look at the matter. A litigant must file her petition within ninety
days of final judgment in state or federal court, accompanied by a
$300 fee that's waivable if the applicant can't pay.

The "cert petition" route has many spurs and detours, depending on the exact posture of the case. For one thing, the defendant may win at some point during the lower court litigation,
putting the *prosecution* in the position of applying for cert. For
another, sometimes defendants consolidate their direct appeal
with the appeal of a state postconviction remedy, sending them
both at once to a state appeals court and setting the table for a
cert petition that asks the Supreme Court to review both outcomes. In unusual situations, a litigant may even forsake the cert
petition process and submit a direct appeal to the Court.[2]

That's just the process for seeking review. The substance of the
cert petition must check certain boxes too. For the Supreme Court
to have proper jurisdiction over the case, the application must raise
a "federal question" by citing a violation of a federal constitutional
or legal principle rather than pure state law. The petition must
also articulate *why* the Court should take the case from among the
thousands jostling for its attention each year. The Supreme Court
tends to accept cases that fall into one of two categories. The first
is when there's a split in the lower courts about how to interpret a
particular law and the Court must mend any confusion. The second concerns cases of national significance, the results of which
will have ramifications that affect people across the country.

Many fact-based claims of innocence by individual criminal defendants don't fit neatly in either category. Supreme Court rules caution that "a petition for a writ of certiorari is rarely granted when the asserted error consists of erroneous factual findings or the misapplication of a properly stated rule of law."[3] The goal for a lawyer drafting a cert petition, then, is to extrapolate from the client's innocence case and convey its broader importance to the Court—to transform a microlevel injustice into a pervasive macrolevel problem.

Suppose you're pitching the Long Island robbery case to the Supreme Court. How would you frame it to hook the Justices? Perhaps make the misidentification of Stephen Schulz a forum on the failings of police lineup procedures and the deprivation of a defendant's federal constitutional right to due process. Maybe characterize the reluctance of Schulz's lawyer to present an alibi defense, much less engage in a hardy pretrial investigation, as a cautionary tale about the holes in the test for ineffective assistance of counsel and the need to close them. Or possibly include *both* arguments in your petition, hoping a double-barreled approach to the legal issues, coupled with latent fears about a wrongful conviction, will blow away the Justices. That's no simple endeavor. Out of the seven thousand to eight thousand cert petitions filed each year, the Justices take about eighty.[4] The Court has become especially circumspect in picking criminal cases. In 2009, more than a third of the cases granted a writ of certiorari involved criminal procedure issues, while just 15 percent covered that turf a decade later.[5]

After the defense submits its cert petition, the government has thirty days in which to file a brief in opposition. Outside interest groups known as amici curiae (friends of the court) also have a chance to file briefs offering their thoughts on why the Court should grant cert.[6] In the innocence context, these entities tend to include innocence projects, criminal justice reform groups, and civil rights organizations. Once the dust settles from briefing, the Court parses through the petitions in search of the chosen few.

The parsing process begins with dispatching the briefs to the Justices' chambers. Seven of the nine Justices currently participate in what's called the cert pool. (Justices Alito and Gorsuch have opted out.)[7] A law clerk for one of the seven Justices in the pool takes an initial look at the briefs and drafts a memorandum advising whether the Court should grant cert. The memorandum is distributed to the pool for analysis by other clerks and, potentially, the Justices. Clerks for the two Justices who aren't in the cert pool conduct their own evaluations and make recommendations directly to their bosses.

If one or more Justices are intrigued by the case, they put it on the "discuss list" as a topic for the next private conference of the Court. If no Justice expresses any interest, the case goes to the "dead list," an unfortunate yet apt name for petitions marked for automatic rejection. Cases on the discuss list, unsurprisingly, are discussed by all nine Justices. If four of the nine are enthralled, cert is granted and the case moves to the Supreme Court docket. The briefing process revs up again during this next phase, known as the merits stage. The sequence of events after that resembles a regular direct appeal, culminating in oral argument before the full Court.

The cert pool has weathered criticism from across the political spectrum.[8] Ken Starr, a conservative lawyer and key figure in the impeachment of President Bill Clinton, has called it a "swamp" and a "Bermuda Triangle." The late Supreme Court Justice John Paul Stevens, a progressive icon, also railed against the system. (Like Alito and Gorsuch today, Stevens bowed out of the cert pool during his tenure.) The criticisms revolve around the notion that the pool gives too much power to Supreme Court law clerks, recent law school graduates whose fancy academic lineage, not litigation experience, has propelled them to those prestigious posts. They also form a homogenous group. One study found that 85 percent of those who secured Supreme Court clerkships from 2005 to 2017 were white, and that there were twice as many men as women.[9]

The fuss over the legitimacy of the cert pool is beside the point, at least for purposes of this book. The effect of the cert pool is that those vying for a cert grant must target their efforts at a cadre of largely white male twentysomethings who have had little exposure to the rough-and-tumble world of criminal practice. For innocence advocates, the challenge is how to educate these precocious gatekeepers about why fact-based, singular injustices deserve coveted spots on the calendar. That's quite a challenge. Even the strongest innocence claims might not make the Supreme Court cut, as a murder case from Texas illustrates.[10]

On April 23, 1996, a young white woman, Stacey Lee Stites, was found strangled to death in the brush of Bastrop County east of Austin. Her fiancé, Jimmy Fennell, a white police officer, was the last person known to have seen her alive. By his telling, they watched television together at their apartment on the night of the twenty-second, and she left for work at three a.m. the next morning.

Vaginal swabs taken from the victim contained three sperm cells that were later traced to Rodney Reed, a local Black man. Although he at first denied knowing Stites, Reed later conceded that they'd been having an affair. The DNA evidence and Reed's prevarication made him the prime suspect and led prosecutors to file murder charges. What clinched the case against him at trial was expert testimony putting the time of death at three a.m. or later, which exculpated the victim's fiancé, Fennell. A jury convicted Reed and voted for the death penalty.

Reed maintained his innocence from the start and has done so ever since. In the years following his conviction, he has also assembled new evidence to prove it. Consider this sampling of the material that Reed has presented in postconviction filings:

Corroboration of the affair. Some of Stites's friends have confirmed that she was in a consensual, clandestine sexual relationship with Reed prior to her death.

Doubts about the time of death. One of the state's expert witnesses admitted that his trial testimony "should not have been used at trial as an accurate statement about when Ms. Stites died." Other analysts have looked at the forensic evidence and interpreted it to show that Stites died on the evening of April 22, not the next morning, putting her in the company of Fennell at the time of the murder.

Mounting circumstantial evidence against Fennell. Several witnesses have reported ominous behavior by Fennell and alarming details about his relationship with Stites.

- Fennell's best friend, a fellow police officer, divulged that Fennell told him he was out drinking the night before the body was found, which contradicted his original position that he had been home with Stites.
- Another officer claimed that, a month before the killing, Fennell used a vulgar racial slur to describe the man with whom Stites was having an affair.
- A third officer observed Fennell at Stites's funeral and overheard him say something to the effect of "You got what you deserved."
- Yet another officer described how Stites's coworkers told him that they would warn Stites whenever Fennell arrived at the workplace so she could avoid interacting with him.
- A salesman signed an affidavit asserting that Fennell had threatened to kill Stites when he was seeking life insurance.
- Law enforcement files revealed that Fennell had a history of violence against women.
- After Stites's death, Fennell served ten years in prison for a sex crime that occurred while he was on duty.

State and federal courts have ignored this evidence of Reed's innocence (and Fennell's guilt). Reed has lost an astonishing *nine* state postconviction filings to date. The Texas Court of Criminal

Appeals stayed his execution in 2019, five days before he was slated to die, to allow evaluation of his latest legal salvo. Reed's tenth state postconviction petition spawned a hearing in Bastrop in 2021, during which his defense team put forward more new evidence of his innocence, including testimony from a man who claimed that Fennell had confessed to the murder.[11]

Stymied so far by the lower courts, Reed has asked the Supreme Court to review his case no fewer than four times.[12] On each occasion the Court refused to issue a writ of certiorari. After the most recent cert denial, in 2020, Justice Sotomayor took the rare step of writing a separate opinion. In reference to the new evidence, she noted that "misgivings this ponderous should not be brushed aside even in the least consequential of criminal cases; certainly they deserve sober consideration when a capital conviction and sentence hang in the balance." She remained "hopeful that available state processes will take care to ensure full and fair consideration of Reed's innocence—and will not allow the most permanent of consequences to weigh on the Nation's conscience while Reed's conviction remains so mired in doubt."

I am less hopeful that Texas will do the right thing or, for that matter, that the Supreme Court will ever hear the merits of Rodney Reed's case. Even if Reed were granted cert, getting an appointment on the Supreme Court's calendar far from guarantees that justice will be served. Only a handful of innocence cases have earned those slots over the years, often with tragic results. Chapter 5 showed how the Supreme Court's 1993 decision in *Herrera* not only effectively condemned a Texas man to death without a full airing of new evidence related to his innocence, but clarified that freestanding innocence claims by themselves may not generally supply the basis for federal habeas corpus relief. The 2009 *Osborne* opinion, from Chapter 7, also portrays the pitfalls in obtaining cert, as the Court refused to recognize a federal constitutional right to postconviction DNA testing in a case out of Alaska.

Herrera and *Osborne* aren't alone in the class of Supreme Court opinions that have set back the movement to overturn wrongful convictions. In his pioneering study of the first two hundred DNA exonerations, Professor Brandon Garrett found that thirty-eight of those defendants had filed cert petitions with the Supreme Court before science freed them.[13] Thirty-seven of those petitions were summarily denied without ever reaching the merits stage. The Court picked just one for full review, a terrible sexual assault case from Arizona.

———

ON THE EVENING OF OCTOBER 29, 1983, A TEN-YEAR-OLD Latino boy named David attended church with his mother in Tucson.[14] Like many kids, he preferred fun and games to religious services, so he ducked out to visit a carnival behind the church. A man kidnapped David and molested him in two different locations over the course of an hour and a half. After returning David to the carnival, the man vowed to kill the boy if he ever breathed a word of the incident to anyone.

Despite the threat, David told his mother what had happened, and she rushed him to a hospital where he was treated for his injuries. A doctor swabbed David's mouth and rectum, made slides of those samples, and gathered specimens of the boy's saliva, blood, and hair. Tucson police put the rape kit in a refrigerator for safekeeping. They also seized the survivor's underwear and T-shirt but didn't refrigerate those items or store them in a temperature-controlled environment.

David described the perpetrator as a middle-aged Black man with "greasy" gray hair, no facial scars, and a unique characteristic—an eye that was almost completely white. He also mentioned details about the assailant's car, a two-door sedan with a loud muffler. These leads proved helpful, and investigators soon had a prime suspect, thirty-year-old Larry Youngblood.

Nine days after the assault, David selected Youngblood's picture from a photo lineup.

Youngblood was a Black man. But he had dry and dark hair, not greasy and gray. He also had a scar on his forehead, walked with a discernible limp, and wore glasses in public. The only thing that really lined up with David's original account of the perpetrator, aside from race, was that Youngblood had a bad eye.

David was not especially confident about his choice. When he first picked Youngblood, he said only that he was "pretty sure." Later he identified a different man from the array as the possible culprit. David's recollection of the car used by his rapist also didn't align with Youngblood's vehicle. The suspect owned a car with four doors, and it didn't even run at the time of the crime because it lacked a battery. When it was operable, it ran quietly.

The day after David's identification of Youngblood, a police criminologist examined the rape kit. Following standard departmental procedure, he did just enough forensic investigation to conclude that sexual contact had occurred. He conducted no further tests, not even a serology test on the rape kit or the victim's clothing to pin down the blood type of the assailant.

The police arrested Youngblood in December 1983, and the state indicted him on charges of child molestation, sexual assault, and kidnapping. The prosecution then asked the criminologist to pursue additional tests; he performed an ABO blood group test on the rectal swab from the rape kit, but it failed to yield any results. The case went to trial a year later with no physical evidence and only a fragile identification from a shaken child witness to implicate Larry Youngblood. The jury deadlocked six to six in 1984, ending in a mistrial.

That could have been the end of the story. Instead, the prosecution geared up for a new trial.

In January 1985, the criminologist turned to David's clothing, which the police had neglected to refrigerate. The examination uncovered a semen stain on the underwear and another on the back of the T-shirt. But the biological samples had deteriorated after more than a year in suboptimal conditions. The scientist's attempts to use the ABO technique to identify the blood type from these samples, as well as a protein molecule test, didn't generate any noteworthy results.

The upshot was that the state couldn't determine the blood type of the assailant or even whether he secreted a blood-type marker into his semen. These determinations could have been made even under the rudimentary scientific techniques of the 1980s *if* the garments had been preserved properly.

So the state took aim at Youngblood once again without any physical evidence to bolster its theory. This time the trial judge issued what's known as an adverse inference instruction. The judge told the jury that if it found that the government had lost or destroyed evidence, it could infer that forensic analysis of the material would have hurt the prosecution's case. After a four-day trial, the jury convened to deliberate, presumably with the adverse inference instruction in mind.

Ninety-five minutes later it rendered its verdict. Guilty.

———————

YOUNGBLOOD GOT A TEN-AND-A-HALF-YEAR PRISON SENTENCE. He appealed his conviction on the grounds that the failure to preserve the biological evidence violated the Due Process Clause of the US Constitution. The Arizona Court of Appeals agreed, concluding that timely testing of David's clothing might have exonerated Youngblood. It held that "when identity is an issue at trial and the police permit destruction of evidence that could eliminate a defendant as the perpetrator, such loss is material to the defense and is a denial of due process." The court didn't find any misconduct on the part of the Tucson police, but it didn't think such a finding was necessary. The panel dismissed the conviction "to avoid an unfair trial, not as punishment" for any behavior by the government.

State officials released Youngblood after three years in prison. He was only provisionally free, however, as his case progressed through the higher courts. First, the Arizona Supreme Court rejected the government's petition for further review. A good sign. Next, prosecutors sought a writ of certiorari from the United States Supreme Court, and that request was among the few granted cert for the October 1988 term. Not such a good sign.

During oral argument that autumn, the Justices' questions for Arizona prosecutors dwelled on the minutiae of the testing process—which items were tested and when, which ones weren't and why, and which forensic tests were available in the crime lab. Their interrogation of Youngblood's counsel had a very different tenor. Justices Sandra Day O'Connor and William Rehnquist focused on the absence of bad faith by Tucson authorities. Rehnquist seemed anxious about the possibility of an open-ended obligation for law enforcement to do everything in its power to guarantee fair trials: to preserve every shred of evidence, to administer all possible scientific tests, to follow each lead, however unpromising. "How broad is this duty?" he asked. "Is the Constitution going to tell prosecutors how they ought to investigate cases?"[15]

The Court issued its decision the following month. By a six-to-three vote, the Justices reinstated Youngblood's conviction and ruled that "unless a criminal defendant can show bad faith on the part of the police, failure to preserve potentially useful evidence does not constitute a denial of due process of law." What a dagger to the heart of Youngblood's case—and to claims of innocence everywhere that hang on subjecting old evidence to new scientific tests.

One might wonder how this squares with *Brady v. Maryland*. As discussed in Chapter 2, a due process violation exists under *Brady* when law enforcement fails to turn over—let alone destroys—exculpatory evidence regardless of whether it was done in good or bad faith. In other words, a prisoner can get a new trial when law enforcement doesn't meet its *Brady* disclosure obligations despite the best of intentions to do so. Well, the Supreme Court distinguished *Youngblood* because the evidence was only *potentially* exculpatory. According to the majority opinion, "The Due Process Clause requires a different result [from *Brady*] when we deal with the failure of the State to preserve evidentiary material of which no more can be said than that it could have been subjected to tests, the results of which might have exonerated the defendant."

That's a lot of legal jargon and doctrinal hairsplitting. Simply put, the destruction of evidence that could possibly clear an innocent suspect doesn't violate the United States Constitution unless the government acted in bad faith, which is very hard to prove in court. The concept of bad faith in American law involves purposeful, usually dishonest behavior.[16] Since Youngblood's case didn't involve deliberate misconduct, just a toxic blend of bad luck and bad investigative choices, the Supreme Court labeled his trial a fair one. Police and prosecutors nationwide now had license to conduct lazy investigations. The Court had also given them a green light to put perishable biological evidence in a box: ignored, forgotten, and untested.

―――――――――

THE SUPREME COURT REMANDED THE YOUNGBLOOD CASE BACK to the Arizona state courts with orders to reassess the matter in light of its opinion. Youngblood retained his freedom pending the outcome of these proceedings—and he had some reason to hope he wouldn't go back to his cell. A bedrock principle of American law is that individual states may afford more protection to their people than federal law provides. The federal Constitution is a floor under which states may not go; states can't offer *fewer* rights than the "Supreme Law of the Land" demands. But there's no ceiling. States may choose, as an expression of their sovereignty under our federalist scheme, to grant *greater* rights to their residents than the Supreme Court has conferred. That's what the Arizona Court of Appeals did on remand. Even if the state's poor handling of the evidence didn't offend federal due process, the court reasoned, it violated Arizona *state* due process.

Youngblood's victory proved fleeting. After prosecutors badgered the highest court in the state to review the decision by the Court of Appeals, the Arizona Supreme Court reinstated the conviction. It ruled that the adverse inference instruction issued at trial sufficed to correct any misstep by the police, essentially saying that absent bad faith by the government, due process in Arizona requires nothing more after the loss or destruction of evidence.

———————

YOUNGBLOOD RETURNED TO PRISON IN 1993. HE STAYED THERE for five more years before his release on parole. He struggled to reacclimate to life outside his cell, though one bright spot was that his original trial lawyer kept fighting to exonerate her client. She drew on her connections to ask the police to test the rectal swab from the rape kit with new, state-of-the-art DNA technology. In 2000, those tests confirmed that Youngblood was innocent.

County prosecutors apologized to Youngblood and promised David's family that they wouldn't rest until they identified the true perpetrator. They ran the DNA profile from the rectal swab through a national database in early 2001. The profile matched that of Walter Cruise, a Black man incarcerated in Texas who had two prior convictions for sexually abusing children in Houston and an arrest in Tucson for similar actions. There was something else too: he was blind in one badly misshapen eye. When confronted with the DNA evidence, Cruise pled guilty to assaulting David and received a twenty-four-year prison sentence.

———————

THE 1983 SEXUAL ASSAULT OF DAVID HAD FAR-REACHING RIP-
ple effects.

David never really recovered from his trauma. He became
addicted to drugs and alcohol, spent time in jail for domestic violence, and had fraught relationships with his parents, who divorced
when he was young. A probation officer once characterized David
as "angry at the whole entire world." In 2004, a train struck and
killed him a few miles down Interstate 10 from where the carnival
had taken place. He was thirty-one years old, nearly the same age
as Larry Youngblood when he was first identified as David's rapist.

Youngblood never recovered either. Despite his exoneration,
he didn't receive any compensation for his wrongful conviction
and resorted to panhandling on the streets of Tucson. Homeless
and unwell, he died of a drug overdose in 2007.

It's also fair to say that criminal law doctrine has never fully recovered from the Supreme Court's *Youngblood* decision. In its wake,
lost and destroyed evidence left thousands of defendants and victims
without recourse to get at the truth.[17] Between 1991 and 2001, New
Orleans got rid of evidence in twenty-five hundred rape cases; in
1992, the New York Police Department demolished large quantities
of evidence to open up room in its warehouse; Houston cited similar
storage constraints to justify obliterating rape kits throughout the
1990s. The timing of these purges is important. The NYPD cleanup
occurred just months after the state's first DNA exoneration, and
Houston's happened on the heels of the governor's decision to pardon a man based on DNA results. Not a single challenge to the evidence discarded during this era in Houston, New Orleans, or New
York City produced a judicial finding of "bad faith." Lower courts
have cited the bad faith test, and its tolerance for government destruction of evidence, to deprive numerous prisoners of relief. DNA
testing later exonerated some of them,[18] as it did Larry Youngblood.

In recent years, many states have intervened with legislation
to counteract the ill effects of *Youngblood*. They've passed laws
that impose strong, affirmative duties on police and prosecutors

to preserve evidence, as discussed in Chapter 7. Not all states have done so, however, and the rules in many others are lousy. The bad faith test from *Youngblood* is still on the books as good law despite calls to turn the page.

———————

THE LARRY YOUNGBLOOD CASE SHOWS HOW FUTILE IT IS TO rely on the United States Supreme Court to catch wrongs left uncorrected by the lower courts. To be fair, the Court has moved the cause of justice forward from time to time during the past thirty years.[19] But not often. The Justices are just as likely to close a path to proving innocence (*Herrera, Osborne, Youngblood*) as to forge a new route or expand an old one. Any dreams of progress also hinge on the willingness of the Court to hear these types of cases, which is a rare event given the fact-based nature of innocence claims and the legions of other cases in the cert pool.

Prospects appear even dimmer for the decades ahead. Former president Donald Trump's appointment of three young conservatives—Justices Amy Coney Barrett, Neil Gorsuch, and Brett Kavanaugh—doesn't bode well for innocence advocates seeking to overturn troublesome precedent, fortify constitutional protections for the innocent, and revamp federal habeas corpus procedures, much less convince the Court to inspect questionable cases where the jury may simply have convicted the wrong person.

Maybe it's foolhardy to depend on *any* court—federal or state, trial or appellate, lowest or highest—to reverse wrongful convictions. Parts I and II of this book present the litany of procedural barriers to doing so. Waivers of the right to appeal a plea deal. Preservation requirements. Deferential standards of appellate review. Harmless error rules. Statutes of limitations. The list goes on and on. Removing or modifying these barriers along the lines I've suggested would help. Another option is to see what remedies exist outside the courtroom.

PART III
EXECUTIVE FUNCTION

9

THE INNOCENT PRISONER'S DILEMMA

How Parole Procedures Fail the
Wrongfully Convicted

THE APPELLATE AND POSTCONVICTION PROCESS GIVES COURTS an opportunity to evaluate innocence claims. But for the reasons advanced throughout this book, they seldom capitalize on it. By recognizing (and even reinforcing) procedural obstacles to litigating these claims, courts uphold many wrongful convictions. The desire for efficiency, the yearning to put an end to litigation, and the wish to pay respect to the rulings of their judicial colleagues supersede the quest for accuracy. If courts truly cared about innocence, the procedures governing such claims wouldn't be so burdensome. Full and fair airings of new evidence would happen more often, exonerations granted more readily, and faith in our criminal justice system restored more broadly.

But the courts don't play the only role in righting injustices. The executive branch also has opportunities to look at possible wrongful convictions. This chapter delves into one of those opportunities, examining how executive officials decide whether to release prisoners on parole and whether those procedures work—or don't work—for the innocent.[1]

MANY STATES HAVE "INDETERMINATE" PUNISHMENT SYSTEMS that ask judges to impose a sentencing range on convicted defendants rather than a fixed term. As prisoners approach the end of their minimum sentence, they normally face a panel of officials appointed by the governor to choose whether they deserve discharge to the outside world on parole. For example, assume a defendant gets a sentence of ten to twenty years' imprisonment. He'd face the parole board at the ten-year mark. If parole was denied, he'd typically confront the board again at regular intervals before the completion of his maximum term.

Granting parole is viewed as an act of grace by the government to a person deemed worthy of a break. Yet it comes with strings attached because parolees stay under government monitoring until their sentence expires. They must check in regularly with parole officers, avoid any criminal activity, even traffic violations, and refrain from out-of-state travel. Any misstep, however petty, may boomerang a parolee back to prison to fulfill what's left of his term. Parolees often struggle to readjust to life in their communities, especially those with yet-to-be-vindicated innocence claims, as the ordeals of Larry Youngblood and Dion Harrell from previous chapters lay bare. Despite its shortcomings, though, parole is a way out of prison for the innocent that doesn't bar them from continuing to seek exoneration in court.

How does an innocent prisoner convince the parole board to grant freedom, qualified as that liberty may be? The answer to this question requires a grasp of the historical backdrop.[2]

THE NAME USED TO DESCRIBE THE CONDITIONAL RELEASE OF A prisoner comes from the French term *parole d'honneur* or "word of honor." From the get-go, parole was directed at the "honorable" prisoner, one who had shown proof of rehabilitation and therefore seemed a safe candidate for release. Parole arose in nineteenth-century English and Irish prisons before migrating across the pond in the 1870s at a time when rehabilitation was the dominant punishment ideology in American penal circles. Rehabilitation rhetoric during that era fused elements of medicine, psychoanalysis, and religion. Corrections officials talked of inmates as "sick" and the goal of the prison system as to "cure." The best treatment, jailers believed, was for prisoners to come to terms with their criminal past. Declining to accept responsibility and acknowledge their guilt was a form of "denial" that meant inmates weren't rehabilitated. It also meant they hadn't repented for their sins, which was another one of the main goals of corrections officials. Consider the nascent label for American prisons in the 1800s: *penitent*iaries.

Parole became a mechanism to incentivize prisoners to accept responsibility for their actions. By accepting responsibility, they could seemingly achieve a trifecta of sorts: (1) display repentance, (2) banish denial from their mindset, and (3) make headway toward curing whatever malady had spurred them to commit crimes to begin with.

That's the philosophy behind parole. Here are some of its effects.

The rise of indeterminate sentencing and the growth of parole transferred power from the judicial to the executive branch. Parole officials could now dictate how long convicted defendants remained in prison. Pleasing them, more than judges, became a key variable in determining inmates' fates. And pleasing them wasn't so simple because, from the outset, boards were stacked with representatives from the law enforcement community who viewed parole as having multiple purposes. One purpose was to dangle the carrot of parole to encourage good behavior and minimize strife within prison walls; another was to alleviate overcrowding and thereby reduce expenses. Board members, then, had a series of interconnected aims. Motivate inmates to avoid fights or other disciplinary infractions, release them if they stayed out of trouble long enough, and keep facilities at desirable occupancy levels.

At one stage in American history, every state utilized a parole system, and almost three-quarters of prison releases were the product of discretionary parole.[3] This changed in the 1970s when the political winds shifted and indeterminate sentencing incurred the wrath of those on both the right and the left. Conservatives attacked minimum sentences as potentially too lenient, while liberals decried the arbitrary and racially biased nature of many parole release decisions. As a 1975 account of the system in New Jersey observed, the average parole recipient in that state was "white and contrite."[4] There were also fears that the uncertainty of the process left inmates on perpetual tenterhooks, lost without the solace afforded by a fixed release date and a set number of days to cross off the calendar. By 2000, sixteen states had eradicated discretionary parole entirely, and four had discarded it for certain violent offenses.

Still, parole has survived in most states and is likely to stay a fixture of the criminal justice landscape.[5] It has even emerged in the 2020s as a component of the "decarceration" movement, a campaign to shrink the prison population that has gathered steam within a diverse set of political constituencies. Advocates include progressives opposed to the very idea of putting humans in cages as well as conservatives leery of excessive public spending who've embraced what's known as the right-on-crime agenda.[6] Parole fits well in the current conversation. It's a time-tested, cost-effective tool for decreasing the number of people in custody. And it's easier to sell to the public than calls to dismantle the prison-industrial complex or otherwise engage in more dramatic reform.

PAROLE MAY BE HERE TO STAY, BUT THE PROCESS THROUGH which boards make release decisions remains largely broken. In deciding whether to grant parole, boards tend to evaluate the in-mate's criminal history, behavior while incarcerated, psycholog-ical makeup, and preparedness for the next phase. Making that decision, based on an appraisal of the paperwork and the person, has traditionally been more art than science. The formula permits unconscious bias to seep into the result, as it has for generations.

Some government officials are aware of this danger and have gravitated toward using algorithms that create individual risk assess-ments to predict whether a person is likely to pose a public safety threat if released.[7] Proponents suggest that these statistical tools yield more equitable outcomes than purely subjective evaluations and safe-guard against unconscious bias. Opponents make the contrary claim that risk assessment models are inherently biased. Their argument is that algorithmic inputs reflect the consequences of law enforcement policies driven by systemic racism; the algorithms rely on factors, like a person's record of previous arrests, in which BIPOC commu-nities are overrepresented because of the scourge of racial profiling and policing priorities that steer patrols to majority-minority neigh-borhoods. In the words of one scholar, "bias in, bias out."[8]

Wherever one stands on whether parole boards should blend qualitative with quantitative methods of evaluation, the data paint a crude picture of how the decision-making process operates in practice.[9] One study of the Colorado parole system described an assembly line–like scheme in which board members dispensed with most cases in a matter of minutes. An account of Nebraska's process is similar, observing that release decisions were "auto-matic," manufactured from rigid eligibility criteria without any individualized appraisal. Some states even allow release decisions to occur without a live appearance by the inmate. Those that per-mit in-person participation all too often make sure the applicant's involvement is trivial. The commission that investigated prison conditions in New York after the notorious 1971 riots at Attica found that parole boards spent, on average, less than six minutes in total to complete their review of an inmate's file, interview the applicant, and reach a decision. A report from Kansas depicted an even speedier process in which officials devoted two to three minutes per parole hearing and resolved as many as 135 cases a day.

As the foregoing primer implies, the parole release decision-making calculus is problematic and presents acute challenges for inmates who claim innocence. First, think about the objectives of parole boards. What most concerns them is *not* an applicant's guilt or innocence—in their view, that issue is best addressed by judges—but whether the person is a public safety risk. Their decisions focus more on how the prisoner performed during his incarceration and is projected to fare going forward as opposed to whether the person might have endured a wrongful conviction.

Second, innocent inmates suffer from the pressure to accept responsibility as a prerequisite to parole. All signs indicate that accepting responsibility (in effect, admitting guilt) increases the likelihood of a positive outcome when applying for parole, while refusing to do so (proclaiming innocence) diminishes the chance for freedom.[10] When I was teaching in Salt Lake City, I visited the state parole board offices to review public records. There I discovered a preprinted "Rationale Sheet" used by Utah parole commissioners when making their release decisions. That form designated *complete acceptance of responsibility* as a mitigating factor and *denial or minimization* as an aggravating one. File after file of inmates deprived of parole contained Rationale Sheets with "X" marked next to "denial or minimization."

Parole commissioners also look for "remorse" on the part of the prisoner. Remorse is intertwined with acceptance of responsibility because it presupposes that the parole applicant admits participation in the act that led to his incarceration. As legal philosopher Jeffrie Murphy explains, remorse is "best understood as the painful combination of guilt and shame that arises in a person when [he] accepts that he has been responsible for seriously wronging another human being."[11] Without this amalgam of responsibility and remorse about the underlying crime, a prospective parolee has little hope of release.

Accepting responsibility and expressing remorse might come easily for guilty prisoners who are genuinely sorry for their crime. Savvy prisoners who lack remorse yet are skilled at summoning crocodile tears might also convince parole boards they've owned up to their misdeeds.[12] Studies suggest not only that parole boards are ill-equipped to differentiate sincere from insincere expressions of remorse, but also that accepting responsibility at a hearing doesn't necessarily correlate with law-abiding behavior down the road.[13]

Most notably, for prisoners who didn't actually commit the crimes they've been convicted of, the emphasis on accepting responsibility and displaying remorse in the parole process creates a quandary that I've termed the Innocent Prisoner's Dilemma:

Option A: Stick to your guns and maintain your innocence in a way that may reduce the likelihood of a parole grant in the short run but doesn't undercut your shot at a future exoneration through appellate and postconviction litigation.

Option B: Feign guilt to boost your chance of parole while harming your prospects for eventual exoneration in court because now there's an admission of guilt on your record.

Exoneration databases are full of examples in which innocent prisoners selected Option A, knowing it would almost invariably prolong their stay in prison.[14] In Chapter 6, I recounted the plight of Audrey Edmunds, the Wisconsin woman wrongfully convicted of shaking a baby to death. Edmunds has written about her mentality when she made her first appearance before the parole board: "Inmates told me I would speak with one person, not a panel, and the parole officer would ask me to admit to the crime and show remorse. . . . But as tempting as the reward might be, it was not an option for me. . . . In my case, admitting guilt would be a lie, and worse, it would be on my record forever."[15]

Edmunds also recalled her experience at the parole hearing, an event that lasted "about three minutes": "A guard led me to a small administration room for the parole hearing. . . . [The parole officer] barely looked at me as she perused my paperwork. My good behavior, excellent job evaluations, and loyal family meant nothing to her. . . . She said that four years were not enough punishment for killing an infant. Parole denied."

Educating parole boards about the Innocent Prisoner's Dilemma can help inmates avoid Edmunds's fate. In fact, the origins of my research into this phenomenon stem from my work in the Manhattan "base house" murder case featured in the opening pages of this book, and my meeting with Bobby Fennell at Otisville Correctional Facility bearing some sobering news. As directors of the Second Look Program at Brooklyn Law School, Will Hellerstein and I didn't see any realistic options for overturning Fennell's wrongful conviction in court. We told our client as much. Other lawyers had exhausted his direct appellate remedies years before, the statute of limitations had passed for federal habeas corpus relief, we couldn't find any new evidence on which to base a coram nobis–type filing, and there wasn't any biological material for DNA testing. Whatever leads had once existed in the 1985 conviction for killing a customer outside a drug den had vanished. We believed that Fennell was innocent of the murder but had no procedure to show it through litigation. We targeted parole as the best avenue to get our client out of Otisville.

The New York State Division of Parole had already denied Fennell's initial application for parole and was slated to revisit his case, coincidentally, just as our investigation was winding up. Fennell had maintained his innocence all along and wasn't about to alter his account. There's no right to counsel at New York state parole hearings. But regulations permit "letters of support," which we saw as an outlet to put our arguments before the board. We wrote a letter that chronicled our efforts in the case, why we thought Fennell was innocent, and why his failure to admit guilt shouldn't be held against him. We stated, "If Mr. Fennell's failure to accept responsibility for the crime for which he has been convicted could serve as a negative factor in his parole application, we would urge the Board to accept it as the only position that a person who has always maintained his innocence, and who the facts strongly suggest is innocent, can logically and in good conscience take."[16]

It worked. The board granted Fennell parole.

The wrongful-conviction rolls also contain many instances where prisoners chose Option B and uttered false admissions of guilt in the hopes of currying favor with the board. Sometimes those efforts paid off with a parole grant, only to accrue long-term liabilities by making it harder to prove innocence through the judicial process. Sometimes they didn't pay off at all, as happened in a baffling case from Utah.

SHERRY ANN FALES WILLIAMS WAS FOUND DEAD ON THE MORNing of November 30, 1984, near a ramp off Interstate 15 in southern Utah.[17] The twenty-one-year-old had lacerations all over her body and no clothing below her waist. An autopsy listed head trauma as the cause of death and noted the presence of defensive wounds, indicating an effort to stave off her attacker.

Forensic evidence gave the first clue about the perpetrator's identity. Crime scene investigators located a cigarette butt in the snow next to Williams. Saliva from the cigarette was later determined to have come from a "type-A secretor," someone with type-A blood who secretes A antigens. An analysis of bodily fluids taken from the rape kit also suggested that the perpetrator was a type-A secretor.

Bruce Dallas Goodman quickly became a suspect. Evidence revealed that he'd started an affair with Williams back in October, and that they'd left Las Vegas together on November 19. Their precise whereabouts after that were unclear. Goodman claimed he had been in California on the thirtieth because Williams had left him to return to her estranged husband. That assertion was corroborated by two alibi witnesses.

Several other people, however, recalled that Goodman had accompanied Williams longer than he'd let on. Two eyewitnesses even placed them together mere hours before the discovery of her corpse. The first, a clerk at a truck stop north of Las Vegas, observed a couple matching their description in the midst of an argument shortly after midnight on November 30. The second, an employee of a casino in Mesquite, Nevada, farther up Interstate 15, saw a duo resembling Goodman and Williams at that location between two a.m. and four a.m. on the thirtieth—and recalled them arguing as well. Finally, Goodman had type-A blood. Armed with this evidence, and little more, prosecutors filed murder charges.

Goodman took his chances at trial, opting to go before a judge rather than a jury. The main evidence against Goodman consisted of (1) a "love gone bad" theory of motive buttressed by (2) tenuous identifications from two strangers placing him in a dispute with the victim well before the body was found miles away in a different state and (3) the fact that he had the same blood type as the person who had left bodily fluids at the crime scene. At trial, there was testimony that 32 percent of the population fell into the category of "A" secretors, further eroding the prosecution case. But the judge found Goodman guilty of murder and gave him an indeterminate prison sentence of five years to life.

The Utah Supreme Court affirmed the conviction on direct appeal by a three-to-two margin. In a dissenting opinion, one justice emphasized the huge time gap—more than five hours—between the sighting in Mesquite and the discovery of Williams's body 180 miles up the highway. The dissenter concluded "this case falls far short of proving that the defendant committed the crime charged."

The minimum sentence for Goodman's murder conviction was just five years, which meant the Utah parole board controlled his fate. The board refused to release Goodman after his first few appearances, presumably in part because he proclaimed innocence and declined to accept responsibility. In 2000, he relented. He "admitted" culpability in an effort to pacify the board.[18] Unmoved, the board denied parole yet again.

Goodman later obtained the help of the Rocky Mountain Innocence Center (RMIC). As I noted in Chapter 3 in the context of Harry Miller's conviction for a Salt Lake City robbery he didn't commit, RMIC handles cases throughout Nevada, Utah, and Wyoming. Unlike the Miller case, Goodman's case had biological evidence in the files. RMIC procured access to that material and submitted the bodily fluids retrieved from the cigarette butt and the rape kit to sophisticated "Y-STR" tests, an advanced form of DNA analysis that hadn't existed at the time of Goodman's trial and that could identify the source with a stunning degree of accuracy. In 2004, those tests revealed profiles for two different men. *Neither* of them was Bruce Dallas Goodman.

What a game changer. The prosecution's theory all along had been that Goodman was a spurned lover who'd acted alone to kill Williams in a fit of pique. The new evidence annihilated that theory.

RMIC was conflicted about how to proceed. I had recently joined the board of directors and participated in the strategy discussions. On the one hand, we preferred to seek relief under Utah's postconviction DNA-testing statute enacted in 2001. That provision would allow a judge to dismiss the case entirely, without the possibility of a retrial, provided we could demonstrate our client was actually innocent. The burden of proof for making that demonstration was very heavy; we'd have to present "clear and convincing" evidence of innocence. Although we thought we had enough, it wasn't a slam dunk. On the other hand, we could pursue recourse through Utah's general postconviction law, which had a coram nobis–like option that permitted a court to reverse a conviction if newly discovered evidence undermined confidence in the verdict. We felt we could meet that standard more easily. Yet the byproduct of meeting the standard was far from ideal: Goodman wouldn't be declared innocent, and the prosecution could retry him.

We went back and forth about our options before landing on the idea of contacting the prosecutors assigned to the case. We knew that our chances under the DNA statute would rise considerably if we could get the prosecutors on board. Maybe we could persuade them to join our motion, or at least soothe their opposition to it. So we reached out to take their temperature— and got burned. Although troubled by the DNA evidence, state prosecutors didn't share our belief that Bruce Dallas Goodman was innocent. Instead, they formulated a novel hypothesis that he had acted with two unknown men to kill Williams, and that the absence of biological evidence didn't absolve him of the crime.

This is where Goodman's "admission" to the parole board came back to harm him. Utah permits the exchange of information between parole boards and prosecutors. As a consequence, damning statements and other negative facts that surface at parole hearings can migrate into prosecutorial responses to postconviction filings. In Goodman's case, prosecutors learned about his statements of guilt at the 2000 parole hearing and cited them as one reason for their hesitancy to deem him innocent. They wouldn't budge even after we explained why innocent prisoners might feign guilt.

The prosecutors pledged to fight any motion under the DNA statute but agree to relief through the postconviction remedy and not retry him if we followed their preferred path. Their rationale was that the new DNA findings created reasonable doubt, not proof of innocence. We suspected this was a face-saving maneuver to spare them public embarrassment and shield the state from civil liability for a wrongful conviction. Their motive didn't really matter, though. What mattered is that we had a tough decision to make.

After evaluating our options again, we came down on the side of the postconviction remedy route. A declaration of innocence was our goal. Even so, freedom for our client without the risk of a retrial was a more urgent objective. A favorable court order under the postconviction remedy would allow our client to leave prison within five days, as compared to the protracted litigation that would inevitably precede a successful effort under the DNA statute. And success was far from certain.

In November 2004, Bruce Dallas Goodman set foot outside Utah's state prison in Draper after nineteen years of incarceration.[19] He only had $120 to his name, and RMIC had to purchase clothing for him to wear.

The years that followed weren't kind to Goodman. Without the official stamp of innocence, he never received compensation for his wrongful conviction, battled to make ends meet, and cycled between county lockup and homelessness in California. He died of a heart attack in November 2014, almost a decade after the day of his release. Utah issued him a posthumous certificate of innocence the next year, paired with a commitment to pay his relatives $100,000 in recognition of the miscarriage of justice in his case, acknowledgment and recompense that came far too late.

THE GOODMAN CASE SHOWS ONE OFFSHOOT OF THE INNOCENT Prisoner's Dilemma. Even if an innocent inmate admits guilt at a parole hearing to gain favor, it doesn't guarantee release on parole. And regardless of whether the admission achieves release, it could ricochet to hurt the prisoner when seeking exoneration in court. It makes sense that innocent prisoners, desperate to escape confinement, might surrender to temptation at a parole hearing and accept responsibility for something they haven't done. They might calculate that the benefit of possible freedom now outweighs the cost of continued imprisonment, all the while hoping that the path to liberty via parole doesn't close off eventual exoneration through the courts. Those calculations can miss the mark, something Bruce Dallas Goodman later discovered to his regret.

One way to counter this dilemma is to relay information about its drawbacks to parole boards, as in Bobby Fennell's case.[20] I've sent letters on many occasions to explain why parole boards shouldn't treat an applicant's assertions of innocence as a negative factor in deciding whether to grant release. I also sometimes advocate for formerly incarcerated people striving to prove their innocence through litigation yet who carry the baggage of past admissions of guilt to the parole board. These attempts have panned out from time to time, giving me hope that parole commissioners and judges are awakening to this situation, and that public awareness is forcing them to reconsider how much emphasis to place on acceptance of responsibility.[21]

To be clear, it's not that parole boards should refuse to consider whether an inmate has accepted responsibility and shown remorse for his actions. Indications that a prisoner has truly come to terms with his offenses may reflect maturation and self-awareness, hints of growth that should constitute a thumb on the scale in favor of release. These statements can also aid crime victims with the healing process.[22] Rather, it's about *how much* pressure that thumb should impose. I think a light touch is warranted, at most, given what we know about the Innocent Prisoner's Dilemma and how difficult it is to distinguish authentic expressions of responsibility and remorse from contrived ones. Parole boards should disentangle remorse from responsibility and give neither much weight in measuring whether to grant parole. Board members should instead look for empathy—search for whether the inmate identifies with the crime victim's suffering at all, or even just feels sorrow about it, irrespective of whether he caused it.

10

NOT JUST MERCY

The Untapped Potential of Clemency

PAROLE IS NOT THE ONLY EXECUTIVE BRANCH REMEDY AVAIL-
able to innocent prisoners. They may also ask the government
for clemency in the form of a pardon or a sentence commutation,
outcomes that are far preferable for the innocent than parole.
Sometimes the *same* officials make both parole and clemency
decisions, but in many jurisdictions these responsibilities are
allocated to different executive actors.[1] Putting aside the exact
setup, clemency typically follows a separate track from parole,
and inmates may seek it regardless of where they are in the parole
process. What the processes share is an utter disregard for claims
of actual innocence.

———

LET'S START WITH AN OVERVIEW OF CLEMENCY'S MAIN FEATURES
and how they differ from parole.

Scope. Clemency normally consists of a *pardon* (full forgiveness for the underlying offense), a *commutation* (reduction in the

prison sentence), or a *reprieve* (temporary delay, or "stay," of a sentence).[2] Once granted, the gift of a pardon or commutation usually can't be rescinded, future misdeeds of its recipient notwithstanding. Those transgressions might trigger new criminal charges, not resuscitate old ones. One exception is that a person whose sentence is commuted is occasionally placed under parole supervision.[3] Otherwise clemency returns its recipient to the free world unencumbered by continued government supervision.

Structure. The US president wields the clemency power at the federal level, guided by the Department of Justice. Governors, administrators, or a combination of the two control it in the states.[4] Most states embrace a hybrid model in which the governor shares clemency responsibility with an administrative board. The bulk of these jurisdictions authorize boards to make nonbinding pardon and commutation recommendations to the governor, while a few require a favorable endorsement from the board before a governor can act. In twelve states, the governor has *complete* autonomy over these decisions. No matter what the precise configuration, governors generally exert much more influence over the clemency process than they do over parole, and with minimal judicial oversight.

Source. Unlike parole, which emerged as an administrative remedy in the nineteenth century, clemency has constitutional underpinnings that predate the nation's founding. The framers of our federal and state constitutions took the concept from England, where monarchs have long used it to pay tribute to loyal subjects and convince the masses of their magnanimity. The framers envisioned clemency not so much as an imperial courtesy to withhold or dispense on a whim, but as a safety net, one last chance to rescue convicted defendants who merit some form of state-sanctioned benevolence.

One thing clemency has in common with parole is that this benevolence seldom extends to prisoners with viable innocence claims, contrary to what some observers believe. In Leonel

Herrera's case, covered in Chapter 5, the US Supreme Court cited the availability of executive clemency in Texas to justify barring him from raising an innocence claim in a federal habeas corpus proceeding.[5] Herrera's claim hinged on newly discovered evidence alleging that his brother Raul had committed the murders of two law enforcement officers that had sent Leonel to death row. In the Court's majority opinion, Chief Justice Rehnquist noted that Herrera had another "forum to raise his actual innocence claim. . . . For under Texas law, petitioner may file a request for executive clemency. Clemency is deeply rooted in our Anglo-American tradition of law, and is the historic remedy for preventing miscarriages of justice where judicial process has been exhausted." The Chief Justice went on to insist that "clemency has provided the 'fail safe' in our criminal justice system. . . . History is replete with examples of wrongfully convicted persons who have been pardoned in the wake of after-discovered evidence establishing their innocence."

The problem is that Rehnquist overstated the extent to which clemency acts as a guardrail for the innocent. It certainly didn't protect Herrera, who was executed with lingering questions about his guilt unanswered. In truth, there are relatively few examples of inmates declared innocent and their records wiped clean by clemency's brush.[6] When executive officials have pardoned prisoners in that manner, it's often because postconviction DNA testing put their innocence in such sharp relief that media attention made it politically expedient to do so.[7]

The data instead show that pardons and commutations usually go to those with sympathetic features to their cases (e.g., women who kill their abusers) and/or their personal profiles (e.g., people with limited education who committed crimes at a young age and took tremendous steps toward self-improvement while incarcerated).[8] Cyntoia Brown exemplifies this phenomenon. A fifteen-year-old runaway conscripted into sex work in Nashville, she shot and killed a client in 2006 who she thought was reaching for a gun.

At trial, the jury didn't buy her claim of self-defense, resulting in a murder conviction and life sentence. While incarcerated, Brown earned her GED, finished college, and mentored at-risk youth. Her case gained attention with the rise of the #MeToo movement and when celebrities, like the pop star Rihanna, flocked to her cause. In 2019, Tennessee's governor commuted her sentence in what he characterized as a "tragic and complex case."[9]

Even accounting for the trends in the data, there's no real rhyme or reason to how most clemency decisions are made. The frequency with which a particular state draws on its pardon power stems more from its idiosyncratic clemency culture than the merits of any batch of applications.[10] And these clemency cultures don't always mirror a state's political reputation. Clemency is rare in famously liberal Massachusetts, and has been for years. The last three governors have issued only six pardons, all toward the end of Governor Deval Patrick's tenure in 2014 and 2015. In the six years after Patrick's last clemency grant, Massachusetts held only *one* commutation hearing, even as 240 applications waited in the queue for evaluation.[11]

Politicians in Massachusetts, perhaps even more than elsewhere, remain scarred by the aftershocks of an event that happened decades ago.[12] In the 1980s, Massachusetts had a work-release program that permitted prisoners to go on furlough for a period of time before returning to their cells. Willie Horton participated in that program, and while on furlough he raped a woman and stabbed her boyfriend. In the 1988 presidential campaign, Republican nominee George H. W. Bush capitalized on this tragedy to portray his Democratic opponent, Massachusetts governor Mike Dukakis, as weak on crime. Political scientists attribute the shellacking that Dukakis later experienced at the polls in large part to the Horton saga.

The "Willie Horton effect" has arguably frightened Bay State officials from granting liberty, in various forms, to prisoners ever since. Nearby Connecticut has a very different track record; the state issued more than seven hundred pardons in 2018 alone. Some reliably "red" states, like Arkansas and Idaho, are also far less stingy on the pardon front than Massachusetts.

In line with these statewide trends, many individual clemency decisions look mercurial when you put them under a microscope, marked just as often by crass calculation or randomness as by grace. Every now and then clemency serves blatant political purposes and little else. Exhibit A: former President Trump's pardon of political bedfellows Steve Bannon, Michael Flynn, Paul Manafort, and Roger Stone, each of whom played a role as an architect of his unexpected 2016 electoral victory and controversial White House agenda. Some of those who benefitted from Trump's last-gasp pardon spree in January 2021 reportedly paid people close to the president thousands of dollars to lobby on their behalf.[13]

The Supreme Judicial Court of Massachusetts summed up the diverse mix of motivations in the clemency cohort more than forty years ago. It observed that executive officials have issued pardons for "highminded purposes" as well as "merely practical purposes of relieving overcrowded prison conditions, rewarding a prisoner's reform or his turning State's evidence, celebrating a holiday, or doing a political favor." The commonwealth's highest court went on to note that "among these various possibilities, the pardon invoked to correct the wrongful conviction of innocent persons is an anomaly which has occurred only rarely."[14]

A rape case from the 1980s demonstrates why the use of clemency "to correct the wrongful conviction of innocent persons" is so anomalous and usually comes about only after science has saved the day.

————————

IN 1982, A BLACK MAN ON A BICYCLE APPROACHED A WHITE woman in a wooded area of rural Hanover County, Virginia.[15]

The man threatened her with a gun and sexually assaulted her. After the attack, the victim rushed to a local hospital, where she told police she would never forget the man's face. She described the assailant as a light-skinned Black man with a medium frame, short hair, and a mustache. There were few other clues to his identity except for one the police glommed on to. According to the victim, the perpetrator claimed he "had a white girl." The investigating officer knew about an eighteen-year-old Black man who lived with a white woman. Based on that leap of logic—that a rapist's boast of an interracial relationship made the only local Black man the officer knew to be romantically involved with a white woman the suspect in the crime—the police began to investigate a churchgoer and volunteer firefighter named Marvin Anderson.

There was a snag with the investigation right out of the gate. Anderson didn't have a criminal record, which meant a mug shot wasn't readily available for viewing by the victim. So the police visited Anderson's job site, where they located an identification card displaying a color photo of him and his employee number. They slipped the card into an assortment of black-and-white pictures of other men, none of which had any numbers, for the victim to examine. She picked Anderson's photo as that of her rapist.

This is what's called a suggestive lineup: when the presentation of one member is so dissimilar from the others that it cries out for selection by the witness. The distinguishing feature in an in-person lineup might be height, race, weight, clothing, or age. In a photo lineup, the shape, size, or hue of the picture can add other differentiating traits. When defense lawyers raise the issue in proper and timely fashion at a pretrial suppression hearing, diligent judges ideally find that suggestive identifications violate due process and exclude them from use at trial. But counsel and judges aren't always up to the task. Even if they are, the Supreme Court allows prosecutors to salvage a suggestive identification by convincing the judge that it was nevertheless "reliable" because of other factors.[16]

Suggestive identifications figure prominently in the wrongful-conviction database. Brandon Garrett's study of the first 250 DNA exonerations in the United States found that mistaken-identification evidence cropped up in 76 percent (190) of them. Of those cases, Garrett determined that at least a third contained lineups that "were biased, or stacked to make the suspect stand out."[17]

The flawed nature of the Marvin Anderson photo array was compounded by what followed. An hour after choosing the picture, the victim observed a live lineup composed of Anderson and several nonsuspects, known as "fillers," who looked like him. Although this may have reflected an effort to avoid another suggestive procedure—because the lineup was structured so that Anderson wouldn't be conspicuous—the die had already been cast. Primed by the earlier photo array, the victim yet again identified Anderson, who was the only participant in the lineup repeated from the array.

Anderson's attorney later moved to suppress the identification evidence. Counsel pointed out that Anderson was the only person depicted in both the array and the lineup, and that he was "dark-skinned." The judge denied the motion on the grounds that "there's been no showing here that the photographs were irregular or were arranged in an irregular way or, uh, were presented in any way to, uh, identify a particular person."

The identification evidence comprised the crux of the prosecution's case against Anderson at trial. The victim reinforced her prior IDs by identifying him from the witness stand and gave an extensive account of the crime. Beyond the harrowing facts surrounding the rape, the victim divulged other memorable (and inflammatory) details, including that the perpetrator forced her to consume fecal matter. Forensic scientists had conducted serology tests on the crime scene evidence but failed to produce any results that could connect Anderson to the assault.

Anderson presented an alibi defense that revolved around testimony that he was washing his car at the time of the attack. Yet his defense didn't put on any evidence related to murmurs in the community that a different man, John Otis Lincoln, had done the crime. The bicycle the rapist had ridden in the run-up to the attack was identified by its owner as having been stolen by Lincoln a half hour before the crime. Anderson begged his attorney to call the bike owner and Lincoln to the stand, a plea that went unheeded.

An all-white jury convicted Anderson of rape, sodomy, abduction, and robbery in 1982. The court then sentenced Anderson, a first-time offender, to 210 years in prison. Harsh sentences like Anderson's are part of the legacy of racial injustice in the South, where Black men have long received disproportionate punishment for sex crimes, especially those involving claims of harm against white women. Even though it's now unconstitutional to give the death penalty for a rape conviction, it was once a common penalty—for Black men at least. Renowned criminologist Marvin Wolfgang found that Black men in the former Confederate and bordering states represented *89 percent* of all people executed for rape between 1930 and 1974.[18]

———————

ANDERSON SPENT FIVE YEARS IN THE VIRGINIA STATE PEN, maintaining his innocence and hoping to catch a break. That break came from an unexpected source. John Otis Lincoln stepped forward in 1988 to admit he'd committed the rape. In a state postconviction hearing that August, Lincoln confessed again, this time under oath in open court. As in many state postconviction proceedings across the country, the hearing took place before the same judge who'd presided over Anderson's trial. That judge branded Lincoln a liar and refused to overturn the conviction.

Anderson fought on from his prison cell with the help of a broad coalition of civil rights activists, church leaders, and state legislators. In 1993, they petitioned Governor Douglas Wilder to pardon Anderson. Despite the flimsy evidence of guilt, Anderson's sterling background, Lincoln's confession, and the exhaustion of judicial remedies, Wilder declined the pardon application for reasons unstated and unknown. It wasn't that the governor was ideologically opposed to showing mercy. That same year he gave clemency to high school (and future professional) basketball star Allen Iverson for a conviction that arose from a bowling alley brawl.[19]

Anderson received parole in 1997 after fifteen years in prison.[20] He went back to Hanover saddled with an ankle monitor. He suffered other indignities, too, among them an early curfew, weekly meetings with his parole officer, and sex offender registration. Prohibited from firefighting, he had to drive by the station every time he went to the few jobs he was able to get, first at a galvanizing plant, later as a trucker restricted to a fifty-mile radius. Although the Innocence Project in New York City had accepted his case back in 1994, they couldn't track down biological evidence for DNA testing. Anderson's parole grant three years later lent even less urgency to that quest. The lawyers and students assigned to Anderson's case believed he was innocent, but they also believed that any evidence that could prove it had been destroyed.

Peter Neufeld, who cofounded the Innocence Project with Barry Scheck, gave it one more shot. He called a friend at the Virginia Department of Forensic Science and asked him to take a final peek at Anderson's file. That phone call led to a startling discovery: a forensic examiner had taped swabs from the rape kit to her worksheets, effectively saving them from destruction under state protocols at the time.

Even so, there was a hang-up. Virginia hadn't yet passed a law that provided access to biological evidence for postconviction DNA testing, and state officials higher up the ranks than Neufeld's pal balked at consenting to those tests for fear it would set a bad precedent. Virginia eventually passed a DNA-testing law in May 2001, which provided a legal avenue to test the swabs from the Hanover rape. Those DNA tests excluded Anderson as the perpetrator and implicated John Otis Lincoln.

DNA results in hand, Anderson went back to the trial court in Hanover. He had a different judge because the one who'd handled his trial had retired. The new judge found him innocent and indicated he should be removed from the sex offender registry. Governor Mark Warner issued an absolute pardon in 2002, announcing, "I am convinced that Mr. Anderson is innocent of the charges for which he was convicted."[21]

––––––––––

MARVIN ANDERSON ULTIMATELY RECEIVED CLEMENCY FROM the governor of Virginia. But only after DNA test results had conclusively proven his innocence and incriminated another man. The pardon materialized twenty years after Anderson's conviction at trial, fourteen years after the true culprit confessed to the crime, and nine years after a prior governor denied his pardon application without explanation.

Pardoning a criminal defendant on actual innocence grounds after scientific evidence like DNA has already cleared his name is low-hanging fruit that's ripe for governors and clemency boards to pluck. It's important that executive officials grab this fruit, and they've done so on occasion.[22] In some cases, the practical effect of a judicial ruling that overturns a wrongful conviction on direct appeal, habeas corpus, coram nobis, or DNA-testing law may be uncertain. A pardon can go a long way toward clarifying that a defendant is officially deemed "innocent" by the state and eligible for wrongful-conviction compensation, or that his conviction is expunged from his record.[23] In other cases, the pardon may be more symbolic, a belt added to the suspenders manufactured by the courts to hold up a declaration of innocence. Symbols matter—for the public, the legal community, and most of all the innocent recipient of the pardon.

But what about cases with compelling innocence claims where the judicial system has failed the defendant? Cases where convictions stay in place due to the procedural obstacles described in this book—things like strict statutes of limitations, rigid preservation rules, deferential standards of review, and narrow interpretations of what equals "new" evidence? Neither clarity nor emphasis is needed in those instances. Bold action by the executive branch through the exercise of its clemency power is called for instead. Yet far too many clemency decisions are characterized by caution, not boldness.

One reason why clemency falls short of being a "fail safe" to help the innocent, as Chief Justice Rehnquist envisioned it in *Herrera*, is its underlying rationale. The long-standing justification for executive clemency—that we need a channel for benevolent leaders to spare regular people—is based more on mercy and forgiveness than innocence. Its origins go back to ancient Greece and Rome.[24] Julius Caesar was renowned for his frequent acts of mercy toward those he'd defeated, and the modern term "clemency" derives from Clementia, the Roman goddess of forgiveness and mercy, who was associated with Caesar at the time.

Although skeptics even then scoffed at this merciful image of clemency, viewing it as an instrument to advance political goals, that notion infused the original American conception of the power.[25] Alexander Hamilton lauded the president's authority to pardon in the Federalist Papers of 1788: "Humanity and good policy conspire to dictate, that the benign prerogative of pardoning should be as little as possible fettered or embarrassed." In 1866, the Supreme Court underscored the "unlimited" nature of the presidential pardon power, one that "cannot be fettered by any legislative restrictions." Echoing Hamilton, the Court declared that the breadth of this power emanated from the "benign prerogative of mercy reposed" in the president.

A corollary of this benign prerogative, that clemency is principally a vehicle to distribute mercy from on high to those down below, is that the power isn't perceived as a way to revisit the fundamental facts of a prisoner's case. Several Supreme Court decisions, including one handed down five years after *Herrera*, insist that clemency is not "an integral part of the . . . system for finally adjudicating guilt or innocence of a defendant."[26] The clemency process is treated as an opportunity not to reassess the accuracy of the convic*tion*, but to evaluate the suitability of the convic*ted* for mercy. It resembles parole in its function as an act of grace bestowed on a deserving person and its assumption that the beneficiary is guilty of the criminal act. It goes without saying that executive officials are poorly positioned to reverse a wrongful conviction through clemency if they're dissuaded—even barred—from examining the facts related to innocence.

Clemency procedures in many jurisdictions make the emphasis on abstract questions of forgiveness and mercy, as opposed to specific ones of guilt or innocence, abundantly clear. Sometimes these rules advise that prisoners must accept responsibility for their crimes in order to gain forgiveness and, by extension, clemency. Consider the official "Information and Instructions on Pardons," published by the United States Department of Justice, which offers support to the president in reaching federal clemency decisions: "Bear in mind that a presidential pardon is ordinarily a sign of forgiveness and is granted in recognition of the applicant's acceptance of responsibility for the crime and established good conduct for a significant period of time after conviction or release from confinement. A pardon is not a sign of vindication and does not connote or establish innocence. For that reason, when considering the merits of a pardon petition, pardon officials take into account the petitioner's acceptance of responsibility, remorse, and atonement for the offense."

Responsibility, remorse, and atonement are terms that should strike a familiar chord from the chapter on parole. This chord is in dissonance with what the actually innocent would likely assert in a pardon petition.

Some states follow the federal approach to clemency.[27] Others nominally permit the consideration of innocence in the assessment process, yet suggest clemency on that basis is rare.[28] A number of jurisdictions go beyond rhetoric and offer procedures through which boards may grant clemency on the specific grounds of actual innocence. These procedures nonetheless tend to contain one of two chief defects. First, many essentially require a prior judicial finding of innocence.[29] Texas, for instance, authorizes "a pardon for innocence" based on "either evidence of actual innocence from at least two trial officials; or the findings of fact and conclusions of law from the district judge in a state habeas action indicating actual innocence." Second, while some states contemplate granting clemency on innocence grounds without a judicial finding to that effect, they still ask the applicant to give executive officials practically irrefutable evidence of innocence.[30] New York will entertain a pardon request when no other administrative or legal remedy exists and there's "overwhelming and convincing proof of innocence not available at the time of conviction."

Even if clemency on the basis of actual innocence is theoretically possible in a particular state, firm eligibility rules and limited transparency diminish the likelihood of such relief in reality.[31] Some states prohibit people from seeking clemency if they have recent disciplinary infractions on their prison record; others oblige inmates to serve a minimum percentage of time in a correctional facility before they qualify for a pardon. State public records laws also largely shield the nuts and bolts of the clemency decision-making process from view.

I applaud states that at least think about pardoning someone due to factual innocence. But their procedures should have fewer barriers to converting that thought into action. Here's what clemency might look like without those hindrances.

Mercy reimagined. There should always be a mechanism for the executive branch to give mercy to prisoners whose personal transformations or sympathetic backgrounds motivate officials to act. But that blueprint for mercy should be revised to encompass cases with credible innocence claims. If governors and clemency boards have genuine doubts about the accuracy of a conviction, then clemency should be available in more than a hortatory or theoretical way. Isn't pardoning someone because of dormant fears of a wrongful conviction just another form of mercy writ large, especially if we conceive of mercy as an expression of kindness and compassion rather than solely forgiveness? Surely an innocent prisoner deserves a reversal of his misfortune regardless of his upbringing or conduct within the prison walls?

To empower clemency officials to act on their doubts about the accuracy of certain criminal convictions, states should ditch the pedantic language of the courtroom, those references to previous judicial rulings or certain quantities of evidence. Let governors and clemency boards make more holistic decisions to aid prisoners when they fear justice may not have been done and that an innocent person remains in prison or, if already released, stained with the mark of a wrongful conviction.

Clear windows. The risk with a more holistic approach to clemency, of course, is that it could provide fertile ground for inequities to flourish—even more than they do at the moment. Racial animus and white privilege could infiltrate clemency decisions guided only by loose standards untethered to the language of the law that omit precise burdens of proof and/or the prerequisite of a judicial finding of innocence. To offset that risk, we could inject greater transparency into the clemency process. Make clemency proceedings and documents public (subject to the privacy interests of applicants), compel executive officials to publish their decisions and explain their reasoning, and demand detailed annual reports. With sunlight peeking through the window of the clemency decision-making process, we could limit the chance that bias will taint the process.

Diverse composition. As noted at the outset of this chapter, most states use a hybrid structure in which governors and administrative boards collaborate in making clemency decisions. The composition of these boards is ordinarily skewed toward law enforcement.[32] In some jurisdictions, the board consists solely of state officials, as in Nebraska, where the Board of Pardons is staffed by the governor, secretary of state, and the attorney general. Even in states that press for broader representation, some boards lack participation by members of the defense community. Take Colorado, where state law requires that its board include the executive directors of the Department of Corrections and the Department of Public Safety along with a crime victim, but nobody with a criminal defense or civil rights background.

Integrating clemency boards with more members who understand the people whose applications they are expected to evaluate would enhance their decisions.[33] Professor Rachel Barkow, a leading clemency scholar, warns that boards must "not be mere arms of law enforcement" and should instead "mix law enforcement interests with those of defense lawyers and former offenders so that each side can learn from the other and increase the likelihood that sound conclusions will be reached and less subject to political attack."[34] Ex-prisoners, defense lawyers, innocence advocates, and academics would all add important voices. Their perspectives could help boards identify the full range of cases that deserve grace, including those with viable innocence claims in which the inmate doesn't sing the tune of responsibility, remorse, and atonement.

I've tried to steer Massachusetts toward many of these suggestions through my work as part of a bar association Clemency Task Force, which drafted a set of reforms in 2021. So far, our proposals have attracted the support of the commonwealth's flagship newspaper, if not the governor or the legislature.[35] I admit these proposed reforms wouldn't quite make clemency the "fail safe" that Chief Justice Rehnquist envisioned. Governors and clemency boards might still feel reluctant to pardon someone a court has not yet exonerated. Implementing more amorphous clemency standards and greater transparency could even have a paralytic effect. Without the political cover afforded by stringent rules and closed doors, inaction might be the default for clemency officials wary of making the *wrong* decision by releasing a person on innocence grounds who later turns out to be guilty or goes on to commit new crimes.

But these changes could inspire a greater number of *right* decisions by making it easier to treat actual innocence as a variable in the clemency process and extend mercy to those whose claims strike executive officials as credible. That's a good thing given the current reticence of governors and clemency boards to fill the void left by the appellate and postconviction process when it comes to freeing the innocent. While clemency may feel somewhat dated and antidemocratic, the "last surviving feature of the divine rights of kings" in the United States,[36] the more tools we have to pry open wrongful convictions the better. By fine-tuning the clemency process, we can fix more mistakes in the system and provide a backup when judges and juries fail to sort the guilty from the innocent, as they so often do.

PART IV
A PATH FORWARD

11

PROSECUTORS WITH CONVICTIONS

The Case for Internal Review Units

I SUSPECT YOU'RE NOT ALONE IF YOU FEEL DESPONDENT AT THIS stage of the book. The roadblocks to litigating innocence claims make judges improbable candidates to rescue innocent prisoners during the appellate and postconviction phases, and the executive branch remedies of parole and clemency are ill-suited to perform this function. The targeted, microlevel reforms suggested throughout these chapters would help, but they may not be enough to advance the movement to free the innocent as far as many of us want it to go. What we need are more ambitious, macrolevel changes to the way innocence claims are treated.

In considering potential structural reforms, let's start with the actors who have the greatest impact on the trajectory of a criminal case from start to finish: prosecutors. Reorienting prosecutors away from "winning" convictions, and toward obtaining justice for all stakeholders, could alter the trajectory of any given case and guide it toward a fair and accurate landing spot. One

concrete means of accelerating that reorientation is to encourage
(1) the election of so-called progressive prosecutors and (2) the
formation of units within DA offices that are dedicated to scrutinizing questionable convictions generated by their own staff.

Before looking at how prosecutors can be part of the solution
of overturning wrongful convictions, it's crucial to explore why
they are part of the current problem. That inquiry requires a deep
dive into the role prosecutors traditionally play in the legal system
and why they tend to perpetuate the status quo after they've got
a conviction.

AS NOTED THROUGHOUT THE BOOK, PROSECUTORS ARGUABLY
wield the most power of any actor in the criminal justice system, even more than judges. They decide whether to file criminal charges at all and what those charges will be. They choose
whether to offer a plea bargain or go to trial. They formulate the
trial strategy and, after a guilty verdict, make sentencing recommendations to the judge. They also have leeway in how to respond to appellate and postconviction innocence claims raised by
prisoners. Those responses influence whether the claims receive a
full airing in open court—and ultimately whether innocent people have their convictions reversed and their freedom restored.
And those responses, in turn, are shaped by the traditional function of the American prosecutor, a function that has a fascinating
backstory.

Since the mid-nineteenth century, courts and legal scholars
have used the term "minister of justice" to refer to the American
prosecutor.[1] The term signifies that prosecutors, as representatives
of the "people" rather than of crime victims or other individuals, are tasked with securing justice for the community, however
amorphous that concept may be. Unlike defense lawyers, whose

sole obligation is to advocate zealously for the accused, prosecutors must juggle two duties. They must strive to advance the government's position by pushing criminal cases forward with gusto while simultaneously ensuring fairness to the accused.

These dual obligations aren't always in harmony. Take the prosecutorial duty to disclose *Brady* material prior to trial, which was covered in Chapter 2. As a matter of professional ethics and constitutional doctrine grounded in the 1963 Supreme Court case *Brady v. Maryland*, prosecutors must disclose any information to the defense that is "favorable" (helpful) to the accused and "material" (of consequence) to guilt or punishment.

Imagine a prosecutor is litigating a murder case. He has two seemingly credible eyewitnesses scheduled to testify, Adam and Barbara, both of whom identified the defendant as the perpetrator shortly after the crime and are prepared to do so again on the stand. On the eve of trial, the prosecutor discovers that Adam has poor eyesight and wasn't wearing his contact lenses at the time of the crime. This is classic impeachment material of a government witness because it would call into question whether Adam accurately identified the accused. A long line of *Brady* cases suggests it should be given to the defense before trial.

But for the trial prosecutor sitting alone in his office pondering whether to disclose this info, the answer might be more complicated. Assume the prosecutor believes he has the right guy, that he has a cold-blooded killer in his sights. Further assume that he believes in the veracity of his other witness, Barbara, and worries the jury will attach so much significance to any evidence about Adam's faulty eyesight that it might spill over and cast doubt on both witnesses. He fears that the seed of doubt, once planted in the minds of the jury, could grow into reasonable doubt about the defendant's involvement and doom the entire prosecution. Add to the mix that Adam has told the prosecutor that his vision is only mildly impaired and his contacts only improve it slightly.

The prosecutor in this example may perceive his dual obligations as in conflict, the duty to fight for the government's position and put "bad guys" in prison at loggerheads with the commitment to fair play. To resolve this tension, it's easy to see the prosecutor imputing little meaning to this newfound information and deciding it isn't material enough to the case to warrant disclosure. It's also easy to picture the prosecutor not even making that calculation, just burying the evidence in a file cabinet under an ends-justify-the-means rationalization. What's harder to conjure, perhaps, is the prosecutor making the ethically and legally proper choice to notify the defense about Adam's vision problems.

Prosecutors frequently face conundrums like this, moments when the dual obligations assigned to them as ministers of justice collide and force them into a vexing decision. All too often prosecutors land on the side of advocacy over fairness. They land on the side of "winning" convictions rather than promoting the more elusive ideal of collective justice.

Why?

I've spent much of my academic career mulling over this question, especially why "good" prosecutors might make ill-advised decisions that hurt innocent defendants.[2] I'm less intrigued by "bad" apples, prosecutors who purposefully circumvent justice, because I think they are rare, and reasonable people would all agree there's no place for government lawyers who intentionally commit misconduct to obtain and maintain convictions. I'm fascinated instead with what triggers an otherwise ethical and deft prosecutor to choose zealous advocacy over fairness, to hide impeachment information in a file cabinet rather than tell the defense and let the chips fall where they may in the courtroom.

I won't pretend I've found the full answer. But my research indicates that three forces can nudge even the most ethically sound prosecutor to make a decision that contributes to a wrongful conviction or lengthens the incarceration of the innocent. These forces are political, practical, and psychological.

THE POLITICS OF PROSECUTION

Chief prosecutors in the United States normally get their jobs through election rather than appointment. Today, voters pick their chief prosecutors at the county and city levels in forty-five states.[3] Once elected, the DA has the authority to hire and oversee her staff of assistant prosecutors, investigators, and other employees. Even in the five outliers that follow an appointment model for local DAs—Alaska, Connecticut, Delaware, New Jersey, and Rhode Island—an elected official, the state attorney general, appoints them.

Elections weren't always the norm. American prosecutors originally occupied a lowly spot on the political ladder, operating as civil servants appointed by public officials. The trend toward electing chief prosecutors emerged during the first half of the nineteenth century, a time marked by a desire to make the government more accountable to the people. By 1861, almost three-quarters of the states elected their chief prosecutors.[4]

The idea then and now is that prosecutors will better respond to the needs of the electorate if they know that their feet will be put to the fire at the ballot box every few years. This makes a lot of sense—in the abstract at least. Situating prosecutors within the civil service apparatus, as is the case with an appointment model, motivates them to please the idiosyncrasies of their superiors more than any other constituency. On a positive note, without fear of losing their jobs by public vote, civil service protections might embolden some prosecutors to stand firm and safeguard the interests of a minority of residents from the whims of a vengeful majority. On a less positive note, the absence of accountability to the public could make appointed prosecutors oblivious or indifferent to the cries of the community. And that doesn't necessarily match up with democratic values. Electing chief prosecutors is arguably a better fit with our populist sensibilities and the notion that citizens' voices should be heard by those who make criminal justice policy.

Regardless of one's views about the best way to choose chief prosecutors, the electoral model predominates, and the brass tacks of prosecutorial politics can get messy. The benefits of electing a chief county prosecutor hinge on informed voters. How many residents, though, actually track criminal justice policy in their counties or even know the name of their DA? I like to put this last question to my students in class, which operates as a random audit. I'm always dismayed to learn that even in this most rarefied of settings, a law school course on criminal justice, a hefty proportion of my students don't know who the DA is in the place where they live.

This sobering truth, that the antennas of potential voters aren't finely attuned to the nuances of regional criminal justice policies, undercuts the rationale for the electoral model. How can we hold our DAs accountable if we aren't paying attention? Public apathy incentivizes chief prosecutors to go for the lowest common denominator when messaging their activities to the community. Historically, that's meant trumpeting "tough-on-crime" tropes. Tout successes in salacious cases, publish conviction rates, and stand shoulder to shoulder with police chiefs at televised press conferences. These themes resonate with a broad swath of the electorate, much of which identifies more with being a potential or actual crime victim than with being a criminal defendant. It should come as no shock that voter turnout is paltry in most prosecutorial elections, and that name recognition and/or party affiliation usually carries the day. One study found that incumbent chief prosecutors win 94 percent of the time and run *unopposed* in more than 80 percent of elections.[5]

This blend of an electoral model with minimal public oversight has huge ramifications for how prosecutors think about postconviction innocence claims. Many DAs have lofty political aspirations that extend beyond county law enforcement and reach into the governor's mansion or the hallowed halls of legislative chambers. How they handle postconviction innocence claims could conceivably impact their career trajectories, or at least they *believe* it could. DAs sometimes fear that appearing open to a prisoner's plea of innocence could be construed as being "soft on crime." They also fret about being "taken for a ride" or "played for a fool" by a guilty defendant who dupes them into joining his campaign for exoneration. (While fools often seem to ascend to power, being played for one by a convicted felon is generally not a political advantage.)

Finally, much like the Willie Horton effect described in Chapter 10, chief prosecutors may agonize over the possibility that if they were to assist with an exoneration, even in a meritorious case, the freed prisoner might go on to commit future crimes and thereby jeopardize their political futures. The Steven Avery case from Wisconsin is a famous warning bell.[6]

Avery spent eighteen years in prison for sexual assault and attempted murder before DNA evidence exonerated him in 2003. His story became a cause célèbre, another chapter in the tome of wrongful convictions and one that reverberated throughout the Upper Midwest. Inspired by Avery's saga, a state legislator formed the Avery Task Force to evaluate criminal justice policy. The subsequent reform package, anointed the Avery Task Force bill, sailed through the Wisconsin legislature in 2005. Only weeks after the bill's passage, authorities arrested Avery for raping and killing a journalist, Teresa Halbach, who'd gone to interview him about his exoneration at the auto salvage yard where he worked. Avery, along with his cousin Brendan Dassey, was later convicted of the homicide. The case eventually became the subject of a wildly popular Netflix documentary series, *Making a Murderer*, which disputed whether Avery killed Halbach. Although Avery and some aficionados of the series continue to deny his involvement in that murder, what's undeniable is that his arrest embarrassed his champions in 2005. The sponsor of the bill hurriedly changed its name to the Criminal Justice Reform Package; efforts by innocence advocates and their allies to hype Avery's 2003 exoneration ceased.

At bottom, many chief prosecutors might calculate that the political risks of being perceived as weak on crime, being tricked by a shrewd inmate, or simply being the person who unlocks the prison gate to someone who later harms others outweigh the benefits of aiding the defense to exonerate a prisoner.

THE PRACTICALITIES OF LAW PRACTICE

Practical considerations surrounding the operation of a government agency aggravate the political variables to further discourage prosecutors from taking innocence claims seriously. District attorneys' offices suffer from resource constraints that make them understaffed and their employees underpaid. As a consequence, most assistant prosecutors carry excessive caseloads. A survey conducted by the US Department of Justice revealed that in 2007 the average state prosecutor closed ninety-four felony cases through convictions, acquittals, dismissals, or other dispositions.[7] *Ninety-four felonies*. That translates to nearly two rapes, murders, robberies, burglaries, or other serious crimes resolved each week by each assistant DA.

There are powerful practical incentives, then, for prosecutors to dispose of their assigned cases quickly and to have those dispositions take the form of a conviction. First, letting cases stay open creates a traffic jam. As new ones enter the system, they clog the arteries of each assistant prosecutor's workflow, and that congestion makes it even harder to close the ever-mounting number of live matters. Second, it's not just that prosecutors feel pressure to close open cases promptly. They feel compelled to convert as many as possible into convictions, anxious that the failure of the office to procure convictions at a high rate could undermine public confidence in its competence and, at the individual level, that a "low" conviction rate could damage an ADA's standing within the organization, possibly even her job security. There must be probable cause to make an arrest and obtain a criminal charge. If prosecutors don't transform those arrests and charges into convictions, what does that say about their judgment in pursuing those cases? In my view, it says little. Only that there's a gap between what probable cause means and what it takes to broker a plea bargain or prove guilt beyond a reasonable doubt at trial. Prosecutors should never be seen as "losing" a case so long as the outcome is fair. Others have a very different opinion: that "winning" convictions is the best measure of success for prosecutors.

Sadly, in a job where performance can be difficult to gauge, convictions have become a metric by which an individual prosecutor and an office as a whole can be assessed. In many locales, data about convictions are the coin of the prosecutorial realm. Tales abound of offices that internally publicize the conviction rates of their lawyers with lists that, like batting average rankings in baseball, feature those with the highest percentage on top. At one office, supervisors posted the names of its prosecutors accompanied by color-coded stickers next to each one—green for those who'd obtained convictions recently and red, a scarlet letter of sorts, for those who hadn't. At another agency, prosecutors were required to write memoranda to their bosses whenever a trial didn't produce an acquittal so as to explain "what went wrong." It's as if that office treated prosecutors who "lost" cases like derelict kindergarteners whose punishment consisted of writing *I will not talk in class* over and over on the chalkboard.

In one county DA's office in Colorado, the leadership even offered annual bonuses to prosecutors who had a conviction rate in felony trials of 70 percent or higher.[8] After rumors of this initiative spread, the cash-for-convictions program caused a firestorm. It also became a stark symbol of the premium that prosecutors, those erstwhile ministers of justice, place on "winning" convictions.

Notwithstanding this story from Colorado, individual prosecutors seldom benefit financially, directly at least, by having high conviction rates. They're usually paid in lockstep based on seniority. Even so, conviction rates may indirectly affect an assistant prosecutor's earnings by serving as a data point for advancement and promotion. Achieving justice is difficult to quantify; conviction rates aren't. It's understandable that chief prosecutors and their deputies may draw on these figures to measure Sally against Sam, to inject objective criteria into a subjective performance review. In a host of prosecutorial agencies, conviction rates serve as a proxy for ability—and a barometer of whether an ADA will rise, plunge, or stagnate within the hierarchy.

Prosecutors have practical reasons to ensure that those convictions, once obtained, remain in place. In most DA offices, appellate and postconviction prosecutors toil in a separate division from those who handle trials.[9] This bypasses the potential conflict of interest that would arise if a prosecutor were tasked with defending her own conviction on appeal and drafting a reply, say, to a defense allegation of prosecutorial misconduct at trial. The chores require different skill sets as well. The quick thinking, decisiveness, and performative aspect of trying a case vary from the deliberative, research-oriented job of writing appellate briefs and postconviction motions. Like their colleagues in the trial unit, though, the workloads of appellate and postconviction prosecutors leave scarce space to inspect the possible innocence of each defendant. They have similar incentives to process as many cases as briskly as possible—and disincentives to scour for the proverbial needle of innocence in the gigantic haystack of cases where the defendant either pled guilty or was found guilty at trial.

Resource constraints therefore have an impact on how prosecutors handle their cases and think about innocence claims. They help make finality and efficiency not just cherished values in the abstract but necessary ones in practice. Secure as many convictions as quickly as possible at trial; then maintain them, again with haste, at the appellate and postconviction level. Recall the conveyor belt analogy from the start of the book. Prosecutors want their cases to emerge from the criminal justice assembly line with their lids on tight.

The motive for prosecutors to keep a lid on convictions manufactured by their office also ties into concerns about future funding streams. When an exoneree sues the state for wrongful-conviction compensation and wins, any monetary award generally comes from the state government's coffers rather than the particular prosecutorial office that litigated the case. Still, chief prosecutors might worry that any wrongful-conviction compensation could *indirectly* affect the fiscal health of the office, especially in offices that rely on state funds to supplement city and county allotments, by leading to a decrease in annual funding. Any reduction would serve as the functional equivalent of a fine, or so prosecutors might fear, imposed because of their part in producing and prolonging a wrongful conviction that cost the state money.

From the vantage point of individual prosecutors, then, expending the effort to unearth a possible wrongful conviction in their midst may come at too great a price to their capacity to process other cases, to future funding for their organization, to their own reputation and that of their colleagues, and to their chance for advancement within the organization.

PSYCHOLOGICAL BARRIERS

Chapter 4 touched on the cognitive biases that affect appeals court judges, biases that for the purposes of that conversation impact how they design the harmless error doctrine. Many of these same phenomena shape prosecutorial behavior at the appellate and postconviction phases, too. Confirmation bias or "tunnel vision" can afflict a prosecutor who looks back at a conviction already obtained by a colleague at trial. Overvaluing information that supports that result, and discounting that which doesn't, is a natural impulse. Guilt has become the status quo. Getting a prosecutor to budge from that default position may require lots of convincing argumentation—and lots of compelling evidence. Like appellate judges reviewing the decisions of their trial counterparts, "conformity effects" may stir appellate and postconviction prosecutors to defer to the tactical and strategic choices made by their trial-division peers at the start of a case. Rocking the boat by second-guessing their crewmates' choices has little allure.

Another cognitive bias permeates how prosecutors act in the appellate and postconviction setting. Most humans try to retain a positive image of themselves as a shield to ward off self-doubt and loathing. Without a positive self-image, to some degree, many of us couldn't go on. Rising from bed in the morning and glancing in the mirror would be too painful. What then happens when you're confronted with negative information about yourself? Well, the cognitive shield works to keep it at arm's length. Scholars label this the aversion to cognitive dissonance—how we tend to think of ourselves as good people, abhor anything that suggests we aren't, and minimize the significance of our bad actions. We aim to neutralize the dissonance created by a clash between our noble view of ourselves and the ignoble reality of our deeds.

Convicting an innocent person violates an ethical prosecutor's view of the job: that a prosecutor should have no part in a wrongful conviction. For a prosecutor, learning that you or a colleague contributed to such a miscarriage of justice challenges that viewpoint. To sidestep cognitive dissonance—the tension between the glossy image of yourself and your team as ministers of justice and the unvarnished truth that you failed to fulfill that commitment—you might cling to the hypothesis of guilt. It's a way to reconcile your beliefs with your actions and those of your comrades. And a way to justify ignoring even the most credible of innocence claims by prisoners.

———

AS WE'VE SEEN, THE PRESSURES FACING PROSECUTORS CAN STEER them toward creating and prolonging wrongful convictions, even prosecutors who seek to act as ministers of justice. The phrase "with power comes responsibility" derives from a famous speech given by former US attorney general Robert H. Jackson in 1940 in reference to the American prosecutor.[10] Yet our district attorneys haven't always exercised their power responsibly, which has led to thousands of miscarriages of justice in this country.

Despite this state of affairs, not all hope is lost. Prosecutors can help get innocent people out of prison because of the power they hold and the fact that many of them want to wield it properly. Power is a double-edged sword with the capacity to protect, not just skewer, the innocent. I'm happy to report that there are signs of progress.

THE PROGRESSIVE PROSECUTION MOVEMENT

At this moment in time, the 2020s, the political, practical, and psychological pressures on prosecutors are in a state of flux, fueled by climbing public awareness of mass incarceration and over-criminalization. An outgrowth of this new consciousness is that voters are taking greater notice of what their district attorneys are doing and looking at their work through a more sophisticated, justice-oriented lens. The old "tough-on-crime" mantra now falls flat in some quarters, outdone by a more measured refrain.[11] The current zeitgeist has also disrupted the variables that have long prodded prosecutors to downplay innocence claims. Doing justice and not merely racking up convictions is a desirable commodity, now more than ever. Aspiring to do justice can enhance a chief prosecutor's political prospects, affect the operations of a DA's office, and mold how assistant prosecutors gaze inward to assess what it means to be a "good" person and lawyer.

This development has altered how some prosecutors grapple with postconviction innocence claims. The rise of so-called progressive prosecutors across the country reflects a novel political landscape, one in which DAs occasionally score points, not lose them, by displaying a willingness to right wrongful convictions.

In my own backyard of Boston, the first Black woman elected to serve as district attorney, Rachael Rollins, has received acclaim in part due to her stance on wrongful convictions. In 2021, she asked the commonwealth's highest court to toss out thousands of drug

convictions tainted by a scandal at the now-shuttered Hinton Crime
Lab in Jamaica Plain, where a disgraced former chemist falsified test
results, engaged in "dry-labbing" (making visual identifications of
narcotics instead of conducting chemical analyses of their proper-
ties), and added cocaine to samples where none was present.[12]

Rollins did something arguably even more dramatic when
she united with two defense attorneys to file a motion to dismiss
the gun-possession conviction of Sean Ellis.[13] It was the only remaining charge that hung over the head of a Black man wrongfully convicted of killing a white police officer, John Mulligan,
outside a Walgreens pharmacy in Boston in 1993. I was in law
school in the area at the time of the murder and recall the vivid,
racially tinged front-page headlines and breathless top-of-the-
hour TV news reports. The media depicted it as an utter tragedy,
the passing of a decorated officer to the scourge of urban gun
violence.

Prosecutors charged two young Black men with the crime and
tried them separately. Ellis's codefendant was convicted of murder and later, after problems arose with his case, pled guilty to
manslaughter. Ellis took a different path. Starting in 1995, the
Suffolk County district attorney's office tried him *three* times for
murder. The first two trials ended with hung juries and mistrials
on the murder charge, although the prosecution came away with
a gun-possession conviction. The third trial produced the murder
conviction long sought by the government.

The headlines and TV accounts had a different tone as Ellis
pursued appellate and postconviction relief. News broke that the
victim, Mulligan, had been a dirty cop with scores of enemies
who had motive to do what Ellis and his codefendant allegedly
had done. Evidence also surfaced that the three detectives who'd
investigated the murder were complicit in Mulligan's corruption
and, to conceal their scheme, had coerced witnesses and hidden evidence to build up the threadbare case against Ellis in the
1990s. These revelations spurred the Supreme Judicial Court of

Massachusetts to reverse the murder conviction and grant Ellis a fourth trial in 2015. Documentary filmmakers lined up to capture Ellis's every move while he prepared for the courtroom yet again. (Their work culminated in the Netflix series *Trial Four*.)

In 2017, the plotline took a sudden turn. Suffolk County district attorney John Pappas announced that his office would not seek a fourth trial because the flawed investigation conducted by three rogue detectives made a murder conviction unlikely. Pappas and the Boston police commissioner, however, stated in no uncertain terms that they still believed Ellis had committed the killing.

Ellis was free and no longer faced murder charges, but he wasn't entirely out of the woods. There was still the gun possession, which stayed on his record since it had occurred in a different trial proceeding than the one that generated the murder verdict. This was when Rollins, who'd succeeded Pappas after her election in 2018, entered the stage. She decided to cooperate with Ellis's defense team and move to reverse the gun conviction. What a bold choice to go against the local law enforcement establishment in a cop-killing case. But Rollins has never been afraid to speak her mind, or to do the right thing even if it incites blowback.

A trial judge agreed with Rollins and granted Ellis a new trial on the gun charge. Then Rollins announced she wouldn't exercise her option to retry him, proclaiming, "Today marks the end of a long and troubling chapter in Boston's history." This made Sean Ellis eligible for wrongful-conviction compensation from the Massachusetts government.[14] In a nutshell, Boston's DA facilitated the effort of a formerly convicted cop killer to sue the state.

Sean and I currently serve together on the board of trustees for the New England Innocence Project, which I joined after I returned to my hometown in 2012 to teach law at Northeastern University. I admire his kind and thoughtful demeanor during our meetings, his can-do attitude, and his ongoing struggle to come to grips with what happened to him. I also admire his respect for

Rachael Rollins, the head of an office that took him to trial not once, not twice, but three times and nearly a fourth.

Rollins's progressive stance in regard to wrongful convictions and other aspects of criminal justice hasn't been met with universal praise. It has earned her quite a few foes, not to mention an ethics complaint submitted by a national police group that accused her of "reckless disregard" for state law.[15] But it has also earned her a promotion: a nomination from President Joe Biden to serve as the federal US attorney for Massachusetts. For district attorneys who harbor similar dreams of career advancement, there are lessons to be drawn from Rollins. One is that taking an open-minded approach to wrongful convictions and acknowledging that prosecutors contribute to those injustices is not the political land mine it once was.[16]

Rollins's efforts in the Sean Ellis case reveal how individual chief prosecutors can make a big difference for the wrongfully convicted. And Rollins is not the only leading district attorney to admit that prosecutors aren't immune from mistakes—that they occasionally charge the wrong person, and that available judicial and executive remedies don't always correct those errors. Progressive prosecutors in places from Philadelphia to Los Angeles, and in between, rose to power in the aftermath of protests following the 2014 murder of an unarmed Black man, Michael Brown, in Ferguson, Missouri.[17] They see their job through a justice lens that neutralizes many of the pernicious political, practical, and professional incentives to secure and maintain wrongful convictions.

The progressive prosecution movement is a victory for justice. It represents a shift toward prosecutors doing the right thing even at the occasional expense of finality, efficiency, and deference to other institutional players. The major problem lies in the potential impermanency of this movement. What will happen when the political winds change?

We've already seen signs of a cold front, a backlash to the notion of the progressive prosecutor. When the president nominates someone for US attorney, it's usually a done deal (provided that the US senators from the particular district approve of the selection). Even though Rachael Rollins received the backing of the two senators from Massachusetts, Republicans in Congress opposed her nomination for US attorney to such a degree that it produced an odd political stalemate. Senator Tom Cotton of Arkansas even went so far as to pen an op-ed in the *Boston Herald* lamenting Rollins's "abysmal record" and portraying her as "uniquely unfit for the role."[18] In December 2021, Republican opposition provoked the Senate to hold its first roll-call vote for a US attorney nominee since 1975. It also forced Vice President Kamala Harris to visit Capitol Hill twice to register her support to break a fifty-fifty tie and pave the way for Rollins's appointment in January 2022.[19]

Consider developments in California, too. A former public defender, Chesa Boudin, became district attorney for San Francisco in 2020. He had ridden the progressive prosecutor wave to election, overcoming what was once almost surely a political detriment: his background as the son of two convicted murderers who belonged to the Weather Underground, a radical left-wing group. Almost immediately after he took office, though, forces converged against him. By the fall of 2021, a recall movement had gained so much momentum, plus roughly eighty-three thousand signatures and $1.4 million, that the local department of elections scheduled a special vote for June 2022.[20] Similar efforts are underway in Southern California. Murmurs of a possible recall surfaced mere weeks after progressive George Gascón assumed his post as Los Angeles County district attorney in 2021. He has so far fended off the cries to recall him, but they refuse to go away.[21]

This counterattack shows that the progressive prosecutor movement might not stand the test of time. A longer-term solution to the scourge of wrongful convictions, perhaps, is for prosecutors to institutionalize their commitment to justice by establishing internal units devoted to investigating possible wrongful convictions within their own jurisdictions. Once added to the fabric of an organization, such units might withstand any political storms.

INTERNAL REVIEW UNITS

A growing number of prosecutorial offices have set up internal divisions called conviction integrity units (CIUs) or conviction review units (CRUs) in which staff evaluate postconviction innocence claims in their county. Some CIUs adopt a proactive model where their team takes the lead in ferreting out possible wrongful convictions within the jurisdiction. Others are more reactive, investigating a matter only after an innocence project or defendant has raised a credible claim. Still others are hybrids, both accepting referrals from outsiders and identifying cases through internal audits. Regardless of the precise structure, when a CIU substantiates the legitimacy of a claim, prosecutors often work to right the wrong by plugging those cases to the courts. By the end of 2020, seventy-four CIUs existed in the United States; their combined efforts contributed to overturning fifty-five wrongful convictions in 2019 and another sixty-three in 2020.[22]

I'm particularly heartened by developments in my old stomping ground, Brooklyn, where the Kings County DA's office has helped vacate thirty wrongful convictions since 2014 and has more in the pipeline.[23] Its conviction review unit has even shown a willingness to butt heads with the police and intervene in controversial cases. Here's one of them.[24]

On New Year's Day 2000, four plainclothes police officers allegedly saw a teenager shoot a revolver into the air in the Crown Heights neighborhood of Brooklyn. They returned fire, prompting the teenager to dash into a nearby building, where he was apprehended.

The officers also recounted the behavior of another person on the scene, a man later identified as twenty-year-old Phillip Almeda (now known as Kadafi Ala). Two officers insisted that while they were responding to the teenager's gunplay with bullets of their own, they observed Ala shooting at them. None of the bullets hit their targets, and investigators recovered nine spent shell casings on the sidewalk along with a gun in an adjacent courtyard.

The police grabbed Ala. According to the police, he made several statements after his arrest that implicated him in the shooting.

Ala went to trial in February 2001. He was acquitted of attempted murder but convicted of three charges of "attempted aggravated assault" of a police officer. Those convictions yielded a total prison sentence of twenty-one years.

Predictably, Ala failed to overturn this conviction through traditional appellate and postconviction procedures. Not only did his case lack evidence suitable for DNA testing, but it was a conviction for firing a weapon *at the police*. Multiple law enforcement officers pinpointed the location of the shooting and the identity of the shooter. The recovery of bullet shells and a forsaken gun appeared to bolster that narrative, and the prosecution presented evidence that Ala himself had admitted his involvement. The cloud of his conviction hovered over him even after he got parole in 2018.

The CRU of the Kings County DA's office commenced a probe into Ala's case. The unit analyzed documents, interviewed police personnel, and enlisted an independent expert to examine the gun retrieved from the courtyard. The CRU then published a report citing troubling details about the conviction and emphasizing how the ballistics evidence didn't back the police version of events. It noted the expert's conclusion that "based on the location of the shell casings and cartridges of the recovered gun, it was highly improbable that they came from the reported firing position of the defendant." For nine casings to wind up on the sidewalk, not in the courtyard, the expert posited that they "would have had to bounce through shrubbery, a chain-link fence and over a two-foot-high brick wall." In addition, the CRU uncovered a number of "inconsistencies" in the evidence that suggested Ala's "post-apprehension statements were not accurately described to the jury." District Attorney Eric Gonzalez used the CRU report as a springboard to ask the court to vacate Ala's conviction; a trial court judge granted that motion in June 2021.

What a good time to take stock. A man prosecuted by the Brooklyn DA's office and convicted of a police shooting was exonerated twenty years later by that very same office. There was no DNA evidence, no shift in the police accounts of the incident, and no new witness or suspect. Just old-fashioned gumshoe investigation, common sense, and the mettle of prosecutors aiming to attain the minister-of-justice ideal.

―――――――――

KUDOS TO PROSECUTORS LIKE ERIC GONZALEZ IN BROOKLYN for taking a justice-oriented approach to their jobs rather than obsessing over "winning" and preserving those conquests. For innocence advocates, getting prosecutors on board with a client's case can be pivotal in convincing the courts that justice may not have been done. Prosecutorial assent, even just to an evidentiary hearing, can legitimate the innocence claim as well as impose subtle pressure on judges. Most judges are probably loath to rebuff a joint invitation from the defense and the government to at least hold an evidentiary hearing on a possible wrongful conviction. Conversely, prosecutorial opposition keeps the case in an adversarial posture. It also provides an excuse, above and beyond a judge's own views about the merits, to deny the defense request.

Without an official line of communication like the one that exists through a CIU, fostering a collaborative relationship between the prosecution and defense is hard to achieve. In the Long Island restaurant-robbery case, my initial overture to the young ADA assigned to Stephen Schulz's appellate and postconviction filings led to a brief meeting out in Riverhead, New York. I implored her to join my motion for an evidentiary hearing. The new evidence, I urged, needed to be vetted in open court to ascertain whether an innocent person was locked up for a crime perpetrated by someone else. I tried to tap into the prosecutor's sense of fair play, her responsibility as a minister of justice. She indulged me for a spell, a passive smile etched across her lips, and ended the meeting by vowing to talk with her supervisor. My follow-up phone calls went to the purgatory of voice mail. The next time I saw her was at the court proceeding where I begged Judge John Copertino for a hearing on Schulz's motion—and where she registered her opposition. My efforts, as noted in Chapter 6, failed miserably. We never got as much as a hearing in state court. At a minimum, CIUs offer a formal outlet to prod prosecutors to look at an innocence claim, a mechanism beyond personal entreaties to the assistant DA trusted with upholding the conviction in the appellate and postconviction arena.

All the same, relying on a select group of prosecutorial offices that profess to be broad-minded about their errors is far from the antidote to the plague of wrongful convictions and the lack of remedies to rectify them. Many CIUs need a makeover. Some operate passively, with nary an exoneration or rigorous investigation under their belts, and seem little more than a link on a website. Others remain a mystery, the nature of their day-to-day activities unclear and data about their work sheltered from public view. Innocence Project cofounder Barry Scheck complains that a portion of these units carry a "brand name that has good public relations value" but may be largely a "fashion accessory" for an elected DA.[25] To make CIUs a vital part of the movement to free the innocent, a centerpiece of its wardrobe so to speak, Scheck recommends they adopt certain "best practices." These include selecting potential cases through both outside referrals and internal audits, brokering information-sharing agreements with the defendants whose convictions they are investigating, integrating nonprosecutors into the case-evaluation process, and publishing data about their work.

Although implementing these practices would improve CIUs on a granular level, I have some larger, more fundamental concerns. To begin with, there's no enforcement mechanism. Prosecutors don't have to establish CIUs, plus there's really no way to know if they're doing it well, despite any nod toward transparency and public reporting.

Also, asking prosecutors to scrutinize cases handled by their peers is a tough assignment. CIU attorneys and investigators may be treated with disdain inside the ranks, in the same way that many police view internal affairs departments as traitors to the law enforcement cause. CIUs are often created by newly elected prosecutors eager to plant their unique flag on the local criminal justice map; some holdover assistant prosecutors may feel suspicious (and defensive) about the venture. When an incoming DA establishes a CRU, the first set of convictions the unit reviews are ones that were secured during a predecessor's watch. That allows the current leadership to distance itself from any prosecutorial missteps exposed by the undertaking, and even to appear more candid and capable than the ancien régime. But at the same time, it may engender animosity from veteran staff. And over the long haul, a CIU will inevitably check out convictions gained during the existing DA's tenure. That enterprise becomes fraught with political peril and potential conflicts of interest. Some CIUs shimmer brightly at first, only for the luster to subside as the founding prosecutor's cases become subject to review and possibly scorn.

Another complication is that CIU support of an innocence claim doesn't guarantee judicial reversal of the conviction because the litigation must still traverse the shoals of appellate and postconviction procedures. Judges—not prosecutors—possess the ultimate legal authority to vacate convictions. While judges normally comply with the wishes of prosecutors who want to overturn a case, as with the Kadafi Ala conviction from Brooklyn, they might not see eye to eye on the merits or on the best way to litigate the matter.

A Missouri case illustrates this danger.[26] St. Louis voters elected Kimberly Gardner as their chief prosecutor in 2017. She'd run on a progressive platform and, true to her word, installed a new conviction integrity unit when she took over. Gardner's CIU investigated the 1995 murder conviction of Lamar Johnson and became convinced he was innocent. The investigation found that a homicide detective had fabricated four police reports in which witness statements offered potential motives for the slaying, most likely that Johnson shot the victim over a drug dispute. All four people mentioned in the reports later swore under oath that they never made those comments. Gardner's team also learned that the only eyewitness who ever connected Johnson to the murder had been paid $4,000 for his cooperation, a detail that had gone undisclosed for more than twenty years. The evidence instead indicated that two other men had killed the victim during a bungled robbery attempt.

In 2019, Gardner took a proactive step to aid Johnson. She filed a motion for a new trial based on newly discovered evidence. A state court in St. Louis denied the motion without a hearing. The court held that Gardner lacked the authority to file that type of motion and, even if she had it, submitting the motion two decades after the conviction wasn't timely.

Gardner and Johnson sought to appeal the decision to the Missouri Supreme Court. They gave several reasons why the judges should take the case: the highest court's need to determine the scope of a lower court's jurisdiction (and a prosecutor's power) under state law, its mandate to review plain errors, and its inherent ability to order new trials under exceptional circumstances. But in March 2021, the state Supreme Court rejected those arguments on the basis that existing procedures afforded no mechanism for appealing the lower court ruling. It asserted that "this case is not about whether Johnson is innocent or whether there exists a remedy for someone who is innocent and did not receive a constitutionally fair trial." The current filing instead "presents only the issue of whether there is any authority to appeal the dismissal of a motion for a new trial filed decades after a criminal conviction became final. No such authority exists; therefore, this Court dismisses the appeal." The court hinted that Johnson should consider pursuing redress through a different remedy, perhaps a state habeas petition, a path that Johnson had previously followed twice in vain.

Missouri lawmakers reacted to the Johnson ruling, and its curtailment of Gardner's authority, within months. In May 2021, the legislature passed a bill to modify state law to empower prosecutors to initiate the process for righting a wrongful conviction when a CIU has found new evidence of innocence.[27] Passing similar measures across the country would give teeth to the CIU bite in convincing appeals courts to rectify a wrongful conviction, a degree of strength that was sorely lacking in the Lamar Johnson litigation.

Speaking of prosecutorial power, a final problem with CIUs is that they enhance the immense clout wielded by district attorneys' offices. Those agencies already have the ability to charge people with crimes, bulldoze defendants into plea bargains or take their cases to trial, champion convictions on direct appeal and in postconviction proceedings, and recommend whether candidates should receive parole or clemency. Unlike the Lamar Johnson case from St. Louis, there's a real risk that a CIU-led prosecutorial assessment of an innocence claim will carry *too much* weight with judges, parole boards, and clemency officials. What signal does it send when a unit declines to proceed with a case? How often will a court ever exonerate a prisoner in a CIU jurisdiction without backing from that unit? Will CIUs effectively become postconviction jury and judge?

On balance, I view CIUs favorably, but with eyes wide open. While not a complete panacea to the many ills that prolong the imprisonment of the innocent, they can heal wounds in individual cases. Together with the progressive prosecution movement, CIUs give reason to believe that some prosecutors truly want to realize the minister-of-justice ideal. And by advocating for justice, prosecutors can correct many wrongs in the legal system given the ample power at their disposal—power they deploy haphazardly and harmfully far too often.

12

COMMISSIONED FOR JUSTICE

A New Model for Handling Innocence Claims

A MORE DRAMATIC CHANGE MAY BE WORTH CONSIDERING, ONE grander than tinkering around the edges of prosecutorial operations as envisioned in Chapter 11. Let's think creatively. How could we change the *structure* of the litigation process to grapple with wrongful convictions more effectively?

We could aim for revolution and seek to get rid of the adversary system entirely or otherwise demolish the appellate and postconviction process. Yet the collateral damage of such a move would seem significant, not to mention the sheer unlikelihood of convincing those in power that our current regime deserves demolition. To stand a realistic chance for success—politically, legally, and practically—I believe any new model must fit within the existing American governmental framework. Think evolution, not revolution.

In the United States, we like to preach about our separation of powers, about our checks and our balances. The balance lies in the disparate roles played by the branches of our government. The legislature legislates (by passing laws), the executive executes (by enforcing those laws), and the judiciary judges (by interpreting their meaning). This differentiation also generates the check. If the legislature enacts an invalid law, the judiciary may strike it down or the executive may choose not to enforce it. If the executive applies the law unfairly, the legislature may pass a new one or the judiciary may rule the conduct illegal. If the judiciary makes an unjust ruling, the legislature may adopt a new statute to counteract it or the executive in many instances may appoint new judges.

As attractive as our governmental design may be, this book has shown how this intricate contraption fails the innocent. If prosecutors charge an innocent person and secure a wrongful conviction, the courts aren't normally capable, or willing, to correct the error. Likewise, executive officials are neither encouraged nor inclined to reexamine the integrity of a conviction through the parole and clemency processes. And legislatures so far have seldom tried to remedy these shortcomings.

So, what if we departed ever so slightly from the model of separate branches and have them join forces to take on wrongful convictions? Each state legislature could form an independent agency authorized to investigate claims of innocence and refer the most meritorious of them to the courts for final review through a special judicial process. With the blessing of the agency, courts would probably take those claims seriously and reverse convictions at high rates.

A few jurisdictions across the world have launched these entities, known as innocence commissions. In their best incarnations, innocence commissions blend the nimbleness of executive decision-making with the deliberative methodology of the courtroom, absent the procedural obstacles that characterize more traditional remedies. They share the mission of CIUs (outlined in Chapter 11) to investigate shaky cases and help prisoners with viable innocence claims overturn their convictions in court, but with greater independence, greater prospects for long-term stability, greater state funding, greater transparency, and fewer adversarial warts. Their proliferation might hold the most promise for identifying the wrongfully convicted and ensuring that their claims are aired in a proper forum.

———

THE INNOCENCE COMMISSION MODEL ORIGINATED WITH A PAIR of tragedies in the United Kingdom.[1] In 1974, bombs detonated at two busy British pubs. One of the bombings, in Birmingham, resulted in twenty-one fatalities; the other, in Guildford, produced seven. A manhunt ensued, with British authorities targeting members of the Irish Republican Army (IRA), an organization committed to using violent means if necessary to wrest control of Northern Ireland away from England. The police arrested six Irish nationals affiliated with the IRA who'd been in Birmingham and were about to board a ferry for Ireland, together with four others deemed responsible for the Guildford attack. The police interrogated each member of the "Birmingham Six" and the "Guildford Four," extracting a series of confessions. Nitroglycerine allegedly found on the hands of the Birmingham Six also linked them to the explosives. All ten suspects were later convicted of murder.

Doubts surfaced about their guilt almost immediately. They insisted that the police had coerced their confessions, and that they didn't know the source of the nitroglycerine. But efforts to get courts to revisit their cases proved futile. Their claims of innocence eventually caused such an uproar that UK home secretary Douglas Hurd took a closer look. What he saw was alarming: confessions induced through beatings at the hands of the police, rampant perjury by law enforcement, and evidence that the substance identified as nitroglycerine was a different (and harmless) chemical compound that likely came from a pack of playing cards the suspects had used during their travels. Hurd referred the cases back to the national Court of Appeal, which quashed the convictions in 1992.

The ten men were freed amid much fanfare. The Guildford Four were even dramatized in the 1993 film *In the Name of the Father*, starring award-winning actor Daniel Day-Lewis. Chastened by these high-profile gaffes, the British government convened a commission to deconstruct what went wrong and weigh changes to prevent future injustices. At the time, the chief recourse for an innocent prisoner who'd lost his appeals was to approach the home secretary directly, as happened with the Birmingham Six and the Guildford Four. Yet the home secretary had an inherent conflict of interest because the executive official in charge of police and prisons in the United Kingdom might naturally hesitate to reverse a case that could cast aspersions on law enforcement leaders within his ambit. Even if the home secretary were inclined to look at a case, he was constrained by a rule that prevented any investigation beyond what the prisoner or his representatives specifically asserted in their request for assistance. These limitations produced a trivial number of referrals to the Court of Appeal over the years, usually only four or five from seven hundred annual applications.

The commission concluded that the system wasn't working well and proposed the formation of a new entity to examine purported miscarriages of justice. In 1995, that proposal gave birth to the Criminal Cases Review Commission (CCRC), an independent agency empowered to investigate suspected wrongful convictions in England, Wales, and Northern Ireland, and send questionable verdicts to the judiciary for mandatory review.[2] It has the capacity to interview new witnesses and use "special legal powers" to gather information from public bodies and private citizens. After a CCRC referral, a panel from the Court of Appeal is assigned to the case and may strike down a conviction if it sees fit to do so.

The concept has a lot going for it. The CCRC's investigative authority allows it to do the fact-intensive legwork that judges aren't poised to do. The organization is also truly independent—of the police, prosecutors, or other government officials. It operates out of Birmingham, which reflects the conscious choice to distance the organization from the national political center of London. Its full-time staff of ninety supports twelve commissioners appointed through national rules governing public service posts, and the staff conduct the heavy lifting of investigating claims across the United Kingdom. The application process for criminal defendants is straightforward, has no filing fee, and doesn't require the involvement of a lawyer. And aware that the CCRC's stamp of approval means something, the Court of Appeal has incentives to treat referred cases with the care they deserve.[3]

Publicly available information suggests that the CCRC process has realized much of its potential to right wrongful convictions.[4] From its opening in March 1997 through September 2021, the CCRC has accomplished the following:

- It has finished review of 27,201 cases. The average time to review the file of an applicant who remained in custody was less than thirty weeks after receipt.
- Based on those completed reviews, the CCRC referred 771 cases to the Court of Appeal. Some of the cases had not yet been heard by the court or had been abandoned at the time of data collection.
- Of the 756 referrals that had been heard, the Court of Appeal granted relief in 527 cases.

Let's unpack these statistics. The CCRC found that 2.8 percent of the cases it investigated (771 of 27,201) were troubling enough to refer to the Court of Appeal. Judges then overturned more than two-thirds of the cases they heard.[5] The thoroughness of the CCRC process, and its credibility as an independent organization, surely contributed to these results.

This story isn't all puppies and rainbows. One could quibble with the proportion (2.8 percent) of cases identified by the CCRC as worthy of further judicial analysis. While that figure is consistent with many scholarly estimates of wrongful conviction rates,[6] consider the denominator. The CCRC only assessed cases initiated by a criminal defendant who filed an application that claimed a miscarriage of justice had occurred. That subset presumably contains a deeper pool of valid innocence claims than the shallower one composed of all convictions nationwide.[7] One possible explanation for the low referral rate is that the CCRC wants to maintain credibility with the courts and therefore is overly cautious. Or it may be that the CCRC is strapped for resources and needs an infusion of funds to better investigate each application.[8]

We know that some legitimate innocence cases have slipped past the CCRC review and referral system. A former postal worker, Victor Nealon, was convicted in 1997 of attempting to rape a twenty-two-year-old woman in Worcestershire, England. He applied to the CCRC twice, in 2001 and 2003, and specifically asked the commission to order DNA testing in his case. The CCRC turned him down both times on the grounds that the request was "speculative." His legal team pressed on despite the CCRC's disinterest—and procured DNA test results on its own that cleared him. After a belated referral from the CCRC, the Court of Appeal reversed Nealon's conviction more than ten years after he initially applied for assistance. CCRC officials wiped the egg off their face with as much aplomb as they could muster, admitting that their first two reviews "could and should have identified there were forensic opportunities that had not been explored."[9] These misgivings about the CCRC's referral rate shouldn't overshadow its achievements in the past quarter century. Its net has caught hundreds of dubious convictions that would have fallen through the otherwise porous review process.

Some jurisdictions, both in the United States and abroad, have embraced a variant of the United Kingdom template by establishing commissions tasked not with remedying individual cases—reviewing their merits and referring them to the courts—but with studying problems in the criminal justice system and proposing changes. Many of these "think tank"–style commissions have sparked notable reforms.[10] A few nations have even replicated the more proactive CCRC model on a wider scale to correct individual miscarriages of justice.[11] One place where the review-and-referral CCRC paradigm hasn't made much headway is in the United States.

With one exception.

I. Beverly "Bev" Lake Jr. served as a judge in North Carolina for many years.[12] He hailed from a well-known conservative family, the scion of a father who ran for governor on a segregationist platform in 1960. Lake had a tough-on-crime reputation burnished by his tendency to wear a pistol in the courthouse and an incident in which he ordered a defendant's mouth to be shut with duct tape.

Shortly after his rise to chief justice of the North Carolina Supreme Court in 2000, Lake became concerned about wrongful convictions. His concerns were kindled by chats with his clerk Christine Mumma, a powerhouse personality with a zest for justice reform, and by Lake's desire to construct a legacy apart from his father's sordid past. Lake and Mumma stayed up late many evenings discussing how to improve criminal justice in their state.

In 2002, Lake invited thirty leaders in the state justice system to Mumma's house for a meal. The guests included prosecutors, defense lawyers, professors, judges, and victims' rights advocates. The North Carolina Actual Innocence Commission emerged from those humble beginnings, from breaking bread to breaking new ground. Its work at first revolved around drafting laws geared toward minimizing wrongful convictions. The commission proposed statutes to compel the recording of police interrogations, standardize eyewitness identification procedures like lineups and photo arrays, and demand the preservation of evidence for DNA testing.

The group decided after a while that recommending incremental reforms wouldn't go far enough to protect innocent North Carolinians, and that broader structural changes were needed. Inspired by the experience in the United Kingdom, the group wrote legislation in 2005 to create a CCRC-style entity to investigate innocence claims and provide relief for those it found viable. After some revisions, the North Carolina General Assembly formed the Innocence Inquiry Commission in 2006. The commission's attributes include the following:[13]

Diverse composition. The commission has eight members, which by law must consist of one trial court judge, one criminal defense attorney, one prosecutor, one sheriff, one victims' rights advocate, one person from the general public, and two other people appointed by the chief justice of the state Supreme Court. The trial judge on the commission serves as its chair. Its work is aided by an executive director, a team of investigators, and other staff.

Innocence lens. The commission only considers "claims of factual innocence" by people convicted of felonies in the state of North Carolina. A claim of factual innocence is defined as one "asserting the complete innocence of any criminal responsibility for the felony" and for which "there is some credible, verifiable evidence of innocence that has not been previously presented at trial or considered at a hearing granted through postconviction relief." Within that category, the commission must prioritize submissions by those who are currently in prison solely due to the challenged felony conviction.

Waiver of rights. As a prerequisite to commission review, the applicant must consent in writing that "the convicted person waives his or her procedural safeguards and privileges, agrees to cooperate with the Commission, and agrees to provide full disclosure regarding all inquiry requirements of the Commission." The waiver rule compels the applicant to give up the privilege against self-incrimination and attorney-client confidences, among other protections, yet only applies to the claim of innocence and not to unrelated legal matters.

Proceedings. The commission has full discretion to decide whether to begin a formal inquiry into the innocence claim. That is, it may screen and dismiss a case without doing any meaningful investigation. If the commission instigates a formal inquiry, it has a range of procedural tools to assist in the process, such as the power to compel witnesses and produce evidence. At the end of the inquiry, the evidence compiled by the staff is disclosed to the full commission at a public hearing. After that hearing, if five or more of the eight voting members of the commission determine there is "sufficient evidence of factual innocence to merit judicial review," the case goes to the courts, along with any findings of fact and the commission's opinion. The rules differ for convictions that come out of a guilty plea. In those instances, all eight voting members must conclude that the case merits further judicial vetting.

If the commission sends a case to the courts, a three-judge panel is then appointed to hold an evidentiary hearing. The panel may consider *all* "credible, verifiable evidence" regardless of whether it was raised in an earlier proceeding. The convicted person's waiver of privileges means he may be called to testify. If all three judges find that the convicted person has proven innocence by "clear and convincing" evidence, they will dismiss the charges. Anything short of a unanimous finding results in the denial of relief. The decision of the three-judge panel is final; there's no right to appeal or otherwise challenge the ruling.

The Innocence Inquiry Commission has reviewed more than three thousand North Carolina cases and produced fifteen exonerations since its inception.[14] Perhaps the most notable exoneration involved two half-brothers who were convicted of a ghastly rape-murder in 1983.[15] That September, eleven-year-old Sandra Buie was found in a soybean field in the tiny town of Red Springs,

clad only in a bra and suffocated by her own underwear. The police located physical evidence but had few firm leads on a suspect
until a teenager told the police about rumors circulating in the
local high school that nineteen-year-old Henry McCollum must
have participated in the crimes because of his "weird" behavior. McCollum, who suffered from cognitive deficits, was in town
from New Jersey visiting his mother.

The police summoned McCollum to the station for questioning. Over the course of four hours, interrogators fed McCollum
details of the crime until he "confessed." He claimed that he and
four other teenagers had escorted the victim to a field, where they
took turns sexually assaulting her before forcing her underwear
down her windpipe until she stopped breathing. He identified his
half-brother Leon Brown and three other Red Springs residents as
his coparticipants. Like his sibling, Brown was cognitively challenged (with an IQ around 50). He confessed shortly after McCollum's interrogation, although he said there were a total of four
participants, not five.

The next day, the police arrested both McCollum and Brown
on charges of capital murder and rape. The other teenagers mentioned in the confessions never faced any charges. Two of them
had strong alibis, and there was no evidence whatsoever connecting the third to the incident.

Case closed.

A few weeks later, though, another girl went missing in Red
Springs. Her corpse was soon discovered; she'd been raped and
strangled. Witnesses insisted the girl had last been seen with a
newcomer to the area, Roscoe Artis. When confronted by the
authorities, Artis confessed. He was convicted in the summer of
1984.

The police never seriously entertained the idea that Artis had
perpetrated the similar crimes against Sandra Buie. Instead, the
case against McCollum and Brown went to trial in the fall of
1984, mere months after Artis's conviction, without any physical

evidence linking the defendants to the crime scene. The prosecution case rested on the confession evidence, paired with testimony from a witness who claimed (1) that he had overheard a conversation between Brown and McCollum prior to the crimes, in which they'd discussed having sex with the victim, and (2) that McCollum later admitted that he and Brown had done the crime. The witness acknowledged that he had neglected to divulge this information during three interviews with the police before the defendants' arrests.[16] McCollum and Brown were tried jointly, convicted, and sentenced to death.

THE CASE MEANDERED THROUGH THE APPELLATE AND POSTCONviction process. In 1988, the North Carolina Supreme Court ordered a new trial, albeit on a rather technical ground: the trial judge hadn't instructed the jury to separately consider the guilt or innocence of each defendant. To avoid replication of that error, the state tried McCollum and Brown anew in separate proceedings. McCollum once again received a death sentence; Brown was spared that fate and ordered to spend the rest of his life behind bars.

Over time, the gruesome details of Sandra Buie's murder became fodder for advocates of capital punishment. Justice Antonin Scalia even referred to those events in an unrelated 1994 Supreme Court opinion. To justify his position in favor of denying review of a death sentence, Scalia cited "the case of the 11-year-old girl raped . . . and then killed by stuffing her panties down her throat. How enviable a quiet death by lethal injection compared with that!"[17]

What a poor example for Scalia to rely on. It turned out that McCollum and Brown by no measure deserved a "quiet death" from a state-administered needle because they were innocent of the Red Springs rape-murder. It also turned out that the North

Carolina Innocence Inquiry Commission played a vital role in exonerating them.

———————

LEON BROWN WROTE THE COMMISSION IN 2009 AND AGREED TO waive his rights and privileges in exchange for review of his case. Staff investigator Sharon Stellato soon detected discrepancies between McCollum's confession and that of Brown, as well as between both confessions and the physical evidence in the case. She also identified gaps in forensic testing of the evidence. The commission opened a formal inquiry in 2010 and began a lengthy campaign to track down the evidence. DNA tests on a bunch of items that were eventually located—the bra, underwear, shoes, hair specimens, and other material—failed to produce useful results.

Stellato set her sights on a final piece of the forensic puzzle, a cigarette butt retrieved near the victim's body. In the early 2000s, McCollum managed to obtain DNA testing of the cigarette. Those tests generated a DNA profile in 2004 that didn't match any on file, including those of McCollum and Brown. Roughly a decade later, the commission convinced law enforcement to run the DNA profile from the cigarette butt through the North Carolina police database. That process yielded a match to Roscoe Artis. Further investigation by the commission unearthed a trail of violent sex offenses by Artis dating back to 1957. One of those crimes was the 1980 murder of a woman found naked below the waist with an object lodged in her throat.

The McCollum-Brown case had a peculiar trajectory after the DNA match to Artis. Instead of taking the road envisioned by the commission's structure—a referral and a hearing before a three-judge panel—the case shifted back to the regular postconviction process. Lawyers for McCollum and Brown, with the cooperation of the local district attorney, chose to present their new evidence at a state postconviction hearing that was conveniently already on the calendar. Stellato served as the sole witness and recounted the details of the commission's investigation. When asked point-blank by the district attorney whether she'd found anything to tie either McCollum or Brown to the rape-murder, she swore that the investigation could not "substantiate any evidence linking them to the crime." Based on the strong evidence of innocence, the court overturned their convictions in 2014, and the governor pardoned them the next year.

McCollum and Brown struggled emotionally, physically, and psychologically after their exonerations. They also suffered financial hardship. North Carolina gave them each $750,000 for the state's role in their trauma. But this compensation largely vanished after their lawyer swindled them out of some of it and pushed them to obtain predatory loans that ate up much of the rest. At long last, in 2021, a jury awarded them $75 million in damages, an amount that many believed to be the largest in North Carolina history for a wrongful-conviction case.[18]

NOTWITHSTANDING ITS PROCEDURAL DETOUR, THE MCCOLLUM-Brown case shows the impact of the Innocence Inquiry Commission on the pursuit of justice in North Carolina. It affords a much-needed venue, above and beyond the hidebound appellate and postconviction process, to air claims of actual innocence. An analysis of the commission's thirteen other exonerations reveals this all too clearly. They are marked by exhaustive investigation, meticulous analysis by staff members, and hearings before unbiased judges.

This is not to say the commission is perfect.[19] The minuscule percentage of exonerations during its existence raises the question of whether, like the CCRC in the United Kingdom, it's far too cautious in sending cases to judicial panels or lacks the funding to handle more than a few investigations at a time. Consider some possible design flaws, too. Asking defendants to relinquish their rights and privileges is a major sacrifice, even if some might deem it a necessary one in light of the commission's truth-seeking mission. Also, given what we now know about the pressures that innocent prisoners face to plead guilty, should North Carolina require unanimity among its eight commissioners to even refer a claim of innocence in a plea case to a judicial panel? And if any case makes it to that three-judge panel, should the convicted person bear such a heavy burden of proving innocence—"clear and convincing" evidence?[20] Think as well about the absence of any right to appeal the decision of that three-judge panel, let alone take issue with the summary dismissal of an application by the commission at the investigative phase.

Together with these distinct concerns, more abstract arguments could be levied against the commission.[21] Critics from the conservative side of the aisle assert that the commission's activities undermine finality and the centrality of the judicial process, impose vast costs on taxpayers, and potentially vindicate guilty people. Attacks from the left focus on the lack of accountability. The scholar David Wolitz has distilled the liberal critique into its essence: that "the commission approach buries claims of actual innocence in the nonappealable, nonjudicial process of an independent state bureaucracy. From this perspective, innocence commissions are simply executive pardon boards in new garb— unaccountable state institutions with absolute discretion to pursue or ignore miscarriages of justice as they please."[22]

Although it's important to respect these criticisms, none of them strike me as compelling enough to discard the North Carolina Innocence Inquiry Commission concept. As an independent entity with robust investigative authority, the commission can do what courts typically can't: it can stray beyond the four corners of the litigants' presentations and seek additional information as it wishes. By specializing in innocence claims alone, the commission can also develop expertise in the field in ways that more generalist courts, much less the executive officials in charge of parole and clemency, could never achieve.[23]

A final point is that sometimes our adversary system just fails to do its job. The axiom of Anglo-American law that the truth will prevail through heated combat between the prosecution and defense at trial—through direct examination and cross-examination, competing closing arguments, and battling experts—isn't always borne out in practice. And when the trial process doesn't properly sort the guilty from the innocent, the usual judicial and executive remedies have proven inadequate to pick up the slack. As this book has underscored, appellate and postconviction procedures erect formidable barriers to correcting wrongful convictions after trial. Executive remedies like parole and clemency are also inept at identifying and sparing innocent prisoners. That's why the inquisitorial approach of a CCRC-style innocence commission is a laudable last resort when the adversary system has fallen shy of justice.

Forfeiting your rights and privileges to enter an innocence commission process over which there's little oversight and no right to appeal is a steep price to pay. But in many cases it's worth what you get in return: an otherwise elusive, last bid at freedom.

CLOSING ARGUMENT

IT TOOK A LONG TIME TO RESOLVE THE LONG ISLAND RESTAURANT-robbery case.

We lost every step of the way in state court. We lost on direct appeal in the Appellate Division, on a coram nobis–type motion at the trial level, and in New York's highest tribunal, the Court of Appeals, where only a blistering dissent from a single judge gave us hope we might prevail in the end. Stephen Schulz lost despite a credible alibi witness along with powerful evidence implicating an alternative suspect who looked just like him and had pled guilty to six similar robberies in the vicinity.

After eight years of litigation, Schulz finally won. It happened on a federal habeas corpus petition when a judge tossed his conviction on constitutional grounds, not innocence. The judge ruled that his lawyer had provided ineffective assistance of counsel by not vigorously pursuing an interview with the robbery victim. The federal judge didn't even consider an independent claim of actual innocence.[1]

Schulz was set free in 2007 and became a long-haul truck driver. One day he called me from a pit stop on his route in Maine to report that he'd had lobster for the first time and found it delicious. Yet while the taste of freedom was sweet, it wasn't lucrative. Without a formal declaration of innocence in his habeas case, he was in a weak posture to recover damages for his wrongful conviction from New York State. He never did.

He now lives in an extended-stay motel in New Jersey with his longtime partner, Lisa, and their dog, Christmas, a rescue they found on December 25 a few years back. He told me recently that when he uses his debit card to buy something, he thinks not about the cost or the dent it puts in his savings. He thinks about how it gives him an alibi just in case the police come around to tag him for a crime he didn't commit, as they once did two decades ago.

Stephen Schulz at least earned his freedom, even if years late and dollars short. Many inmates whose stories dot these pages also had complicated endings to their cases. Freed but not declared innocent; released but deported; exonerated but uncompensated. Some died a few years after leaving their cells, unable to exorcise the demons hatched by their wrongful convictions. And those are the lucky ones. What about the unknown and unknowable corps of innocent inmates who have not yet made it outside the prison gates? Age, illness, and procedural barriers to exoneration all conspire to make it unlikely most of them ever will. Some might return to their communities, without being exonerated, after serving out their sentences. But for those condemned to die for their crimes, even that unsatisfactory outcome is a fantasy.

SINCE 1973, AT LEAST 186 INNOCENT PRISONERS HAVE BEEN EXonerated from death row in the United States. Put another way, for approximately every nine executions, there's one exoneration.[2]

Some people might interpret these statistics to suggest that the system "works," that appellate and postconviction procedures filter out weak capital cases. Other observers have a different take.

They think the disturbing number of exonerations in capital cases points to the intrinsic fallibility of our criminal justice system even when the ultimate punishment, death, is on the line and extra safeguards are supposed to be in place. Given the poor safety record of these procedural precautions, there's no reason to think proven exonerations represent the full universe of innocent defendants slated to die. How many wrongful capital convictions have morphed into wrongful executions? How many people await the same fate unless we abolish the death penalty or completely revamp capital appellate and postconviction procedures?

The Death Penalty Information Center (DPIC), a nonprofit research and advocacy group, lists twenty cases where a possibly innocent person was executed.[3] One concerns the execution of Cameron Todd Willingham for crimes related to a 1991 fire that caused the death of his three small children.[4] Fire investigators initially deemed it arson based on the alleged presence of an accelerant. Arson experts later debunked that theory and found evidence indicating that the fire had accidental origins. The state of Texas nevertheless killed Willingham in 2004. To this day serious doubts swirl about his guilt, with commentators citing several possible sources of the fire, including misuse of a space heater in the children's bedroom.

Like the Willingham case, so far none of the cases cited by DPIC as potential wrongful executions feature the silver bullet of DNA evidence that could conclusively exclude the executed person as the culprit in the underlying crimes. One reason is that the government has little interest in pursuing posthumous DNA testing after an execution. Even innocence projects and their allies may feel hard-pressed to allot scarce resources to such a pursuit when so many of their living clients remain incarcerated and need aid.[5] But a remarkable case pending in Tennessee could change everything.

———

AROUND 10:30 P.M. ON JULY 11, 1985, NINETEEN-YEAR-OLD
Lance Corporal Suzanne Collins went for a jog near the military
base where she lived on the outskirts of Memphis.[6] Her dead,
naked body was found eight hours later in a nearby park. She'd
been struck a minimum of one hundred times, strangled, and violated by a tree branch.

Investigators found a pair of men's underwear and other
clothing at the crime scene. Two Marines reported they'd crossed
paths with Collins while she was running the night before. They
also recalled that moments after seeing her, they had to dodge a
brown station wagon that darted out from her direction. Officers
later stopped a man driving a station wagon resembling that description, although it was dark green, not brown.

The driver, Sedley Alley, lived on the base with his wife, who
was employed by the armed forces. Alley had a military background too, one that ended with a discharge for drug and alcohol
abuse. The police interrogated Alley, who'd been drinking that
night, about the Collins murder. At first he denied any knowledge
of it and asked for a lawyer. Twelve hours later, though, he confessed in writing, an admission of guilt that he later insisted had
been coerced. The chief problem was that most of the available
evidence clashed with Alley's account:

- His confession claimed he'd struck Collins with his car
  at a particular spot and used a screwdriver to stab her.
  But the location he mentioned wasn't the one cited by
  the two Marine witnesses, and the autopsy gave no
  indication that Collins had been hit with a vehicle or
  stabbed.
- None of Collins's blood, hair, or fingerprints were found
  on Alley. There were slight streaks of blood on the
  driver's-side door of his wagon, which came back as
  type O blood, the most common in the nation and the
  same as both Alley and Collins.

- Tire tracks at the crime scene didn't match those from the wheels on Alley's station wagon, and shoe prints observed at the location didn't line up with his footwear.
- Most notably, a third witness who saw someone with a station wagon near the site of Collins's murder described a shorter man (five feet six to five feet eight) with a different color and style of hair (short brown) than the six-feet-four Alley, who sported a long red mane at the time.

Still, the case went forward against Alley based on the confession and the limited circumstantial evidence. Police and prosecutors ignored the mountain of other evidence signaling Alley's innocence. The judge and jury at Alley's trial ignored it as well, convicting him of murder and sentencing him to death.

––––––––––

THE INNOCENCE PROJECT OF NEW YORK CITY TOOK UP ALLEY'S cause as he languished on death row, his case bogged down in the appellate and postconviction process. In May 2006, the organization persuaded the Tennessee Board of Probation and Parole to ask the governor to delay Alley's looming execution to allow for DNA tests on the crime scene evidence. These tests could confirm Alley's guilt or innocence and pinpoint the true perpetrator by running the genetic profile through the federal Combined DNA Index System (CODIS) database. If the process produced a "hit" in the database, the Collins murder would be solved, all nagging doubts put to rest.

Governor Phil Bredesen granted Alley a fifteen-day reprieve to give the courts a chance to consider the Innocence Project's request under the state's Post-Conviction DNA Analysis Act of 2001. That law, like others discussed in Chapter 7, gives prisoners access to biological evidence from their cases for DNA testing in certain circumstances. Those circumstances vary from state to state, and the Tennessee judiciary offered an extremely narrow interpretation of their statute. The Court of Criminal Appeals ruled that the law wasn't concerned with establishing the guilt of an alternative perpetrator—"the DNA Act does not require further investigation into the identity of third party DNA." Rather, in the eyes of the court, the law was only concerned with whether any DNA results, if known at the time of trial, would have caused the government to forego prosecution or a jury not to convict. It determined that any DNA testing in the Alley case wouldn't meet that high bar given the "overwhelming" evidence of guilt at trial, the possible contamination of the evidence due to the passage of time, and the inability of the defense to link some of it directly to another assailant.

Five days later, the United States Supreme Court denied Alley's cert petition seeking further review. A day after that, on June 28, 2006, Tennessee executed Alley by lethal injection.

———

In 2011, the highest court in Tennessee, the state Supreme Court, heard a different case that afforded a new opportunity to examine the state's postconviction DNA-testing law.[7] It took that opportunity to correct the flawed analysis by the Court of Criminal Appeals and overrule the *Alley* decision, although far too late to benefit the case's namesake. The Tennessee Supreme Court found that the DNA Act advanced two goals, not just the one put forth earlier by its judicial brethren: "first, to aid in the exoneration of those who are wrongfully convicted and second, to aid in identifying the true perpetrators." It was now clear that, if Alley were still alive, he could receive DNA testing of the evidence to determine innocence or guilt *and* seek to identify the actual killer under Tennessee law. The question was: Did his death make such a process moot?

Alley's daughter put that question to the test. In 2019, April Alley succeeded in petitioning the probate court to become executor of her father's estate and, as his personal representative, received authorization to exercise all rights held by her father, arguably including those under the state's Post-Conviction DNA Analysis Act. With the assistance of the Innocence Project, later that year she filed a motion formally requesting DNA testing of a range of items that could prove Alley's innocence, or substantiate his guilt, once and for all.

This wasn't a shot in the dark. By that point, the defense team's investigation had shed light on several leads about the true perpetrator. They had information that a man recently charged with rape and homicide might be a serial offender and had evidently taken courses at the same training school as Suzanne Collins back in 1985. There were also long-standing questions about whether Collins's boyfriend at the time, who admitted having seen her on the night of her jog and drove a dark station wagon, might have done the crime. As Barry Scheck, cofounder of the Innocence Project, stated shortly after filing April Alley's motion, "All we need to do is test the DNA. The DNA will tell us who committed the crime."

It is that simple. DNA testing—of the underwear, the tree branch, any number of other things—could very well tell us who killed Suzanne Collins. The identity of the person responsible for that tragedy is a mystery, despite the execution of the man convicted of doing it. Procedural barriers have so far prevented DNA tests from happening.[8] In November 2019, the county court rejected April Alley's motion on behalf of her father's estate. The Tennessee Court of Criminal Appeals upheld that decision in May 2021 on the grounds that the estate lacked "standing" to litigate a claim under the Post-Conviction DNA Analysis Act. Why, exactly? Well, the appellate court found that the plain language of the law restricts eligibility to convicted "persons," and that an estate is not technically a person. Since April Alley filed the motion as the representative of her father's estate, not in her individual capacity, she was procedurally barred from seeking relief. The Innocence Project vowed to pursue further review in the state Supreme Court. It remains to be seen whether Tennessee will ever do the right thing and figure out whether the state executed an innocent man.

———

THE ALLEY CASE ECHOES A THEME THAT HAS REVERBERATED throughout this book. In our criminal justice system, the institutional focus on finality, efficiency, and deference to trial-level decisions comes at the expense of accuracy. Nothing could be more final than an execution, and few capital cases have more profound questions about accuracy than Alley's. After conviction, the presumption of innocence disappears. A new presumption of guilt forms and hardens over time. On direct appeal, procedural rules concerning preservation, deferential standards of review, and harmless error make this presumption virtually immovable. The rest of the postconviction process isn't much more flexible. Habeas corpus elevates claims grounded in constitutional and jurisdictional issues over factual ones. Even coram nobis, a remedy constructed to scrutinize factual mistakes, has procedural hurdles strewn across its path. The entity at the pinnacle of the judicial hierarchy, the United States Supreme Court, has exhibited minimal interest in innocence cases; when it has shown interest, prisoners usually don't fare well.

Executive officials could bridge the gap left by the courts. But the principal remedies available to them aren't envisioned as chances to look at whether courts got it wrong on the question of guilt or innocence. Instead, executive officials view parole and clemency as acts of grace for prisoners who've displayed model behavior or otherwise possess socially desirable character traits.

People classified that way aren't necessarily those who are innocent of the crimes that led them to their current residence.

Tweaking appellate, postconviction, and executive procedures along the lines I've suggested would make it easier for prisoners' cries of innocence to get heard. Encouraging the election of progressive prosecutors and the formation of conviction integrity units within DAs' offices would be another step forward. In particular, establishing innocence commissions to investigate wrongful convictions in every state could improve the situation considerably, assuming that route to exoneration is not also littered with impregnable procedural barriers.

But altering the procedural landscape facing innocent prisoners poses a challenge. First, the most direct way to foment change is to spur legislatures to amend the procedures that govern in this area, and the lack of political will is a real impediment. Although criminal justice reform is all the rage, the public's appetite has its limits. One of those limits is the fear of guilty defendants convicted of violent offenses exploiting procedural "loopholes" to get out of prison. Convincing people about the wisdom of, for example, streamlining federal habeas corpus procedures is a tall order, even if you can get voters and legislators to focus on the topic. Second, legislative amendments to the litigation process would remain subject to judicial interpretation, leaving open the possibility that courts would simply interpret the new rules to function in a manner akin to the old ones. Likewise, changes to the executive branch remedies of parole and clemency would only be as good as the officials in charge of implementing them.

Eliciting empathy from prosecutors, judges, executive officials, and the public at large might be the most effective solution in the long run. Whatever your views are about imprisonment—whether you believe it should be used extensively, occasionally, or not at all—those ensnared by the carceral state aren't so different from you and me. They enjoy tasting lobster and celebrating birthdays over Zoom with friends far and wide. Many committed the crimes that landed them behind bars. Others didn't. Prisoners with viable innocence claims deserve painstaking, transparent evaluations by neutral decision makers. They deserve a system that values accuracy over finality, efficiency, and deference. They deserve to live in a country where—with all due respect to my first-year law professor—substance wins over procedure.

ACKNOWLEDGMENTS

WHEN MY OLDEST DAUGHTER, MILI, WAS IN PRESCHOOL, SHE used to tell her chums that "Daddy does footnotes." She has since grown into a precocious teenager. I suppose I have evolved, too—from footnotes to endnotes at least. I could never have made that leap, from the rigidity of law scholarship to the relative freedom of a trade book, without the encouragement of my wife, Sharissa Jones, who gave me the idea to write for a general audience; the support of Mili; and the unbridled enthusiasm of our dynamic youngest daughter, Clementine.

So many other people deserve thanks.

I am indebted to my former clients, some of whose stories dot these pages, for fueling my passion for criminal justice reform. I cherish the close relationships that I have maintained with three of them in particular—Fernando Bermudez, Stephen Schulz, and David Wong. Agent extraordinaire Sam Stoloff had a hand in nearly every facet of this book. He helped shape the proposal, guide it to the ideal publisher, and tweak the manuscript. I cannot thank my friend and criminal law colleague Sasha Natapoff enough for introducing me to Sam, cheering me on throughout the writing process, and imparting her characteristically wise (and brutally honest) advice on an early draft. The team at Basic Books is simply incredible. I am grateful to Brian Distelberg for acquiring the book and playing a key role in refining the concept; Kyle Gipson for his outstanding editing and dedication to his craft; Katie Carruthers-Busser for overseeing the production process with skill; and Kelley Blewster for exceptional copyediting.

A slew of colleagues gave terrific guidance and feedback. Several close collaborators on other writing projects—my partners-in-criminal-law Michael Meltsner, Joshua Dressler, George Thomas, and Kevin McMunigal—spent hours reviewing the draft manuscript and making invaluable suggestions. My former teammate with the Second Look Program at Brooklyn Law School, Will Hellerstein, has been a tremendous ally, mentor, and confidante for more than two decades. The participants at Duke Law School's 2020 "Criminal Law Books" workshop served as a constructive sounding board while I molded my ideas for this project. A handful of dear pals on the Northeastern faculty and criminal justice comrades in other locales provided tremendous insight on earlier versions: Libby Adler, Lara Bazelon, Rashmi Dyal-Chand, Brandon Garrett, Stephanie Hartung, Margo Lindauer, Nina Morrison, and Jessica Silbey. Northeastern University and my wonderful dean, James Hackney, gave generous research funding, not to mention a half-year sabbatical, that allowed me to complete this project.

A fleet of talented students delivered vital research assistance as well: Abby Armstrong, Xenovia Bartholomew, Azra Carrington, Antonio Coronado, Rachel Crosby, Laura Follansbee, Julia Gaffney, India Rose Goldberg, Joy Holden, Mohammed Jagana, Eric Jensen, Sreenidhi Kotipalli, Kasey Lam, Lucy Litt, MaryRose Mazzola, and Alexandra Wood. I often say that teachers learn as much from their students as their students learn from them. That was certainly my experience with this remarkable team.

My brother Jono, his wife, Marnie Davidoff, and their children, Gabriel and Mirabelle, provided much-needed moral support from New York City, as did my relatives in Nebraska—the Jones family—and my dear friends Rich Dubois, Joel Goldberg, John Haddad, and Andy Sheffer.

Finally, the lessons learned from my novelist mother, Mameve, and my attorney father, Howard, informed every word in this book. My mother taught me to love writing and appreciate the power of narrative; my father taught me to relish the intricacies of legal analysis and admire the capacity of law to advance justice. Mameo and Bowie: I miss you each and every day.

NOTES

OPENING STATEMENT

1. For a description of the Robert Fennell case, see "In the Matter of the Application for Parole of Robert Fennell," November 21, 2001 (on file with author); People v. Perry (Joseph), 148 A.D.2d 1017 (N.Y.1st Dept.1989); Daniel S. Medwed, "The Innocent Prisoner's Dilemma: Consequences of Failing to Admit Guilt at Parole Hearings," 93 *Iowa Law Review* 491, 518–523 (2008).

2. For information about the origins of the Second Look Program and how innocence projects tend to choose cases, see Daniel S. Medwed, "Actual Innocents: Considerations in Selecting New Cases for a New Innocence Project," 81 *Nebraska Law Review* 1097 (2003). For a list of the various innocence projects in the United States that are members of the Innocence Network, a consortium of organizations that do this work across the globe, see "Network Member Organization Locator and Directory," Innocence Network, accessed January 5, 2022, https://innocencenetwork.org/directory.

3. As law professor David Dow once wrote about capital punishment, "Typically when politicians and the media use the phrase 'legal technicality' to decry a decision that results in a new trial for, or the release of, a convicted offender, what they mean is that a criminal who did in fact commit a crime has been released for a trivial reason. It is worth noting, however, that these so-called technicalities can also—and at least as often do—prevent people who did not commit a crime

from proving that they are innocent." See David R. Dow, *Executed on a Technicality: Lethal Injustice on America's Death Row* (Boston: Beacon Press, 2005), xv.

4. The Innocence Project in New York City keeps a running tally of DNA exonerations. See "Exonerate the Innocent," Innocence Project, accessed December 8, 2021, www.innocenceproject.org/exonerate/. For a more complete list of exonerations, including those generated by non-DNA evidence, see the National Registry of Exonerations, a project run by a group of scholars. Home page, National Registry of Exonerations, accessed January 5, 2022, www.law.umich.edu/special /exoneration/Pages/about.aspx. For an interesting discussion of the shortcomings of these data, and of the definition of "wrongful conviction" more generally, see Carrie Leonetti, "The Innocence Checklist," 58 *American Criminal Law Review* 97 (2021).

5. George C. Thomas III, "Where Have All the Innocents Gone?," 60 *Arizona Law Review* 865, 865 (2018): "Estimates have ranged from 0.027% to 15%; most estimates are in the 0.5% to 2% range." See also D. Michael Risinger, "Innocents Convicted: An Empirically Justified Factual Wrongful Conviction Rate," 97 *Journal of Criminal Law and Criminology* 761 (2007), putting the error rate at 3.3 to 5 percent for capital rape-murder cases; Marvin Zalman, "Qualitatively Estimating the Incidence of Wrongful Conviction," 48 *Criminal Law Bulletin* 221, 230 (2012), evaluating assorted studies and placing the general probable error rate at 0.5 to 1 percent; and Marvin Zalman and Robert J. Norris, "Measuring Innocence: How to Think About the Rate of Wrongful Conviction," 24 *New Criminal Law Review* 601 (2021).

6. See "Death Penalty Overhaul," Hearing Before the S. Comm. on the Judiciary, 107th Cong., June 18, 2002 (statement of Barry Scheck): "The vast majority (probably 80%) of felony cases do not involve biological evidence that can be subjected to DNA testing"; and Nina Martin, "Innocence Lost," *San Francisco Magazine*, November 2004, 78, 105, noting that "only about 10 percent of criminal cases have any biological evidence—blood, semen, skin—to test."

7. See Samuel R. Gross et al., *Race and Wrongful Convictions* (National Registry of Exonerations, March 7, 2017), www.law.umich .edu/special/exoneration/Documents/Race_and_Wrongful _Convictions.pdf. It's not far-fetched to say that the systemic devaluation of Black lives, whether manifested in wrongful convictions or incidents of police brutality, descends from slavery. Scholars have even shown how a direct line exists between the slave patrols of the 1800s and the modern system of American policing. See, e.g., Michelle

Alexander, *The New Jim Crow: Mass Incarceration in the Age of Colorblindness* (New York: New Press, 2010).

8. See Medwed, "Actual Innocents."

1. SOME BARGAIN

1. For background information about this case, see Maurice Possley, "Davontae Sanford," National Registry of Exonerations, last updated October 27, 2020, www.law.umich.edu/special/exoneration/Pages/casedetail.aspx?caseid=4913; and Lara Bazelon, "Ending Innocence Denying," 47 *Hofstra Law Review* 393, 412–415 (2018).

2. This attorney lost his license to practice law in 2018 after it emerged that he had forged another lawyer's signature on court documents. Ed White, "Lawyer Accused of Forging Filing Signature Disbarred," *Detroit Free Press*, February 14, 2018.

3. State v. Sanford, 844 N.W.2d 725, 725 (MI. 2014).

4. Sanford filed several civil lawsuits against the government. In 2020, as part of one of those lawsuits, the Michigan state police disclosed preliminary findings from tests conducted by a private lab indicating that there was blood from one of the victims found on Sanford's shoe. Although the police cautioned that those findings were unconfirmed—and the defense cited concerns about the methodology of the blood test—it still comprises an odd addendum to an odd case. Ed White, "Detroit Wrongful Conviction Case Takes Strange Twist with Blood on Shoe Test," *Detroit Free Press*, January 10, 2020.

5. States differ on whether an innocence claim may serve as the basis for withdrawing a guilty plea. See Peter A. Joy and Kevin C. McMunigal, "Post-Conviction Relief After a Guilty Plea?," 35-SUM *Criminal Justice* 53, 54 (2020). On the one hand, jurisdictions tend to "agree that a defendant can challenge the validity of the process that generated the guilty plea, sometimes referred to as an intrinsic challenge." On the other hand, states vary in the extent to which they allow challenges to a guilty plea for claims "unrelated to the process that generated the guilty plea. Such a claim is sometimes referred to as an extrinsic challenge."

6. I compiled these statistics based on a search of the database in the National Registry of Exonerations and use of the term "guilty pleas" to separate plea cases from trial ones. See "Detailed View," National Registry of Exonerations, accessed August 14, 2021, www.law.umich.edu/special/exoneration/Pages/browse.aspx. A previous report produced by that organization noted that approximately 15 percent of documented exonerations (261 of 1,702) involve guilty pleas. *Innocents Who Plead*

Guilty (National Registry of Exonerations, November 24, 2015), www.law.umich.edu/special/exoneration/Documents/NRE.Guilty .Plea.Article1.pdf.

7. Daniel S. Medwed, "Actual Innocents: Considerations in Selecting New Cases for a New Innocence Project," 81 *Nebraska Law Review* 1097 (2003).

8. I previously discussed some of the main points, cases, and arguments described in this chapter in Daniel S. Medwed, *Prosecution Complex: America's Race to Convict and Its Impact on the Innocent* (New York: New York University Press, 2012), 52–68.

9. See Lindsey Devers, *Plea and Charge Bargaining* (Bureau of Justice Assistance, Department of Justice, January 2011), https://bja.ojp .gov/sites/g/files/xyckuh186/files/media/document/PleaBargaining ResearchSummary.pdf. A 2018 report by the National Association of Criminal Defense Lawyers concluded that a trial "now occurs in less than 3% of state and federal criminal cases." National Association of Criminal Defense Lawyers, *The Trial Penalty: The Sixth Amendment Right to Trial on the Verge of Extinction and How to Save It* (2018), 5.

10. For a description of this case, see Daniel S. Medwed, "Up the River Without a Procedure: Innocent Prisoners and Newly Discovered Non-DNA Evidence in State Courts," 47 *Arizona Law Review* 655, 662–664 (2005). See also Medwed, *Prosecution Complex*, 55–56.

11. This is Stephen Schulz's recollection of how he learned about Anthony Guilfoyle and communicated that information to his lawyer.

12. The defense lawyer later claimed he had wanted to interview the witness before she took the stand, but that the prosecution prevented him from doing so. Schulz v. Marshall, 528 F.Supp.2d 77, 80–81 (E.D.N.Y. 2007).

13. See People v. Schulz, 829 N.E.2d 1192 (N.Y. 2005).

14. For a thoughtful discussion of the history of plea bargaining, see George Fisher, "Plea Bargaining's Triumph," 109 *Yale Law Journal* 857 (2000). As law professor Al Alschuler put it, "the guilty-plea system has grown largely as a product of circumstance, not choice." See Albert W. Alschuler, "The Prosecutor's Role in Plea Bargaining," 36 *University of Chicago Law Review* 50 (1968).

15. Santobello v. New York, 404 U.S. 257, 261 (1971). See also Fisher, "Plea Bargaining's Triumph."

16. Human Rights Watch, *An Offer You Can't Refuse: How US Federal Prosecutors Force Drug Defendants to Plead Guilty* (2013), 2. Prosecutors also sometimes penalize defendants who turn down a plea offer by bringing additional, and more serious, criminal charges

against them. See, e.g., Paige A. Nutini, "What Practitioners Should Know About Navigating the Prosecutor's 'Trial Tax,'" *ABA Journal*, April 25, 2019.

17. A study taken more than fifty years ago asked prosecutors which factors might spur them to plead out a case. The only factor they could all agree on was having a weak case. See Josh Bowers, "Punishing the Innocent," 156 *University of Pennsylvania Law Review* 1117, 1152–1153, n. 182 (2008).

18. In many jurisdictions, prosecutors may invite a criminal defendant to either plead "no contest" (an agreement not to fight the charges but without an admission of guilt) or enter a peculiar type of plea based on a 1970 Supreme Court case, *North Carolina v. Alford*. See Medwed, *Prosecution Complex*, 66–67; and Caroline H. Reinwald, "A Deal with the Devil: Reevaluating Plea Bargains Offered to the Wrongfully Convicted," 96 *North Carolina Law Review Forum* 139 (2021). An *Alford* plea expands on the no-contest concept, permitting a defendant to assent to the charges while still denying guilt. These tools have stirred quite a bit of controversy. To their credit, they allow for the innocent to refrain from admitting guilt. This can have beneficial ripple effects, including no past statement on the record that could be used against the defendant at a subsequent civil trial, for instance, if a person charged with the crime of murder later faces a wrongful death civil suit from the victim's family. They are also, arguably, an artful alternative for innocent defendants feeling pressure to accept a traditional guilty plea. Still, there's an arbitrariness to how and when prosecutors utilize these options and judges accept them. Not all states allow them, not all prosecutors draw on them consistently, and not every judge views them kindly. Even more, I'm puzzled by the fact these procedures exist at all. Doesn't an *Alford* plea formally put the court on notice that the case is weak and the defendant may very well be innocent? If so, why do we encourage the defendant to nevertheless acquiesce to the criminal charges and incur a punishment? Doesn't the fact that we tolerate no-contest and *Alford* pleas at all point to a larger flaw in the system, a system that treats guilt or innocence as incidental to the broader goal of processing cases, ideally convictions, as quickly as possible?

19. See Stephanos Bibas, "Plea Bargaining Outside the Shadow of Trial," 117 *Harvard Law Review* 2463 (2004).

20. See George C. Thomas III, "Two Windows into Innocence," 7 *Ohio State Journal of Criminal Law* 575, 591 (2010).

21. Brady v. Maryland, 373 U.S. 83 (1963).

22. See United States v. Ruiz, 536 U.S. 622 (2002).

23. See, e.g., National Association of Criminal Defense Lawyers and New York State Association of Defense Lawyers, *The New York State Trial Penalty: The Constitutional Right to Trial Under Attack* (2021), 56, describing the "Excellence Initiative" in New York State, in which judges were given a series of "Standards and Goals" to resolve felony cases within 180 days after indictment. For the latest research and data regarding caseflow management, see "Caseflow Management," National Center for State Courts, accessed January 7, 2022, www .ncsc.org/services-and-experts/areas-of-expertise/caseflow-and-work flow-management. See also "Judicial Selection: Significant Figures," Brennan Center for Justice, October 4, 2021, www.brennancenter .org/our-work/research-reports/judicial-selection-significant-figures.

24. See, e.g., Robert K. Calhoun, "Waiver of the Right to Appeal," 23 *Hastings Constitutional Law Quarterly* 127 (1995).

25. In his dissent to a 2019 opinion that upheld their use in New York State, Court of Appeals judge Rowan Wilson noted that "for many defendants, the harsh and chilling effect of appellate waivers results in the deprivation of their constitutional and statutory rights, far from anything one could, other than with great irony, call a game." People v. Thomas, 34 N.Y. 3d 545, 587 (2019).

26. See National Association of Criminal Defense Lawyers and New York State Association of Defense Lawyers, *The New York State Trial Penalty*, 20–21; People v. Batista, 167 A.D.3d 69, 82 (N.Y.2d Dept. 2018). Although appeal waivers may be justified, in part, as a way to protect scarce judicial resources, they may merely shift judicial review away from the substance of the case to the process through which the waiver was obtained. As Judge Wilson wrote in his New York Court of Appeals dissent in *Thomas*, "Rather than conserving judicial resources, appellate waivers consume the time of prosecutors, defense counsel and the court in attempting to create a record that might satisfy our appellate waiver jurisprudence. All that time and effort would be saved were appellate waivers banned." People v. Thomas, 34 N.Y. 3d 545, 597 (2019).

27. Much to my surprise, decriminalization has become politically popular, and even surfaced as an issue in the 2020 presidential campaign. See, e.g., Matt Cohen, "How Decriminalizing Sex Work Became a 2020 Campaign Issue," *Mother Jones*, July 5, 2019, www.motherjones.com/politics/2019/07/how-decriminalizing -sex-work-became-a-2020-campaign-issue/.

28. The information about Alaska's attempt to abolish plea bargaining comes from the following sources: "Alaska Ending Plea Bargaining to Raise Confidence in Justice," *New York Times*, July 12, 1975; Jill Burke, "Will Alaska's Plea Bargaining Plan Serve Justice,

or Cause It to Grind to a Halt?," *Anchorage Daily News*, August 14, 2013; Douglas D. Guidorizzi, "Should We Really 'Ban' Plea Bargaining?: The Core Concerns of Plea Bargaining Critics," 47 *Emory Law Journal* 753, 774–777 (1998); and Teresa White Carns and John A. Kruse, "Alaska's Ban on Plea Bargaining Reevaluated," 75 *Judicature* 310 (April/May 1992). While Alaska is the only jurisdiction that has tried to ban plea bargaining statewide, several smaller governmental entities have sought to do so on a more localized level. See, e.g., Robert A. Weninger, "The Abolition of Plea Bargaining: A Case Study of El Paso County, Texas," 35 *UCLA Law Review* 265 (1987).

29. See Medwed, *Prosecution Complex*, 60–66.

30. The "trial tax" also seems to affect negotiations *after* a prisoner has been exonerated and prosecutors are considering whether to pursue a retrial. In such instances, prosecutors frequently offer enticing plea deals, maybe even to "time served," in order to retain convictions. See Keith A. Findley et al., "Plea Bargaining in the Shadow of a Retrial: Bargaining Away Innocence," *Wisconsin Law Review* (forthcoming; draft dated October 18, 2021, on file with author), indicating "the data reveal that, in post-conviction litigation involving defendants with a high likelihood of being actually innocent and wrongly convicted, prosecutors offered plea bargains in 23 percent of the cases. Moreover, when prosecutors made plea offers, the plea concessions they offered were uniformly steep."

31. For a discussion of practices in Italy, see Michal Vitiello, "Bargained-for-Justice: Lessons from the Italians?," 48 *University of Pacific Law Review* 247 (2017); and William T. Pizzi and Mariangela Montagna, "The Battle to Establish an Adversarial Trial System in Italy," 25 *Michigan Journal of International Law* 429 (2004).

32. Even two scholars who otherwise seem skeptical about the extent to which the innocent plead guilty proposed minimizing the gap between plea and potential posttrial sentences, and suggest that "practically speaking, imposing limits on sentence bargains would not be particularly difficult. Courts could be instructed to reject plea bargains if the proposed sentence is substantially lower than that imposed in similar circumstances following a full trial." Oren Gazal-Ayal and Avisham Tor, "The Innocence Effect," 62 *Duke Law Journal* 339, 394–396 (2012).

33. I, along with many others, have chimed in to this discussion. See Daniel S. Medwed, "Brady's Bunch of Flaws," 67 *Washington and Lee Law Review* 1533 (2010); Medwed, *Prosecution Complex*, 35–51.

34. For a thorough and compelling discussion of the need for pre-plea disclosure, see Colin Miller, "The Right to Evidence of Innocence Before Pleading Guilty," 53 *UC Davis Law Review* 271 (2019).

35. See, e.g., Federal Rules of Civil Procedure, Rule 16, empowering courts to order pretrial conferences for purposes such as "expediting disposition of the action" and "facilitating settlement."

36. See Jenia Iontcheva Turner, "Judicial Participation in Plea Negotiations: A Comparative Review," 54 *American Journal of Comparative Law* 199 (2006). For an interesting analysis of the recent rise in judicial involvement in plea negotiations, a trend that has gone largely unnoticed, see Nancy J. King and Ronald F. Wright, "The Invisible Revolution in Plea Bargaining: Managerial Judging and Judicial Participation in Negotiations," 95 *Texas Law Review* 325 (2016).

37. See National Association of Criminal Defense Lawyers and New York State Association of Defense Lawyers, *The New York State Trial Penalty*, 40.

2. PRESERVED FOR REVIEW

1. See Daniel S. Medwed, "Up the River Without a Procedure: Innocent Prisoners and Newly Discovered Non-DNA Evidence in State Courts," 47 *Arizona Law Review* 655 (2005). New trial motions of this nature are conceptually similar to the postconviction coram nobis remedy covered in Chapter 6.

2. For a discussion of some of the cognitive biases that might push people to stick with their original decisions, see Chapter 4.

3. Davila v. Davis, 137 S.Ct. 2058, 2066 (2017).

4. For a primer on the preservation doctrine, see Ursula Bentele and Eve Cary, *Appellate Advocacy: Principles and Practice*, 4th ed. (Newark, NJ: LexisNexis, 2004), 77–103; and William Cassel and Anneliese Wright, "Preservation of Error for Appellate Review," *Nebraska Law Bulletin*, January 6, 2010.

5. These are known as *Anders* briefs, in recognition of a Supreme Court case in which an attorney appointed to handle a criminal appeal sought to abandon the case after determining that any appellate challenge would be frivolous. The Court ruled that, to do this, an appointed attorney must review the trial record and any relevant law, file a brief with the court explaining why an appeal would lack merit, move to withdraw as the attorney in the case, and provide the client with a copy of the brief. Anders v. California, 386 U.S. 738 (1967).

6. The description of this case is based on the appellate decision upholding Turner's conviction, Turner v. State, 719 S.W.2d 190 (Tex. Ct. Crim. Apps. 1986); "Keith Turner," National Registry of Exonerations, last updated November 26, 2016, www.law.umich.edu/special /exoneration/Pages/casedetail.aspx?caseid=3701; and Glenna Whitley,

"Chains of Evidence," *Dallas Observer*, August 2, 2007, www.dal lasobserver.com/news/chains-of-evidence-6375827.

7. This scientific testimony did not account for the possibility that the survivor's own blood group markers may have masked the perpetrator's, thereby casting doubt on the inferences drawn by the findings.

8. Specifically, the prosecutor asked Turner whether he had made any statements about his alibi "after that day" and "while on bond," i.e., after his arrest and release.

9. Part of the answer to this question hinges on the harmless error doctrine. As analyzed in Chapter 4, showing the existence of a trial error is ordinarily insufficient to gain relief on appeal; the defendant usually must show both that an error occurred and that it was not harmless in affecting the outcome.

10. For a discussion of the plain error doctrine, see Bentele and Cary, *Appellate Advocacy*, 103–116.

11. For insight into how these issues are addressed in New York, see People v. DeLee, 26 N.E.3d 210 (N.Y.2014). This area of the law is complicated, and jurisdictions differ in how they tackle the issue. Some courts distinguish between "legally" inconsistent verdicts (which are reversible) and "logically" inconsistent verdicts (which are permissible). In the words of the Illinois Supreme Court, "Verdicts of guilty of crime A but not guilty of crime B, where both crimes arise out of the same set of facts, are legally inconsistent when they necessarily involve the conclusion that the same essential element or elements of each crime were found both to exist and not to exist." People v. Frias, 457 N.E.2d 1233, 1235 (Ill. 1983). That's what occurred in my case—the jury found the element of DWI to exist with respect to one count and not with respect to another, even though both counts stemmed from the same incident. In contrast, logically inconsistent verdicts are those that "acquit and convict a defendant of crimes composed of different elements, but arising out of the same set of facts." People v. Klingenberg, 665 N.E.2d 1370, 1373 (Ill. 1996). See also State v. Tully, 110 A.3d 1181, 1192–1193 (R.I. 2015). The United States Supreme Court has long tolerated inconsistent verdicts at the federal level. As Justice Oliver Wendell Holmes Jr. put it, "Consistency in the verdict is not necessary. Each count in an indictment is regarded as if it was a separate indictment. . . . That the verdict may have been the result of compromise, or of a mistake on the part of the jury, is possible. But verdicts cannot be upset by speculation or inquiry into such matters." Dunn v. United States, 284 U.S. 390, 393–394 (1932).

12. The account of this case derives from a series of judicial opinions as well as profiles of Donald Gates. Gates v. D.C., 66 F.Supp.3d

1 (D.C. 2014); Gates v. U.S., 481 A.2d 120 (D.C.App. 1984); and Maurice Possley, "Donald Eugene Gates," National Registry of Exonerations, last updated November 20, 2015, www.law.umich.edu /special/exoneration/Pages/casedetail.aspx?caseid=3233.

13. The information in this paragraph about the role played by flawed forensic evidence in wrongful convictions comes from "DNA Exonerations in the United States," Innocence Project, accessed January 7, 2022, https://innocenceproject.org/dna-exonerations-in-the -united-states/; and "Overturning Wrongful Convictions Involving Misapplied Forensics," Innocence Project, accessed January 7, 2022, https://innocenceproject.org/overturning-wrongful-convictions -involving-flawed-forensics/.

14. See "Informing Injustice: The Disturbing Use of Jailhouse Informants," Innocence Project, March 6, 2019, https://innocenceproject .org/informing-injustice/. For a brilliant book by the country's leading expert on informants, see Alexandra Natapoff, *Snitching: Criminal Informants and the Erosion of American Justice* (New York: New York University Press, 2009).

15. At best, a defense lawyer could (and should) make a boilerplate pretrial request for all *Brady* material and hope that satisfies the preservation requirement if the evidence surfaces prior to the direct appeal. See, e.g., People v. Vilardi, 76 N.Y.2d 67 (1990).

16. For thoughts on why prosecutors disregard this obligation, see Daniel S. Medwed, "Brady's Bunch of Flaws," 67 *Washington and Lee Law Review* 1533 (2010); Daniel S. Medwed, *Prosecution Complex: America's Race to Convict and Its Impact on the Innocent* (New York: New York University Press, 2012), 35–51.

3. IN DEFERENCE

1. For a useful discussion of the various standards of appellate review, see Ursula Bentele and Eve Cary, *Appellate Advocacy: Principles and Practice*, 4th ed. (Newark, NJ: LexisNexis, 2004), 119–247.

2. People v. Schulz, 829 N.E.2d 1192 (N.Y. 2005); and People v. Schulz, 5 A.D.3d 799 (App. Div.2d Dept. 2004), first layer of appellate review.

3. Gates v. U.S., 481 A.2d 120, 124 (D.C. Apps. 1984).

4. For a helpful and clear articulation of how standards of review work, see "Identifying and Understanding Standards of Review," The Writing Center, Georgetown University Law Center, 2019, www.law .georgetown.edu/wp-content/uploads/2019/09/Identifying-and -Understanding-Standards-of-Review.pdf.

5. Gideon v. Wainwright, 372 U.S. 335 (1963). For background information about Clarence Gideon and his case, see "Facts and Summary: Gideon v. Wainwright," United States Courts, accessed January 6, 2022, www.uscourts.gov/educational-resources/educational-activities/facts-and-case-summary-gideon-v-wainwright; and Jack King, "Clarence Earl Gideon: Unlikely World-Shaker," *The Champion*, June 2012, 58.

6. The Supreme Court case law regarding when a defendant has a right to assigned counsel can be confusing. See Scott v. Illinois, 440 U.S. 367 (1979), which holds that there is no right to counsel in misdemeanor cases if just a possibility of imprisonment exists; Argersinger v. Hamlin, 407 U.S. 25 (1972), holding that a defendant cannot be subjected to actual incarceration without being provided counsel; and Douglas v. California, 372 U.S. 353 (1963), which extends the right to counsel for indigent defendants to the appeal-as-of-right stage.

7. McMann v. Richardson, 397 U.S. 759, 771 (1970), emphasis added.

8. Strickland v. Washington, 466 U.S. 668 (1984).

9. See David Von Drehle, *Among the Lowest of the Dead: The Culture of Death Row* (Westminster, MD: Times Books, 1995), 134, 254; and Jesus Rangel, "Confessed Murderer of 3 Executed in Florida," *New York Times*, July 14, 1984.

10. See Joshua Dressler et al., *Criminal Procedure: Principles, Policies and Perspectives*, 7th ed. (St. Paul, MN: West Academic, 2020), 1096, n. 10.

11. For some early examples of these cases, see Jeffrey L. Kirchmeier, "Drink, Drugs, and Drowsiness: The Constitutional Right to Effective Assistance of Counsel and the Strickland Prejudice Requirement," 75 *Nebraska Law Review* 425 (1996).

12. Kirchmeier, "Drink, Drugs, and Drowsiness," 426–427. For more information about this alarming case, see Ex parte McFarland, 163 S.W.3d 743 (Tex. Crim. App. 2005); and Stephen B. Bright, "Independence of Counsel: An Essential Requirement for Competent Counsel and a Working Adversary System," 55 *Houston Law Review* 853, 865–866 (2018).

13. Jon B. Gould et al., "Predicting Erroneous Convictions," 99 *Iowa Law Review* 471, 503 (2014).

14. For background information about this case, see Miller v. State, 226 P.3d 743 (Ut. Ct. Apps. 2010); and Stephanie Denzel, "Harry Miller," National Registry of Exonerations, accessed January 7, 2022, www.law.umich.edu/special/exoneration/Pages/casedetail.aspx?caseid=3468.

15. See "The Role of Race in Misidentifications," Innocence Project, August 11, 2008, https://innocenceproject.org/the-role-of-race-in

-misidentification/; Laura Connelly, "Cross-Racial Identifications: Solutions to the 'They All Look Alike' Effect,'" 21 *Michigan Journal of Race and Law* 125 (2015); and Bryan Scott Ryan, "Alleviating Own-Race Bias in Cross-Racial Identifications," 8 *Washington University Jurisprudence Review* 115 (2015).

16. The description of the American jury in this paragraph stems from Bennett L. Gershman, "Contaminating the Verdict: The Problem of Juror Misconduct," 50 *South Dakota Law Review* 322, 322 (2005).

17. Batson v. Kentucky, 476 U.S. 79 (1986). Arizona recently became the first state in the nation to ban peremptory challenges, in both civil and criminal jury trials, starting in January 2022. As the chief justice of the Arizona Supreme Court proclaimed in a statement announcing the change, "Eliminating peremptory strikes of jurors will reduce the opportunity for misuse of the jury selection process and will improve jury participation and fairness." See Brenna Goth, "Arizona Bans Use of Peremptory Strikes in State Jury Trials," *Bloomberg Law*, August 30, 2021.

18. See Flowers v. Mississippi, 588 U.S. __ (2019); Nicholas Bogel-Burroughs, "After 6 Murder Trials and Nearly 24 Years, Charges Dropped Against Curtis Flowers," *New York Times*, September 4, 2020; and Dressler et al., *Criminal Procedure*, 1244–1247.

19. Federal Rule of Evidence, Rule 606(b).

20. Tanner v. United States, 483 U.S. 107 (1987).

21. Tanner v. United States, 483 U.S. 107, 120–121 (1987).

22. See Ken Otterbourg, "Darrell Jones," National Registry of Exonerations, last updated June 2, 2021, www.law.umich.edu/special/exoneration/Pages/casedetail.aspx?caseid=5584; Bruce Gellerman, "Freed After 32 Years in Prison, Darrell Jones Will Be Tried Again in 1986 Murder Case," WBUR, May 20, 2019, www.wbur.org/news/2019/05/20/darrell-jones-murder-case-retrial; Bruce Gellerman, "Darrell Jones Is Found Not Guilty in Murder Retrial," WBUR, June 12, 2019, www.wbur.org/news/2019/06/11/darrell-jones-acquitted; Stephanie Roberts Hartung, "After 32 Years in Prison, Darrell Jones' 'Not Guilty' Retrial Verdict Was Long Overdue," *Cognoscenti*, WBUR, June 12, 2019, www.wbur.org/cognoscenti/2019/06/12/darrell-jones-retrial-innocence-project-stephanie-roberts-hartung; and Tom Relihan, "Judge Overturns Conviction in 30-Year-Old Brockton Murder Case," *Patriot Ledger* (Quincy, MA), December 20, 2017, www.patriotledger.com/news/20171220/judge-overturns-conviction-in-30-year-old-brockton-murder-case.

23. Peña-Rodriguez v. Colorado, 580 U.S. ___ (2017); Dressler et al., *Criminal Procedure*, 1367–1368.

24. Jackson v. Virginia, 443 U.S. 307 (1979). Although *Jackson* technically involved a challenge to a conviction at a federal habeas corpus proceeding (the subject of Chapter 5) after the completion of the direct appeal, it has salience for direct appeals too.

25. Coleman v. Johnson, 566 U.S. 650, 651 (2012), citing Cavazos v. Smith, 565 U.S. 1 (2011).

26. For an example of weight-of-the-evidence review in New York, see People v. Bleakley, 508 N.E.2d 672 (N.Y. 1987), and New York Criminal Procedure Law § 470.15.5.

27. See State v. Booker, 1988 WL 86417 (Ohio App. 8 Dist. 1988). This case concerned Donte Booker, who was convicted of sexual assault and other crimes near Cleveland. The Ohio Court of Appeals for the Eighth District upheld his conviction and found that the verdict was neither legally insufficient nor against the weight of the evidence. Postconviction DNA testing, however, later cleared him. See "Donte Booker," National Registry of Exonerations, last updated January 27, 2015, www.law.umich.edu/special/exoneration/Pages/casedetail.aspx?caseid=3033.

28. The concept of the thirteenth juror goes back centuries and was described by English legal commentator William Blackstone in the 1700s. Weight-of-the-evidence review is often exercised by trial judges as well. See Cassandra Burke Robertson, "Invisible Error," 50 *Connecticut Law Review* 161 (2018).

29. For a detailed account of what went wrong in the investigation and prosecution of Jeffrey Deskovic, see the following report prepared at the direction of Westchester County (NY) district attorney Janet DiFiore: "Report on the Conviction of Jeffrey Deskovic," June 2007, www.westchesterda.net/Jeffrey%20Deskovic%20Comm%20Rpt.pdf. I also discussed this case in Daniel S. Medwed, *Prosecution Complex: America's Race to Convict and Its Impact on the Innocent* (New York: New York University Press, 2012), 107–109, 114.

30. People v. Deskovic, 607 N.Y.S.2d 957 (App. Div. 2d Dept. 1994). I have reviewed the appellate brief to ascertain the precise "contentions" that Deskovic's attorney raised on appeal. Although many of the issues could have been presented more explicitly, counsel noted the "conjecture ridden summation" and mentioned that "the weight of properly admissible evidence failed to connect Appellant to the crime." Brief of Defendant-Appellant, People v. Deskovic, No. 90-01563, at 2, 58 (on file with author).

31. See Clark Nelly, "Are a Disproportionate Number of Federal Judges Former Government Advocates?," Cato Institute, May 27, 2021, www.cato.org/study/are-disproportionate-number-federal-judges-former-government-advocates: "[Former President Donald] Trump

appointed over *ten times* as many former prosecutors as former defense attorneys. As a result, the ratio of prosecutors to defense attorneys on the bench today is almost exactly four to one." See also Editorial Board, "The Homogenous Federal Bench," *New York Times*, February 6, 2014, discussing President Obama's judicial appointments and noting, "At the appellate level, only 4 out of 56 nominees were public defenders and 21 were prosecutors." President Biden appears to be in the process of changing this classic narrative. See, e.g., Mark Shearman and Darlene Superville, "Biden's Judges: More Diverse and More of Them," *U.S. News and World Report*, August 2, 2021, www.usnews.com/news/politics/articles/2021-08-02/bidens-judges-more-diverse-and-more-of-them.

32. For a compelling argument against the "neutral umpire" model of judging and in favor of greater empathy from those behind the bench, see Kim M. Wardlaw, "Umpires, Empathy, and Activism: Lessons from Judge Cardozo," 85 *Notre Dame Law Review* 1629 (2010).

4. FOUL PLAY

1. For a discussion of the history of the harmless error doctrine, see Daniel Epps, "Harmless Error and Substantial Rights," 131 *Harvard Law Review* 2117, 2126–2129 (2018); Roger A. Fairfax Jr., "A Fair Trial, Not a Perfect One: The Early Twentieth-Century Campaign for the Harmless Error Rule," 93 *Marquette Law Review* 433 (2009); Brandon L. Garrett, "Innocence, Harmless Error, and Federal Wrongful Conviction Law," 2005 *Wisconsin Law Review* 35, 56–62 (2005); and Justin Murray, "Policing Procedural Error in the Lower Criminal Courts," 89 *Fordham Law Review* 1411 (2021).

2. See Fairfax, "A Fair Trial, Not a Perfect One," 436, nn. 12–13.

3. For a discussion of the different federal tests for constitutional and nonconstitutional error, see Anne Bowen Poulin, "Tests for Harm in Criminal Cases: A Fix for Blurred Lines," 17 *University of Pennsylvania Journal of Constitutional Law* 991, 1004–1006 (2015).

4. Chapman v. California, 386 U.S. 18 (1967). Some constitutional errors are even considered "structural errors" that trigger a reversal of the conviction without any harm analysis at all.

5. See Federal Rule of Criminal Procedure, Rule 52(a).

6. Kotteakos v. United States, 328 U.S. 750, 759 (1946).

7. Roger Traynor, *The Riddle of Harmless Error* (Columbus: Ohio State University Press, 1970), 50.

8. See Harry T. Edwards, "To Err Is Human, but Not Always Harmless: When Should Legal Error Be Tolerated?," 70 *New York*

University Law Review 1167, 1171–1172, 1185 (1995). See also generally Garrett, "Innocence, Harmless Error, and Federal Wrongful Conviction Law."

9. See, e.g., Keith A. Findley and Michael A. Scott, "The Multiple Dimensions of Tunnel Vision in Criminal Cases," 2006 *Wisconsin Law Review* 1291 (2006).

10. See Elizabeth Kolbert, "Why Facts Don't Change Our Minds," *New Yorker*, February 20, 2007.

11. For a discussion of the status quo bias, see Daniel S. Medwed, "The Prosecutor as Minister of Justice: Preaching to the Unconverted from the Post-Conviction Pulpit," 84 *Washington Law Review* 35, 51–53 (2009).

12. William Samuelson and Richard Zeckhauser, "Status Quo Bias in Decision Making," 1 (1) *Journal of Risk and Uncertainty* 7–59 (March 1988).

13. See, e.g., Daniel S. Medwed, "Deterrence Theory and the Corporate Criminal Actor: Professor Utset's Fresh Take on an Old Problem, 1 *Virginia Journal of Criminal Law* 329, 331–332 (2013).

14. Emily M. West, *Court Findings of Prosecutorial Misconduct Claims in Post-Conviction Appeals and Civil Suits Among the First 255 DNA Exonerations* (Innocence Project, August 2010, updated October 2010), www.innocenceproject.org/wp-content/uploads/2016/04/pmc_appeals_255_final_oct_2011.pdf; and Daniel S. Medwed, *Prosecution Complex: America's Race to Convict and Its Impact on the Innocent* (New York: New York University Press, 2012), 103–118.

15. See R. Michael Cassidy, *Prosecutorial Ethics* (St. Paul, MN: West Academic, 2005), 101–107.

16. See Medwed, "The Prosecutor as Minister of Justice;" Medwed, *Prosecution Complex*, 104–105, 108.

17. The description of this case is based on People v. Evans, 399 N.E.2d 1333 (Ill.App.Ct.1st Dist.2d Div. 1979); and Rob Warden, "Michael Evans," National Registry of Exonerations, accessed January 8, 2022, www.law.umich.edu/special/exoneration/Pages/casedetail.aspx?caseid=3208.

18. The case was even more complicated than this summary suggests. A third man, James Davis, was originally charged with crimes related to the murder, but charges were dropped. Also, prior to his joint trial with Terry, Evans had a bench trial before a judge that resulted in a conviction that was almost immediately vacated after it turned out the prosecution had failed to disclose that the star witness had received money from the state, ostensibly for relocation expenses.

19. As the American Bar Association has pointed out, "Prosecutorial conduct in argument is a matter of special concern because of the

possibility that the jury will give special weight to the prosecutor's arguments, not only because of the prestige associated with the prosecutor's office, but also because of the fact-finding facilities presumably available to the office." Commentary, Criminal Justice Standards Commission, American Bar Association, *Standards for Criminal Justice: Prosecution and Defense Function Standards*, 3rd ed. (Washington, DC: American Bar Association, 1993), 3–5.8.

20. See, e.g., Shari Seidman Diamond and Neil Vidmar, "Jury Room Ruminations on Forbidden Topics," 87 *Virginia Law Review* 1857, 1864 (2001): "Researchers have examined the effect on mock jurors of simple admonitions that instruct the jury to disregard psychologically compelling but inadmissible testimony. The results provide support for practitioner intuitions: Simple admonitions often fail to unring the bell."

21. The description of this case is based on State v. Brown, 1983 WL 6945 (Ohio Ct. Apps. 6th Dist. 1983); "Danny Brown," National Registry of Exonerations, last updated July 21, 2018, www.law.umich .edu/special/exoneration/Pages/casedetail.aspx?caseid=3059; Jennifer Feehan, "Man's Wrongful-Imprisonment Lawsuit Dismissed," *Toledo Blade*, February 9, 2018; and Jeff Gerritt, "Released from Prison, Danny Brown Still Isn't Free," *Toledo Blade*, February 14, 2016.

22. "Judges Dedicate Room to Handwork," *Sentinel-Tribune* (Bowling Green, OH), February 10, 2020, www.sent-trib.com/news /judges-dedicate-room-to-handwork/article_f4774ea0-4c49-11ea -bab1-b3735834c1dc.html.

5. THE NOT-SO-GREAT WRIT

1. See Herrera v. Collins, 506 U.S. 390 (1993); and "Man in Case on Curbing Use of New Evidence Is Executed," *New York Times*, May 13, 1993.

2. For a brief history of habeas corpus and its connection with fact-based claims, see Daniel S. Medwed, "Up the River Without a Procedure: Innocent Prisoners and Newly Discovered Non-DNA Evidence in State Courts," 47 *Arizona Law Review* 655, 674–675 (2005).

3. U.S. Const. Art. I, Sec. 9, cl. 2.

4. For a discussion of the background to the Guantanamo Bay cases, see "Guantanamo Litigation-History," *Lawfare*, accessed January 8, 2022, www.lawfareblog.com/guantanamo-litigation-history. See also Samantha Pearlman, "Human Rights Violations at Guantánamo Bay: How the United States Has Avoided Enforcement of International Norms," 38 *Seattle University Law Review* 1109 (2015).

5. See, e.g., Boumediene v. Bush, 553 U.S. 723 (2008).

6. See the Supremacy Clause, U.S. Const., Art. VI, cl. 2.

7. For a concise discussion of the history of habeas corpus in the United States, see Ursula Bentele and Eve Cary, *Appellate Advocacy: Principles and Practice*, 4th ed. (Newark, NJ: LexisNexis, 2004), 341–342. Courts were reluctant to use habeas beyond its relatively narrow contours throughout much of American history, allowing it to operate as a "sleeping giant" until it awakened in the middle of the twentieth century. See, e.g., Diane P. Wood, "The Enduring Challenges for Habeas Corpus," 95 *Notre Dame Law Review* 1809, 1812 (2020), quoting Lewis Mayers. Scholars often cite a Supreme Court case, Brown v. Allen, 344 U.S. 443 (1953), as a watershed moment. *Brown* involved a consolidated review of several cases in which Black defendants had been tried for murder and sentenced to death in North Carolina state court before juries that were allegedly selected in a racially discriminatory manner. The upshot is that the Supreme Court issued an opinion that paved the way for state prisoners to seek habeas corpus review more easily in federal court to test the constitutional validity of their convictions, even if state courts had already reviewed and rejected those same constitutional claims. See, e.g., Wood, "The Enduring Challenges for Habeas Corpus."

8. Springstein v. Saunders, 164 N.W. 622, 624 (Iowa 1917).

9. Anderson v. Gladden, 383 P.2d 986, 991 (Or. 1963).

10. The Supreme Court later held that for an innocence claim to serve as a "gateway" to allow review of defaulted claims, the petitioner must show that given the new evidence, "it is more likely than not that no reasonable juror would have found petitioner guilty beyond a reasonable doubt." See Schlup v. Delo, 513 U.S. 298, 327 (1995). In one high-profile case, the Court found that DNA evidence satisfied this test. See House v. Bell, 547 U.S. 518 (2006). For a thoughtful discussion of the intersection between innocence and federal habeas corpus, including the actual innocence "gateway," see Brandon L. Garrett and Lee Kovarsky, *Federal Habeas Corpus: Executive Detention and Post-Conviction Litigation* (St. Paul, MN: Foundation Press, 2013), 151–162.

11. See, e.g., Wayne R. LaFave et al., "Freestanding," "Standalone," or "Bare" Innocence Claims, 7 *Criminal Procedure* § 28.3(e), 4th ed. (December 2019 Update). In the high-profile Troy Davis case from Georgia, a majority of Supreme Court Justices found his claim of actual innocence compelling enough to order an evidentiary hearing. The federal district judge who presided over that hearing acknowledged that, while actual innocence may serve as a basis for relief in

a habeas action, Davis had failed to "clearly" show his innocence. See Joshua M. Lott, "The End of Innocence? Federal Habeas Corpus Law After *In Re Davis*," 27 *Georgia State University Law Review* 443, 468 (2011).

12. For the chief laws that govern federal habeas corpus procedures, see 28 U.S.C. § § 2244, 2254. As Stephanie Hartung has observed, Congress passed the AEDPA in the early days of the "innocence movement," and legislators may not have been cognizant of the full consequences for innocent prisoners. Stephanie Roberts Hartung, "Post-Conviction Procedure: The Next Frontier in Innocence Reform," in *Wrongful Convictions and the DNA Revolution: Twenty-Five Years of Freeing the Innocent*, ed. Daniel S. Medwed (New York: Cambridge University Press, 2017), 254.

13. This sample was of noncapital cases. The grant rate was much higher—thirty-five times higher—in death penalty cases. See Nancy J. King et al., *Final Technical Report: Habeas Litigation in U.S. District Courts: An Empirical Study of Habeas Corpus Cases Filed by State Prisoners Under the Antiterrorism and Effective Death Penalty Act of 1996 (Executive Summary)* (Bureau of Justice Statistics, August 2007).

14. See, e.g., McQuiggin v. Perkins, 569 U.S. 383, 386–387 (2013), recognizing an actual innocence exception to statute of limitations constructed by the AEDPA. For an interesting discussion of how innocence has emerged as a key part of federal habeas jurisprudence and scholarship in the area, see Leah Litman, "Legal Innocence and Federal Habeas," 104 *Virginia Law Review* 417 (2018).

15. See Deskovic v. Mann, 210 F.3d 354 (2d Cir. 2000); and Deskovic v. Mann, No. 97-2946, 2000 WL 511034 (2d Cir. April 26, 2000).

16. For an example of this, please see this book's Closing Argument.

17. The following description of the Audrey Edmunds case is based primarily on Alexandra Gross, "Audrey Edmunds," National Registry of Exonerations, last updated June 2, 2018, www.law.umich.edu /special/exoneration/Pages/casedetail.aspx?caseid=3201; and Edmunds v. Deppisch, 313 F.3d 997 (7th Cir. 2002).

18. See Chapter 6 of this book for a thorough examination of these types of remedies. For the chief postconviction remedy in Wisconsin, see Wis. Stat. Ann. § 974.06 (2021).

19. The data cited in this paragraph stem from Daniele Selby, "8 Facts About Incarcerated and Wrongfully Convicted Women You Should Know," Innocence Project, March 1, 2020, www.innocenceproject .org/women-wrongful-conviction-incarceration-facts-iwd2020/.

20. For a fascinating and important exploration of the intersection between race and gender in the wrongful-conviction dataset, see Elizabeth Webster and Jody Miller, "Gendering and Racing Wrongful Conviction: Intersectionality, 'Normal Crimes,' and Women's Experiences of Miscarriage of Justice," 78 *Albany Law Review* 973 (2015).

21. For a description of the Fernando Bermudez case, see Decision and Order, People of the State of New York v. Fernando Bermudez, Supreme Court of the State of New York, County of New York (Hon. J. Cataldo), November 9, 2009, https://law.justia.com/cases/new-york /other-courts/2009/2009-52302.html; Daniel S. Medwed, *Prosecution Complex: America's Race to Convict and Its Impact on the Innocent* (New York: New York University Press, 2012), 82–83; and Report and Recommendation, Bermudez v. Portuondo, 00 Civ. 4795 (LAP) (KNF) (S.D.N.Y. March 29, 2004) (Hon. J. Fox).

22. "Southern District Names New Chief Magistrate Judge," *New York Law Journal*, January 19, 2012.

23. A team led by Barry Pollack and Leslie Risinger deserves credit for this development.

24. For information about this case, see the following federal and state judicial opinions: Jackson v. Day, 121 F.3d 705 (5th Cir. 1997); Jackson v. Day, 1996 WL 225021 (E.D.La. 1996); Jackson v. Day, 1996 WL 8083 (E.D.La. 1996); and State v. Jackson, 570 So.2d 227 (La.App. 5th Cir. 1990). See also "Willie Jackson," National Registry of Exonerations, last updated July 10, 2014, www.law.umich.edu /special/exoneration/Pages/casedetail.aspx?caseid=3319.

25. See Daniele Selby, "Why Bite Mark Evidence Should Never Be Used in Criminal Trials," Innocence Project, April 26, 2020, www .innocenceproject.org/what-is-bite-mark-evidence-forensic-science/.

26. See Chapter 3 of this book for a discussion of the issues related to claims of ineffective assistance of counsel.

27. Much of this evidence had been previously presented in a post-conviction hearing in state court that failed to provide relief for Jackson well before he sought the remedy of habeas corpus in federal court.

28. In this paragraph, I have simplified Friendly's argument in some respects. His self-proclaimed "thesis is that, with a few important exceptions, convictions should be subject to collateral attack only when the prisoner supplements his constitutional plea with a colorable claim of innocence." Henry J. Friendly, "Is Innocence Irrelevant? Collateral Attack on Criminal Judgments," 38 *University of Chicago Law Review* 142 (1970), 142.

29. Stephanie Hartung has made a convincing proposal in favor of a separate "innocence track" in federal habeas corpus litigation. This

approach would allow incarcerated people to raise viable claims of innocence without being subject to all the AEDPA's procedural restrictions. It's also a compromise that could address the courts' historic concerns about finality while providing appropriate review when innocence claims appear to have merit. See, e.g., Stephanie Roberts Hartung, "Habeas Corpus for the Innocent, 19 *University of Pennsylvania Journal of Law and Social Change* 1, 35 (2016); and Stephanie Roberts Hartung, "Missing the Forest for the Trees: Federal Habeas Corpus and the Piecemeal Problem in Actual Innocence Cases," 10 *Stanford Journal of Civil Rights and Civil Liberties* 55 (2014).

6. THE ANCIENT WRIT OF CORAM NOBIS

1. See Chapter 5, note 13.

2. For more information about coram nobis, see Daniel S. Medwed, "Up the River Without a Procedure: Innocent Prisoners and Newly Discovered Non-DNA Evidence in State Courts," 47 *Arizona Law Review* 655, 669–674 (2005).

3. See Daniel F. Piar, "Using Coram Nobis to Attack Wrongful Convictions: A New Look at an Ancient Writ," 30 *Northern Kentucky Law Review* 505, 507 n. 20 (2003), quoting Blackstone.

4. Anderson v. Buchanan, 168 S.W.2d 48, 55 (Ky. 1943), Sims, J., dissenting.

5. For a tremendous multivolume resource about the intricacies of state postconviction procedures, see Donald E. Wilkes Jr., *State Postconviction Remedies and Relief Handbook with Forms* (Eagan, MN: Thomson Reuters, 2018).

6. See Opening Statement and Chapter 2 of this book.

7. John Henry Wigmore, 5 *Evidence in Trials at Common Law*, § 1367, ed. James H. Chadbourn (Boston: Little, Brown, 1974), 32.

8. This discussion of the David Wong case derives from Daniel S. Medwed, "Anatomy of a Wrongful Conviction: Theoretical Implications and Practical Solutions," 51 *Villanova Law Review* 337 (2006); and Daniel S. Medwed, *Prosecution Complex: America's Race to Convict and Its Impact on the Innocent* 69–76 (New York: New York University Press, 2012).

9. See Shawn Armbrust, "Reevaluating Recanting Witnesses: Why the Red-Headed Stepchild of New Evidence Deserves Another Look," 28 *Boston College Third World Law Journal* 75 (2008).

10. The hazards of Rikers are well documented. They include undertrained and overwhelmed guards, deteriorating infrastructure, and gangs galore. In 2019, the New York City Council pledged to

dismantle Rikers by 2026 and usher in an era of "humane incarceration." Heather Leopere, "Prison Abolition and the Fight to Close Rikers," *Columbia Political Review*, December 3, 2019, www.cpreview.org/blog/2019/12/prison-abolition-and-the-fight-to-close-rikers.

11. For a discussion of the deferential standards of review that appeals courts apply to trial-level decisions, see Chapter 3 of this book.

12. This discussion of the Frank Sterling case is based on the following sources: People v. Sterling, 787 N.Y.S.2d 846 (Monroe Co. Ct. (N.Y.), 2004); People v. Sterling, 700 N.Y.S.2d 883 (N.Y. App. Div. 4th Dept. 1999); Decision and Order, People v. Sterling, Supreme Court, State of New York, Monroe County, Wisner, J., May 12, 1997 (on file with author); People v. Sterling, 619 N.Y.S.2d 448 (App. Div. 4th Dept. 1994); James R. Acker, "The Flipside Injustice of Wrongful Convictions: When the Guilty Go Free," 76 *Albany Law Review* 1629, 1636–1639 (2012–2013); Steven M. Cytryn, "Guilty Until Proven Innocent: Providing Effective Relief to the Actually Innocent in New York," 10 *Cardozo Public Law, Policy and Ethics Journal* 469, 484–486 (2012); and "Frank Sterling," Innocence Project, accessed January 8, 2022, www.innocenceproject.org/cases/frank-sterling/.

13. I floated many of these proposals in Medwed, "Up the River Without a Procedure," 686–715.

14. Tennessee Code Ann. § 40-30-102 (2021).

7. THE SILVER BULLET OF SCIENCE

1. Although DNA testing is remarkably accurate, and a far more reliable method of identifying the perpetrator of a crime than, say, fingerprinting, it is far from perfect. Consider the famous case of Josiah Sutton, a Houston man wrongfully convicted of kidnapping and sexual assault in 1999 after faulty DNA tests erroneously implicated him. For a discussion of the Sutton case and possible problems with the silver bullet of DNA, see Matthew Shaer, "The False Promise of DNA Testing," *The Atlantic*, June 2016, www.theatlantic.com/magazine/archive/2016/06/a-reasonable-doubt/480747/.

2. See Opening Statement, note 4.

3. The discussion of this case derives from Maurice Possley, "Dion Harrell," National Registry of Exonerations, last updated January 21, 2021, www.law.umich.edu/special/exoneration/Pages/casedetail.aspx?caseid=4959; Harrell v. N.J. Department of Treasury, 2020 WL 898124 (N.J. Super. App. Div. February 25, 2020); Ian J. Postman, "Re-examining Custody and Incarceration Requirements in Postconviction DNA Testing Statutes," 40 *Cardozo Law Review* 1723,

1726–1727 (2019); and S. P. Sullivan, "In Reversal, N.J. Will Now Pay Innocent Man Locked Up for Years on Rape Conviction," *NJ .com*, July 8, 2020, www.nj.com/news/2020/07/in-reversal-nj-will-now-pay-innocent-man-locked-up-for-years-on-rape-conviction.html.

4. Harrell struggled after his exoneration. State officials fought his claim for wrongful-conviction compensation, insisting that he should have filed it shortly after his release from prison, not after the reversal of his conviction. The parties finally reached a settlement just months before he died suddenly in 2021 at age fifty-three, cause of death unknown. See S. P. Sullivan, "N.J. Man Dies Suddenly After Winning Decades-Long Fight to Clear His Name and Help Wrongfully Convicted," *NJ.com*, January 22, 2021, www.nj.com/news/2021/01/nj-man-dies-suddenly-after-winning-decades-long-fight-to-clear-his-name-and-help-wrongfully-convicted.html.

5. District Attorney's Office v. Osborne, 557 U.S. 52 (2009).

6. District Attorney's Office v. Osborne, 557 U.S. 52, 73 (2009). See also Daniel S. Medwed, *Prosecution Complex: America's Race to Convict and Its Impact on the Innocent* (New York: New York University Press, 2012), 151.

7. See Matt Miller, "Juneau Man Wants DNA Tested, Seeks Review of Nearly 30-Year-Old Homicide Conviction," KTOO, July 13, 2012, www.ktoo.org/2012/07/13/juneau-man-wants-dna-tested-seeks-review-of-30-year-old-homicide-conviction/.

8. The following discussion of these impediments derives largely from my own review of the various state postconviction DNA statutes; "Access to Post-Conviction DNA Testing," Innocence Project, accessed January 9, 2022, www.innocenceproject.org/causes/access-post-conviction-dna-testing/; Justin Brooks and Alexander Simpson, "Blood Sugar Sex Magik: A Review of Postconviction DNA Testing Statutes and Legislative Recommendations," 59 *Drake Law Review* 799 (2011); and Postman, "Re-examining Custody and Incarceration Requirements."

9. For an excellent book about the broken misdemeanor system in the United States, see Alexandra Natapoff, *Punishment Without Crime: How Our Massive Misdemeanor System Traps the Innocent and Makes America More Unequal* (New York: Basic Books, 2018).

10. See Colin Miller, "Why States Must Consider Innocence Claims after Guilty Pleas," 10 *UC Irvine Law Review* 671 (2020).

11. Some states have abandoned these sunset provisions over the years, often at the last minute. See, e.g., "Michigan's Post-Conviction DNA Testing Law Set to Expire if State Senate Doesn't Act," Innocence Project, October 3, 2008, https://innocenceproject.org

/michigans-post-conviction-dna-testing-law-set-to-expire-if-state
-senate-doesnt-act/. Remnants still exist, though. In Florida, people
convicted of a felony at trial may seek DNA testing at any time, while
in guilty plea cases, only those who pled guilty prior to July 1, 2006,
may pursue relief at all. See Florida Statutes Annotated § 925.11(2)
(2021). The rationale for sunset provisions is to afford an opportunity
for older cases in which DNA testing was not available on the front
end, but to basically close the door to more recent convictions.

12. For instance, Iowa's law specifies that the defendant must eventually pay for the test if the results are unfavorable, but seemingly
fails to mention who absorbs the initial cost. Iowa Code §§ 81.10(3)
(a), 81.13(4) (2021). See also Brooks and Simpson, "Blood Sugar Sex
Magik," 829–833.

13. Regrettably, judges sometimes use their discretion in a manner
that limits access to DNA testing and deprives defendants of an opportunity to prove their innocence. For an example of this in North Carolina, see Joseph Neff, "A DNA Test Might Help Exonerate This Man.
A Judge Won't Allow It," Marshall Project, March 18, 2019, www
.themarshallproject.org/2019/03/18/a-dna-test-might-help-exonerate
-this-man-a-judge-won-t-allow-it.

14. For more information about the flaws in state evidence retention
and preservation laws, see Krista A. Dolan, "Creating the Best Practices
in DNA Preservation: Recommended Practices and Procedures," 49 No.
2 *Criminal Law Bulletin* ART 6 (2013); and Christina Martin, "DNA
Storage Banks: The Importance of Preserving DNA Evidence to Allow
for Transparency and the Preservation of Justice," 91 *Chicago-Kent Law
Review* 1173 (2016). See also Medwed, *Prosecution Complex*, 151–153.

15. See, e.g., Revised Code Washington Annotated § 10.73.170 (6)
(2021): "Notwithstanding any other provision of law, upon motion
of defense counsel or the court's own motion, a sentencing court in a
felony case may order the preservation of any biological material that
has been secured in connection with a criminal case, or evidence samples sufficient for testing, in accordance with any court rule adopted
for the preservation of evidence. The court must specify the samples to
be maintained and the length of time the samples must be preserved."

16. My discussion of this case derives from conversations with Nina
Morrison; the hearing transcript of Dismissal of Conviction, People of
the State of New York v. Felipe Rodriguez, Supreme Court of the State
of New York, County of Queens, Criminal Term, Part K-11, Indictment No. 1568-89, December 30, 2019 (on file with author); Arthur
Browne, "His Gift of Life Reborn: Freed after 27 Years on Shaky Murder Rap, a Dad Fights for Exoneration on a Very Merry Christmas,"

New York Daily News, December 24, 2017; Arthur Browne, "NYC Man Wrongfully Imprisoned 27 Years for Savage Murder of Mom Finally Exonerated," *New York Daily News*, December 30, 2019; and Maurice Possley, "Felipe Rodriguez," National Registry of Exonerations, last updated November 5, 2021, www.law.umich.edu/special/exoneration/Pages/casedetail.aspx?caseid=5660.

17. As Chapter 10 explains in more detail, clemency usually involves a request to an executive branch official or agency asking the state to pardon an offender (to offer forgiveness and erase the conviction) or commute a prisoner's sentence (reduce it and grant freedom).

18. See Chapter 2 for a more extensive discussion of *Brady*.

8. THE SUPREMES

1. The following discussion is based principally on Rules of the Supreme Court of the United States, Part III: Jurisdiction on Writ of Certiorari, Rules 10–16.

2. There are several narrow ways in which litigants may file a direct appeal with the Supreme Court, but they generally involve civil cases. See 28 U.S. Code § 2101. Getting review of *federal* criminal convictions differs slightly in that there's only one stage of appellate review (the circuit court of appeals) below the Supreme Court, and litigants can't chase any state postconviction remedies along the way.

3. See Rules of the Supreme Court of the United States, Part III, Rule 10.

4. For a helpful description of this process, see "Supreme Court Procedure," *SCOTUSblog*, accessed January 8, 2022, www.scotusblog.com/reference/educational-resources/supreme-court-procedure/.

5. Memorandum from Abby Armstrong to Daniel Medwed, "Research on Cert Grants," February 9, 2021 (on file with author), citing information gathered from Washington University (St. Louis) Law's Supreme Court Database, http://scdb.wustl.edu.

6. At the certiorari stage, amici typically only consist of those in favor of cert. If cert is granted, opposing interests have the opportunity to file amicus briefs about the merits of the case. See "Supreme Court Procedure."

7. See Adam Liptak, "Gorsuch, in Sign of Independence, Is Out of Supreme Court's Clerical Pool," *New York Times*, May 1, 2017.

8. For a discussion of these criticisms, see Barbara Palmer, "The 'Bermuda Triangle'? The Cert Pool and Its Influence over the Supreme Court's Agenda," 18 *Constitutional Commentary* 105 (2001).

9. Mark Joseph Stern, "The Supreme Court Is Terrible at Hiring Diverse Law Clerks, but Neil Gorsuch Is Surprisingly Good at It," *Slate*, April 16, 2018, https://slate.com/news-and-politics/2018/04/the-supreme-court-is-terrible-at-hiring-diverse-law-clerks-but-neil-gorsuch-is-surprisingly-good-at-it.html.

10. This overview of the Rodney Reed case stems principally from "10 Facts About Rodney Reed's Case You Need to Know," Innocence Project, October 11, 2019, https://innocenceproject.org/10-facts-you-need-to-know-about-rodney-reed-who-is-scheduled-for-execution-on-november-20/; and Justice Sonia Sotomayor's opinion related to the denial of a writ of certiorari in Reed v. Texas, 140 S.Ct. 686, 686–690 (2020).

11. See David Barer, "Rodney Reed Case: Newly-Obtained List Shows 41 Potential Witnesses in Upcoming Hearing," KXAN, June 18, 2021, www.kxan.com/investigations/rodney-reed-case-newly-obtained-list-shows-41-potential-witnesses-in-upcoming-hearing/.

12. See Reed v. Texas, 140 S.Ct. 686 (2020); Reed v. Texas, 138 S.Ct. 2675 (2018); Reed v. Stephens, 135 S.Ct. 435 (2014); and Reed v. Texas, 534 U.S. 955 (2001).

13. Brandon L. Garrett, *Convicting the Innocent: Where Criminal Prosecutions Go Wrong* (Cambridge, MA: Harvard University Press, 2011), 196.

14. This account of the Larry Youngblood case derives from the following sources: Arizona v. Youngblood, 488 U.S. 51 (1988); Norman C. Bay, "Old Blood, Bad Blood, and Youngblood: Due Process, Lost Evidence, and the Limits of Bad Faith," 86 *Washington University Law Review* 241 (2008); Marc Bookman, "Does an Innocent Man Have the Right to Be Exonerated?," *The Atlantic*, December 6, 2014, www.theatlantic.com/national/archive/2014/12/does-an-innocent-man-have-the-right-to-be-exonerated/383343/; and "Larry Youngblood," Innocence Project, accessed January 9, 2022, https://innocenceproject.org/cases/larry-youngblood/.

15. See Bay, "Old Blood, Bad Blood, and Youngblood," 252–253.

16. I concede that the definition of "bad faith" is far more complex and nuanced than this description suggests. For an interesting foray into the elusive and elastic nature of the phrase, see David E. Pozen, "Constitutional Bad Faith," 129 *Harvard Law Review* 885 (2016).

17. The information about police purging evidence from storage facilities stems from Bookman, "Does an Innocent Man Have the Right to Be Exonerated?"

18. A case from West Virginia illustrates this phenomenon. A man sexually assaulted a woman jogging in Charleston in 1982. After the

attack, she immediately ran to the hospital, where medical personnel collected biological evidence. The survivor later identified Larry Holdren as her assailant. Holdren put up an innocence defense and asked the state to test the biological evidence, but the hospital had not preserved it properly. Holdren was convicted and later raised a number of claims in the appellate and postconviction process, including a claim that the loss of this evidence violated his due process rights. A panel of judges from the Fourth Circuit Court of Appeals rejected the due process argument contained in Holdren's appeal of a habeas corpus denial, relying on *Youngblood*, and holding that the physicians did not act in bad faith when they failed to preserve the evidence. Holdren persisted with his efforts to locate biological evidence for testing, and the prosecution allowed him to test the victim's sweatshirt. Subsequent tests revealed the presence of semen that did not come from Holdren. He was exonerated in 2000, more than five years after the Fourth Circuit had rejected his claim. See Holdren v. Legursky, 16 F.3d 57 (4th Cir. 1994); and "Larry Holdren," Innocence Project, accessed January 8, 2022, https://innocenceproject.org/cases/larry-holdren/.

19. Some of the Supreme Court's post-*Herrera* jurisprudence reinforces the idea that viable innocence claims may, in certain circumstances, trigger review of claims in federal habeas corpus actions that are otherwise procedurally barred. Paul House was convicted of a gruesome murder in Tennessee but later cobbled together evidence pointing to his innocence, including DNA evidence. Tennessee state courts repeatedly parried his efforts to obtain freedom, so he sought relief in the federal courts via habeas corpus. The case went up to the Supreme Court, which concluded in 2006 that if this evidence had been presented at trial, no reasonable juror would have convicted him. Although the Court did not exonerate House, it remanded the case to a lower federal court for review on the basis that House had met the innocence "gateway" test from *Herrera*, i.e., that the presence of a credible innocence claim revived any procedurally defaulted constitutional claims in his case and made them cognizable for judicial review. House v. Bell, 547 U.S. 518 (2006). He was freed in 2008. See "Paul House," Innocence Project, accessed January 9, 2022, https://innocenceproject.org/cases/paul-house/.

9. THE INNOCENT PRISONER'S DILEMMA

1. Many of the ideas in this chapter originally stem from a 2008 article I wrote: Daniel S. Medwed, "The Innocent Prisoner's Dilemma: Consequences of Failing to Admit Guilt at Parole Hearings," 93 *Iowa*

Law Review 491 (2008). It was the last major article I wrote before I applied for (and secured) tenure, a mammoth sixty-seven-page, 321-footnote opus that few people have likely read cover to cover—aside from the unfortunate souls on my tenure committee. See also Daniel S. Medwed, " 'In Denial': The Hazards of Maintaining Innocence after Conviction," in *Wrongful Allegations of Sexual and Child Abuse*, ed. Ros Burnett (Oxford, UK: Oxford University Press, 2016), 204–214.

2. See Medwed, "The Innocent Prisoner's Dilemma," 497–504, for an overview of the history of parole.

3. The bulk of this paragraph stems from Nicole Bronnimann, "Remorse in Parole Hearings: An Elusive Concept with Concrete Consequences," 85 *Missouri Law Review* 321, 326 (2020); see also Medwed, "The Innocent Prisoner's Dilemma."

4. See Medwed, "The Innocent Prisoner's Dilemma," 507 n. 66.

5. Alexandra Harrington, "The Constitutionalization of Parole: Fulfilling the Promise of Meaningful Review," 106 *Cornell Law Review* 1173, 1193 (2021): "Currently, forty states have some form of discretionary parole for at least some people."

6. See "The Conservative Approach to Criminal Justice Reform," Right on Crime, accessed January 10, 2022, www.rightoncrime.com: "Right on Crime is a national campaign of the Texas Public Policy Foundation that supports conservative solutions for reducing crime, restoring victims, reforming offenders, and lowering taxpayer costs."

7. See, e.g., Julia Angwin et al., "Machine Bias," ProPublica, May 23, 2016, www.propublica.org/article/machine-bias-risk-assessments-in-criminal-sentencing; and Cade Metz and Adam Satarino, "An Algorithm That Grants Freedom, or Takes It Away," *New York Times*, February 7, 2020.

8. Sandra G. Mayson, "Bias In, Bias Out," 128 *Yale Law Journal* 2218 (2019). See also Johana Bhuiyan, "LAPD Ended Predictive Policing Programs amid Public Outcry. A New Effort Shares Many of Their Flaws," *The Guardian*, November 8, 2021, discussing how "data-driven programs" used by the Los Angeles Police Department "validated existing patterns of policing and reinforced decisions to patrol certain neighborhoods over others, leading to the over-policing of Black and brown communities in the metropole."

9. See Medwed, "The Innocent Prisoner's Dilemma," 510, 547.

10. For examples of cases where inmates were denied parole because they maintained innocence and therefore declined to accept responsibility, see Medwed, "The Innocent Prisoner's Dilemma," 514 n. 92.

11. Jeffrie G. Murphy, "Remorse, Apology, and Mercy," 4 *Ohio State Journal of Criminal Law* 423, 438 (2007).

12. See Medwed, "The Innocent Prisoner's Dilemma," 538: "In fact, one study of the Georgia parole system concluded that parole officers 'erred' more frequently in their decisions made after prisoner participation at parole hearings—with errors measured by the number of parole revocations and disciplinary infractions later attained by the candidates—than those made before personally interviewing the applicant" (internal citations omitted).

13. Researchers in one study tracked 144 prisoners convicted of sex crimes in England. The parole board branded about one-third of those inmates "in denial" and therefore "high-risk." Yet ultimately only one of those "high-risk" individuals was ever reconvicted of a sex offense after release. In contrast, 17 of the 97 subjects who were deemed "non-deniers" were later reconvicted of a sex crime. See Medwed, "The Innocent Prisoner's Dilemma," 536–537.

14. For a moving account of a person with a compelling innocence claim who refused to "admit" guilt to the parole board and remained locked up at the age of seventy-eight, see Tom Robbins, "He Says He's No Murderer. That's Why He's Still in Prison," *New York Times*, December 2, 2021.

15. Audrey Edmunds and Jill Wellington, *It Happened to Audrey: A Terrifying Journey from Loving Mom to Accused Baby Killer* (Green Bay, WI: TitleTown Publishing, 2012), 145–146.

16. See "In the Matter of the Application for Parole of Robert Fennell," November 21, 2001 (on file with author).

17. For a description of this case, see Medwed, "In Denial," 209–211; Medwed, "The Innocent Prisoner's Dilemma," 523– 528; Daniel S. Medwed, *Prosecution Complex: America's Race to Convict and Its Impact on the Innocent* (New York: New York University Press, 2012), 159-161; and State v. Goodman, 763 P.2d 786 (Utah 1988).

18. See Associated Press, "DNA Tests Set Man Free After 19 Years," *Los Angeles Times*, November 10, 2004: "After insisting for years that he was innocent, Goodman accepted responsibility for the crime at a parole hearing in 2000, but said he did not remember it. His attorney, Josh Bowland, said Goodman was just trying to win favor with the parole board."

19. For information about the day of Goodman's release and how he fared in later years, see Aaron Falk, "Conviction Tossed After 19 Years, Freed Man Wants Utah to Pay Up," *Salt Lake Tribune*, October 11, 2012; and John Ferak, "Murder Cases Often Go Cold After Exonerations," *Post-Crescent* (Appleton, WI), May 18, 2017, www.postcrescent.com/story/news/investigations/2017/05/18/murder-cases-often-go-cold-after-exonerations/100019208/.

20. My research about the Innocent Prisoner's Dilemma has fortunately (and surprisingly) attracted attention to the issue. See, e.g., Rob Harris and Trymaine Lee, "The 'Innocent Prisoner's Dilemma,'" *New York Times*, June 4, 2010, video, www.nytimes.com/video /nyregion/1247467961918/the-innocent-prisoner-s-dilemma.html. Several appellate courts have also cited my paper in their opinions. See, e.g., Newman v. Beard, 617 F.3d 775, 786 (3rd Cir. 2008); Commonwealth v. Clark, 528 S.W.3d 342, 348 (Ky. 2017); and Deal v. Massachusetts Parole Board, 142 N.E.3d 77, 88 (Ma. 2020).

21. See, e.g., Frances Robles, "Parole Is Granted in a 1995 Killing Investigated by Brooklyn Detective," *New York Times*, November 1, 2013.

22. See, e.g., Stephanos Bibas and Richard A. Bierschbach, "Integrating Remorse and Responsibility into Criminal Procedure," 114 *Yale Law Journal* 85, 87 (2004).

10. NOT JUST MERCY

1. See, e.g., "Mission," State of Utah Board of Pardons and Parole, accessed May 5, 2021, https://bop.utah.gov.

2. For a description of the various types of clemency, see Daniel T. Kobil, "The Quality of Mercy Strained: Wresting the Pardoning Power from the King," 69 *Texas Law Review* 569, 575–578 (1991). In addition to pardons, commutations, and reprieves, Kobil mentions the use of clemency to remit fines and forfeitures and to grant amnesty. Amnesty technically differs from pardons in that it does not represent forgiveness for the infraction, but rather is a means to overlook the crime and absolve the person of any penalty. It ordinarily applies to large groups of people and often takes place before any conviction. The practical effects of a pardon and amnesty, however, are essentially the same, and the choice between them is often dictated by political factors. For instance, as Kobil writes, "in justifying his grant of amnesty to those who evaded service in Vietnam, President Carter argued that their crimes were not forgiven, as they might have been through a pardon, only forgotten" (577).

3. This occurred in the Cyntoia Brown case; see note 9 to this chapter.

4. The information in this paragraph derives from "Clemency Procedures by State," Death Penalty Information Center, accessed January 11, 2022, https://deathpenaltyinfo.org/facts-and-research/clemency /clemency-by-state; and Sarah Lucy Cooper and Daniel Gough, "The Controversy of Clemency and Innocence in America," 51 *California Western Law Review* 55, 73 (2014).

5. Herrera v. Collins, 506 U.S. 390 (1993).

6. See, e.g., Laura Schaefer and Michael L. Radelet, "Have Mercy: New Opportunities for Commutations in Death Penalty Cases," 42 *Human Rights Magazine* 18 (2017), which notes that "we now know of 156 individuals who have been released from death rows because of evidence of innocence—and only one, Earl Washington in Virginia, first saw his death sentence commuted before receiving a full pardon."

7. See "Brief of Eleven Individuals Who Have Received Clemency Through DNA Testing as Amici Curiae in Support of Respondent," District Attorney's Office for the Third District v. Osborne, No. 08-06, 2009 WL 271057 (U.S.) (Appellate Brief), February 2, 2009.

8. Some scholars have disputed Rehnquist's assertion that clemency is a "fail safe" that has come to the aid of many innocent prisoners. See, e.g., James R. Acker and Catherine Bonventre, "Protecting the Innocent in New York: Moving Beyond Changing Only Their Names," 73 *Albany Law Review* 1245, 1350–1353 (2010); and Nicholas Berg, "Turning a Blind Eye to Innocence: The Legacy of Herrera v. Collins," 42 *American Criminal Law Review* 121 (2005). For a strong empirical assessment of who receives clemency, see Michael Heise, "Mercy by the Numbers: An Empirical Analysis of Clemency and Its Structure," 89 *Virginia Law Review* 239 (2003).

9. See, e.g., Bobby Allyn, "Cyntoia Brown Released After 15 Years in Prison for Murder," NPR, August 7, 2019, www.npr .org/2019/08/07/749025458/cyntoia-brown-released-after-15-years -in-prison-for-murder.

10. For information about clemency grants in the states (Arkansas, Connecticut, Idaho, and Massachusetts) mentioned in this passage, see Maria Cramer, "As 2 Felons Earn Pardons, Time for Others Runs Short," *Boston Globe*, January 2, 2015; "Massachusetts Restoration of Rights and Record Relief," Restoration of Rights Project, last updated June 9, 2021, https://ccresourcecenter.org/state-restoration-profiles /massachusetts-restoration-of-rights-pardon-expungement-sealing/; and "50-State Comparison: Pardon Policy and Practice," *Restoration of Rights Project*, last updated November 2021, https://ccresourcecenter .org/state-restoration-profiles/50-state-comparisoncharacteristics -of-pardon-authorities-2/.

11. See Editorial Board, "State Parole Board, Clemency Process Need Reform," *Boston Globe*, April 5, 2021. Governor Patrick also commuted one person's sentence, which was the last favorable clemency decision in Massachusetts for many years. The Massachusetts Parole Board held one commutation hearing in October 2020 and another in June 2021. Both hearings resulted in favorable outcomes for the applicants, with the board in each instance recommending

a sentence commutation to Governor Charlie Baker. See Deborah Becker, "Parole Board Recommends Commutation for William Allen," WBUR News, September 16, 2021, www.wbur.org/news/2021/09/16/massachusetts-clemency-parole-allen-dejuneas-murder. In January 2022, Baker acted on those recommendations and commuted the sentences of William Allen and Thomas Koonce. See Matt Stout and Shelley Murphy, "Baker Approves Commutation Requests for Two Convicted of Murder," *Boston Globe*, January 12, 2022. The Massachusetts Parole Board held four additional clemency hearings in December 2021, "fueling optimism among legal observers that the state could embrace clemency for the first time in years." Matt Stout and Shelley Murphy, "Will Charlie Baker Commute a Convicted Murderer's Life Sentence?," *Boston Globe*, January 9, 2022.

12. See, e.g., Peter Baker, "Bush Made Willie Horton an Issue in 1988, and the Racial Scars Are Still Fresh," *New York Times*, December 3, 2018; and John Pfaff, "The Never-Ending 'Willie Horton Effect' Is Keeping Prisons Too Full for America's Good," *Los Angeles Times*, May 14, 2017.

13. See, e.g., Nicole Lewis et al., "Trump's Pardons Show the Process Has Always Been Broken," The Marshall Project, January 19, 2021, www.themarshallproject.org/2021/01/19/trump-s-pardons-show-the-process-has-always-been-broken; and Michael S. Schmidt and Kenneth P. Vogel, "Prospect of Pardons in Final Days Fuels Market to Buy Access to Trump," *New York Times*, January 17, 2021. Cf. Heise, "Mercy by the Numbers," at 304, noting "that many standard political factors assumed to influence clemency decisions might be overstated."

14. See Commonwealth v. Vickey, 412 N.E.2d 877, 881 (Ma. 1980).

15. This discussion of the Marvin Anderson case comes from Kate Andrews, "This Man Is Innocent," *Richmond Magazine*, May 26, 2011; Brandon L. Garrett, *Convicting the Innocent: Where Criminal Prosecutions Go Wrong* (Cambridge, MA: Harvard University Press, 2011), 57–58; Kristen Gelineau, "Saving Grace," *Washington Post*, October 9, 2005; Maria Glod, "Cleared Va. Man to Be Pardoned," *Washington Post*, August 21, 2002; and "Marvin Anderson," National Registry of Exonerations, last updated March 8, 2019, www.law.umich.edu/special/exoneration/Pages/casedetail.aspx?caseid=2995.

16. Manson v. Brathwaite, 432 U.S. 98 (1977); and Neil v. Biggers, 409 U.S. 188 (1972).

17. Garrett, *Convicting the Innocent*, 8–9, 48–50, 57–59.

18. Margaret Burnham, "Retrospective Justice in the Age of Innocence," in *Wrongful Convictions and the DNA Revolution: Twenty-Five Years of Freeing the Innocent*, ed. Daniel S. Medwed (New York:

Cambridge University Press, 2017), 291. In 1977, the Supreme Court outlawed the death penalty for rape crimes as a violation of the Constitution's prohibition against cruel and unusual punishment. Coker v. Georgia, 433 U.S. 584 (1977).

19. See David Nakamura, "Wilder Releases Va. Prep Star Iverson from Jail," *Washington Post*, December 31, 1993: "In a surprise move, Virginia Gov. L. Douglas Wilder granted Iverson, 18, conditional clemency, which allows Iverson to resume his high school education but bars him from participating in organized sports."

20. It appears that Anderson faced the parole board several times prior to 1997, "and each time he faced the parole board, having declared his innocence to the interviewer, Marvin was turned down." See Andrews, "This Man Is Innocent."

21. Virginia's complicated history with clemency continues to resonate today. Within a month's time in the summer of 2021, Governor Ralph Northam of Virginia issued absolute pardons on the grounds of actual innocence in *three* different cases. Eric Williamson, "Third Innocence Project Client Receives Absolute Pardon," *UVA Lawyer*, August 17, 2021, www.law.virginia.edu/news/202108/third -innocence-project-client-receives-absolute-pardon.

22. For example, after DNA tests excluded the genetic profile of Michael Evans, the Chicago man whose story of wrongful conviction for raping and killing a nine-year-old girl appeared in Chapter 4, and prosecutors dismissed the charges against him, Illinois governor Rod Blagojevich pardoned him. See "Brief of Eleven Individuals Who Have Received Clemency." Recently, Tennessee governor Bill Lee fully exonerated Adam Braseel, a man convicted of a 2006 murder, after new fingerprint evidence pointed to another person as the culprit. See Melissa Brown, "Gov. Bill Lee Grants Clemency to 17 People, Introduces New Review for School Zone Drug Offenses," *Tennessean*, December 2, 2021.

23. In fact, after Governor Warner pardoned Anderson, the commonwealth passed legislation to compensate him for his damages: $200,000 and a $460,000 annuity. See 2003 Va. Acts Ch. 826. The precise legal consequences of a pardon differ from state to state. A pardon in some states serves to essentially erase the conviction from a person's record. See, e.g., In the Matter of the Petition of L.B., 848 A.2d 899, 900 (N.J. Super.2004), suggesting that a pardon in New Jersey restores the recipient's rights and makes the conviction eligible for expungement. In others, the relief is more limited. In Nevada, a pardon eliminates most collateral consequences of a conviction, including restrictions on having a gun or obtaining other state licenses, but does

not "erase the conviction," and it may still factor into sentencing as a predicate crime if the person is subsequently convicted of an offense. Nev. Rev. State. § 213.090 (2021).

24. For a fascinating discussion of the history of the clemency power, see Cooper and Gough, "The Controversy of Clemency and Innocence in America," 58–71.

25. See Alexander Hamilton, "The Command of the Military and Naval Forces, and the Pardoning Power of the Executive," *Federalist*, no. 74, March 25, 1788; and Ex parte Garland, 71 U.S. 333, 380 (1866).

26. See, e.g., Evitts v. Lucey, 469 U.S. 387, 393 (1985); and Ohio Adult Parole Authority v. Woodard, 523 U.S. 272, 274 (1998).

27. See Massachusetts Executive Clemency Guidelines 4.2.1, issued by Governor Charles D. Baker, February 21, 2020: "The Governor will rarely grant clemency to a petitioner who has not clearly demonstrated acceptance of responsibility for the offense for which the petitioner is seeking clemency."

28. See Cooper and Gough, "The Controversy of Clemency and Innocence in America," 87–88, noting the examples of Georgia and Virginia.

29. See Cooper and Gough, "The Controversy of Clemency and Innocence in America," 92–94. In North Carolina, a person may earn a "pardon of innocence" when they've been convicted, incarcerated, and later ruled innocent. A pardon of innocence is defined as "granted when an individual has been convicted and the criminal charges are subsequently dismissed. Application for this type of Pardon allows an individual to petition the Governor for a declaration of innocence when the individual has been erroneously convicted and imprisoned and later determined to be innocent." See North Carolina Department of Public Safety, "Glossary of Terms," accessed January 11, 2022, www.ncdps.gov/adult-corrections/governors-clemency-office/glossary-of-terms.

30. Montana and South Dakota explicitly allow for consideration of actual innocence as part of the clemency calculus. Tennessee has a distinct clemency "exoneration" procedure through which the governor may pardon a person if the facts, circumstances, and newly discovered evidence constitute "clear and convincing evidence" the person did not commit the crime. See Cooper and Gough, "The Controversy of Clemency and Innocence in America," 82–94.

31. See Cooper and Gough, "The Controversy of Clemency and Innocence in America," 74–81, 84–86.

32. See Cooper and Gough, "The Controversy of Clemency and Innocence in America," 81–84.

33. See Rachel E. Barkow, "The Politics of Forgiveness: Reconceptualizing Clemency," 21 *Federal Sentencing Reporter* 153, 155–156 (2009). See also Cooper and Gough, "The Controversy of Clemency and Innocence in America," 81.

34. Barkow, "The Politics of Forgiveness," 156.

35. See Editorial Board, "State Parole Board, Clemency Process Need Reform."

36. See Paul J. Larkin Jr., "Guiding Presidential Clemency Decision Making," 18 *Georgetown Journal of Law and Public Policy* 451, 456 (2020).

11. PROSECUTORS WITH CONVICTIONS

1. This phrase is often credited to George Sharswood in his 1854 paper, "An Essay on Professional Ethics," Making of America, accessed January 4, 2022, https://quod.lib.umich.edu/m/moa/AJF2351.0001.001?rgn=main;view=fulltext.

2. In this chapter, much of the discussion of the political, practical, and psychological factors that influence prosecutorial decision-making stems from my previous research in the area. See Daniel S. Medwed, *Prosecution Complex: America's Race to Convict and Its Impact on the Innocent* (New York: New York University Press, 2012); Daniel S. Medwed, "The Prosecutor as Minister of Justice: Preaching to the Unconverted from the Post-Conviction Pulpit," 84 *Washington Law Review* 35, 51–53 (2009); and Daniel S. Medwed, "The Zeal Deal: Prosecutorial Resistance to Post-Conviction Claims of Innocence," 84 *Boston University Law Review* 125 (2004).

3. See Ronald F. Wright, "Beyond Prosecutor Elections," 67 *SMU Law Review* 593, 598–599 (2014).

4. For the background surrounding the election of American prosecutors, see Michael J. Ellis, "The Origins of the Elected Prosecutor," 121 *Yale Law Journal* 1528 (2012). See also Steven Zeidman, "Virtuous Prosecutors?," 25 *CUNY Law Review Forum* 1 (2022).

5. See Wright, "Beyond Prosecutor Elections," 600–601.

6. There are many sources available concerning Avery's exoneration as well as his subsequent arrest, conviction, and battle to clear his name. The most notable is the Netflix documentary series *Making a Murderer* (2015–2018), available at www.imdb.com/title/tt5189670/. See also Medwed, *Prosecution Complex*, 131.

7. Steven W. Perry and Duren Banks, *Prosecutors in State Courts, 2007-Statistical Tables* (US Department of Justice, Bureau

of Justice Statistics, December 2011), https://bjs.ojp.gov/content/pub
/pdf/psc07st.pdf.

8. Jessica Fender, "DA Chambers Offers Bonuses for Prosecutors
Who Hit Conviction Targets," *Denver Post*, March 23, 2011.

9. Some states enlist an entirely different agency, such as the state
attorney general's office, to field appeals and postconviction motions
in cases that county DA offices handled at the trial level. See, e.g.,
"Appellate Department," Attorney General Sean D. Reyes, Office
of the Utah State Attorney General, last updated August 17, 2018,
https://attorneygeneral.utah.gov/about/dept/appellate/.

10. Robert H. Jackson, "The Federal Prosecutor: An Address at
the Second Annual Conference of United States Attorneys," April 1,
1940, accessed January 3, 2022, www.justice.gov/sites/default/files
/ag/legacy/2011/09/16/04-01-1940.pdf.

11. For examples of contemporary approaches to prosecution, from
both the left and the right side of the political spectrum, see, e.g.,
the websites for the organizations Fair and Just Prosecution, https://
fairandjustprosecution.org, and Right on Crime, https://rightoncrime
.com (both accessed January 4, 2022).

12. Andrea Estes, "Rollins Moves to Overturn Thousands of Convictions Based on Testing at Now-Closed State Drug Lab," *Boston
Globe*, July 9, 2021.

13. See, e.g., John Ellement, "Judge Throws Out Remaining Gun
Charge Against Sean Ellis in 1993 Killing of Boston Police Officer,"
Boston Globe, May 4, 2021; Rick Sobey, "Sean Ellis After Rachael
Rollins Supports New Trial: 'Now I Can Get On with My Life,'"
Boston Herald, March 17, 2021; and Adrian Walker, "Suffolk DA
Rollins Files Motion to End the Long-Running Prosecution of Sean
Ellis," *Boston Globe*, March 17, 2021.

14. See Ellement, "Judge Throws Out Remaining Gun Charge,"
which notes that "Ellis's appellate attorney, Rosemary Scapicchio,
said the removal of the felony conviction creates the opportunity for
Ellis to apply for compensation as a wrongfully convicted person."

15. Sean Philip Cotter and Joe Dwindell, "National Police Group
Knocks Incoming DA Rachael Rollins," *Boston Herald*, December 28,
2018.

16. As Rollins said in the context of her effort to help another man,
Tyrone Clark, overturn a 1974 rape conviction, "We are not afraid in
this administration to look back and see if we got it right or wrong."
See Shelley Murphy, "Suffolk Prosecutors Support Bid for New Trial
by Convicted Rapist," *Boston Globe*, September 7, 2021.

17. See Emily Bazelon and Jennifer Medina, "He's Remaking Criminal Justice in L.A., but How Far Is Too Far?," *New York Times Magazine*, November 17, 2021.

18. Tom Cotton, "Cotton: Biden Pick Rachael Rollins Poses Threat to N.E. If Confirmed," *Boston Herald*, October 17, 2021.

19. Jim Puzzanghera, "Senate Confirms Rachael Rollins to be US Attorney for Massachusetts, Making Her the First Black Woman to Hold the Office in State History," *Boston Globe*, December 8, 2021. See also Shelley Murphy, " 'A Very Good Day': Rachael Rollins Sworn In as US Attorney," *Boston Globe*, January 10, 2022.

20. Trisha Thadani, "Recall of District Attorney Chesa Boudin Heads to San Francisco Voters in June," *San Francisco Chronicle*, November 9, 2021; and Trisha Thadani, "Recall of S.F. D.A. Chesa Boudin Likely to Head to Voters, with Many More Signatures Submitted than Needed," *San Francisco Chronicle*, October 22, 2021.

21. James Queally, "Effort to Recall L.A. County DA George Gascón Fizzles Out, but a Retry Is Coming," *Los Angeles Times*, September 16, 2021; and Bazelon and Medina, "He's Remaking Criminal Justice in L.A."

22. The National Registry of Exonerations reported that eight new CIUs were formed in 2020, and in early 2021 another five appeared to be operational. See *Annual Report* (National Registry of Exonerations, March 31, 2021), 18, www.law.umich.edu/special/exoneration/Documents/2021AnnualReport.pdf. See also "Conviction Integrity Units," National Registry of Exonerations, accessed January 11, 2022, www.law.umich.edu/special/exoneration/Pages/Conviction-Integrity-Units.aspx; and *Annual Report* (National Registry of Exonerations, March 31, 2020), www.law.umich.edu/special/exoneration/Documents/Exonerations_in_2019.pdf. See also Medwed, *Prosecution Complex*, 135–141.

23. See Troy Closson, "A Detective Was Accused of Lying. Now 90 Convictions May Be Erased," *New York Times*, April 6, 2021; and Eric Gonzalez, "Reckoning with Wrongful Convictions: Lessons Learned from an Examination of 25 Wrongful Convictions in Brooklyn, New York," 35 *Criminal Justice* 4 (2021).

24. Ben Brachfeld, "DA Vacates Conviction of Man Who Served 19 Years, 30th Such Judgement Overturned Since 2014," *Brooklyn Paper*, June 30, 2021; Brooklyn District Attorney's Office, "Brooklyn District Attorney Moves to Vacate Conviction of Man Who Served Nearly 19 Years in Prison for Firing at Police," press release, June 30, 2021; and *Report on the Conviction of Phillip Almeda* (Conviction Review Unit, District Attorney, Kings County, June 2021), www.brooklynda.org/wp-content/uploads/2021/06/Phillip-Almeda.Publication-6.2021.pdf.

25. Barry C. Scheck, "Conviction Integrity Units Revisited," 14 *Ohio State Journal of Criminal Law* 705, 705–706 (2017).

26. See Missouri v. Johnson, Appeal from the Circuit Court of the City of St. Louis, Supreme Court of Missouri, No. SC98303 (Hogan, J. March 2, 2021). See also Joel Currier, "Missouri Supreme Court Denies New Trial in 1994 Murder Case," *St. Louis Post-Dispatch*, March 2, 2021; Editorial Board, "Opinion: Missouri Is Inhibiting the Ability of Local Prosecutors to Correct Wrongful Convictions," *Washington Post*, June 20, 2021; Meaghan Flynn, "To Win a Murder Conviction, Police and Prosecutors Made Up Evidence and Secretly Paid a Witness, St. Louis DA Finds," *Washington Post*, July 26, 2019; and Jordan Smith, "Missouri Prosecutors Lack the Power to Right a Wrongful Conviction," *The Intercept*, March 14, 2021, https://theintercept.com/2021/03/14/missouri-prosecutor-wrongful-conviction-lamar-johnson/.

27. Tony Messenger, "Messenger: Missouri Legislature Gives Prosecutors a Path to Seek Justice," *St. Louis Post-Dispatch*, May 14, 2021. Prosecutors in Missouri have already started to utilize this law. See Sam Zeff and Luke X. Martin, "Using New Missouri Law, Jackson County Prosecutor Files Motion to Free Kevin Strickland after 43 Years," KCUR, August 30, 2021, www.kcur.org/news/2021-08-30/jackson-county-prosecutor-kevin-strickland-should-not-remain-in-prison-a-day-longer; and Heather Hollingsworth and Margaret Stafford, "Missouri Man Exonerated in 1979 Killings, Releasing Him from Prison After 4 Decades," *USA Today*, November 23, 2021.

12. COMMISSIONED FOR JUSTICE

1. This summary of the origins of the Criminal Cases Review Commission comes from "How It All Began," Criminal Cases Review Commission, accessed January 13, 2022, https://ccrc.gov.uk/how-it-all-began/; and John Weeden, "The Criminal Cases Review Commission (CCRC) of England, Wales, and Northern Ireland," 80 *University of Cincinnati Law Review* 1415, 1415–1418 (2013).

2. Much of the information about the CCRC comes from the organization's official website. See "About Us," Criminal Cases Review Commission, accessed January 4, 2022, https://ccrc.gov.uk/about-us/what-we-do/.

3. See, e.g., *Tailored Review of the Criminal Cases Review Commission* (Ministry of Justice, based on data through the end of 2017), https://assets.publishing.service.gov.uk/government/uploads/system/uploads/attachment_data/file/777176/tailored-review-of-the-criminal-cases-review-commission.pdf.

4. See "Facts and Figures," Criminal Cases Review Commission, accessed November 14, 2021, https://ccrc.gov.uk/facts-figures/.

5. I am grateful to my UK criminal law colleague Carole McCartney for interpreting the CCRC's facts and figures and explaining that the phrase "appeals have been allowed" means that these convictions were quashed, and a form of relief granted. To be sure, some may have just resulted in a new trial or a sentence reduction. Referrals also do not always trigger judicial relief. The court rejected the appeal in nearly a third of the carefully winnowed cases tagged by the CCRC for reexamination.

6. See note 5 to this book's Opening Statement, discussing estimates in a nation with a similar legal system, the United States.

7. The agency's average annual referral rate has also dipped below 2.8 percent every year since 2016. Westminster Commission on Miscarriages of Justice, *In the Interests of Justice: An Inquiry into the Criminal Cases Review Commission* (March 2021), 12–13, https://appgmiscarriagesofjustice.files.wordpress.com/2021/03/westminster-commission-on-miscarriages-of-justice-in-the-interests-of-justice.pdf.

8. In 2015, the agency's former chair stated that the CCRC received "the biggest cut that has taken place in the criminal justice system.... For every £10 that my predecessor had to spend on a case a decade ago, I have £4 today." Westminster Commission on Miscarriages of Justice, *In the Interests of Justice*, 27.

9. See Westminster Commission on Miscarriages of Justice, *In the Interests of Justice*, 10; and John Hall, "Postman Who Spent 17 Years in Prison After Wrongful Conviction for Attempted Rape Says He Is a 'Greater Person' for Being Victim of Miscarriage of Justice," *Daily Mail* (UK), January 1, 2014.

10. Many of these commissions came about in reaction to an especially egregious wrongful conviction. See, e.g., Margaret Burnham, "Retrospective Justice in the Age of Innocence: The Hard Case of Rape Execution," in *Wrongful Convictions and the DNA Revolution: Twenty-Five Years of Freeing the Innocent*, ed. Daniel S. Medwed (New York: Cambridge University Press, 2017), 302–303. In the United States, this general "think tank" type of innocence commission has surfaced in a range of states, including California, Connecticut, Florida, Illinois, Louisiana, New York, Oklahoma, Pennsylvania, Texas, Virginia, and Wisconsin. See Mary Kelly Tate, "Commissioning Innocence and Restoring Confidence: The North Carolina Innocence Inquiry Commission," 64 *Maine Law Review* 531, 536–542 (2012).

11. See, e.g., Ulf Stridbeck and Philos Svein Magnussen, "Prevention of Wrongful Convictions: Norwegian Legal Safeguards and the

Criminal Cases Review Commission," 80 *University of Cincinnati Law Review* 1373, 1381 (2013), noting that Norway followed the United Kingdom's lead and established a similar entity in 2004.

12. My description of the origins and operations of the North Carolina Actual Innocence Inquiry Commission derives from a range of media and scholarly sources. See Eli Hager, "A One-Man Justice Crusade in North Carolina," Marshall Project, July 29, 2015, www.themarshallproject.org/2015/07/29/a-one-man-justice-crusade-in-north-carolina; Jerome M. Maiatico, "All Eyes on Us: A Comparative Critique of the North Carolina Innocence Inquiry Commission," 56 *Duke Law Journal* 1345 (2007); Robert P. Mosteller, "N.C. Innocence Inquiry Commission's First Decade: Impressive Successes and Lessons Learned," 94 *North Carolina Law Review* 1725 (2016); Christine C. Mumma, "The North Carolina Actual Innocence Commission: Uncommon Perspectives Joined by a Common Cause," 52 *Drake Law Review* 647 (2004); Tate, "Commissioning Innocence and Restoring Confidence"; George C. Thomas III, "Where Have All the Innocents Gone?," 60 *Arizona Law Review* 865 (2018); and David Wolitz, "Innocence Commissions and the Future of Post-Conviction Review," 52 *Arizona Law Review* 1027 (2010).

13. The commission is structured as an independent entity housed within the court system for administrative purposes only. For the laws that cover the commission's operations, see North Car. Gen. Ass. Stat. Ann. §§ 15A-1460—15A-1471 (2021). See also "Rules and Procedures," North Carolina Innocence Inquiry Commission, accessed January 13, 2022, https://innocencecommission-nc.gov/wp-content/uploads/2021/04/rules-and-procedures.pdf.

14. See home page, North Carolina Innocence Inquiry Commission, accessed November 14, 2021, https://innocencecommission-nc.gov.

15. Information about the McCollum and Brown case comes from Mosteller, "N.C. Innocence Inquiry Commission's First Decade," 1815–1828; Joseph Neff, "They Did Thirty Years for Someone Else's Crime. Then Paid for It," *New York Times*, April 7, 2018; Maurice Possley, "Henry McCollum," National Registry of Exonerations, last updated August 13, 2021, www.law.umich.edu/special/exoneration/Pages/casedetail.aspx?caseid=4492; and Maurice Possley, "Leon Brown," National Registry of Exonerations, last updated August 13, 2021, www.law.umich.edu/special/exoneration/Pages/casedetail.aspx?caseid=4493.

16. Unbeknownst to the defense until much later, the witness had also taken a polygraph before trial during which his statements that he knew nothing about the crime were found truthful by the examiner.

17. Callins v. Collins, 510 U.S. 1141, 1143 (1994) (Scalia, J., concurring).

18. Andrew Carter, "Jury Awards Wrongfully Convicted NC Brothers $75 Million in Federal Civil Rights Case," *News and Observer* (Raleigh, NC), May 15, 2021; "North Carolina Bar Suspends License of Lawyer Who Defrauded Death-Row Exonerees," Death Penalty Information Center, March 29, 2021, https://deathpenaltyinfo.org /news/north-carolina-bar-suspends-license-of-lawyer-who-defrauded -death-row-exonerees; and Neff, "They Did Thirty Years for Someone Else's Crime."

19. For a discussion of the general pros and cons of the North Carolina Innocence Inquiry Commission, see Barry C. Scheck, "Conviction Integrity Units Revisited," 14 *Ohio State Journal of Criminal Law* 705, 711–712 (2017). For some suggested reforms to the commission's operations, see Mosteller, "N.C. Innocence Inquiry Commission's First Decade," 1865–1869; and Wolitz, "Innocence Commissions and the Future of Post-Conviction Review," 1077–1081.

20. As Wolitz mentions, perhaps the commission could yet again borrow from the United Kingdom, where courts tend to employ an "unsafe verdict" standard and overturn cases where there's a "lurking doubt." See, e.g., Wolitz, "Innocence Commissions and the Future of Post-Conviction Review," 1080, observing that "Under the unsafe verdict standard, a reviewing court will vacate a conviction if the court 'entertains a "lurking doubt" that the defendant was rightly convicted, or where the court is not "sure" that the defendant was "rightly convicted."'" For the argument why American courts should more generally draw upon an unsafe verdict test, see D. Michael Risinger, "Unsafe Verdicts: The Need for Reformed Standards for the Trial and Review of Factual Innocence Claims," 41 *Houston Law Review* 1281 (2004).

21. See Wolitz, "Innocence Commissions and the Future of Post-Conviction Review," 1053–1072.

22. Wolitz, "Innocence Commissions and the Future of Post-Conviction Review," 1070.

23. For an additional discussion of the commission's strengths, see Mosteller, "N.C. Innocence Inquiry Commission's First Decade," 1860–1865.

CLOSING ARGUMENT

1. Schulz v. Marshall, 528 F.Supp.2d 77 (E.D.N.Y. 2007). In fact, in a footnote to the last line of its opinion, the court praised prosecutors for their diligence in helping to reinvestigate the case, even if

it did not resolve Schulz's innocence claim, and noted once again in support of its ruling that "even in the absence of conclusive proof of actual innocence, there is a reasonable likelihood that, but for defense counsel's constitutional errors, the result of the trial would likely have been different" (102 n. 18).

2. "Innocence by the Numbers," Death Penalty Information Center, accessed November 9, 2021, https://deathpenaltyinfo.org/policy-issues/innocence/innocence-by-the-numbers. See also "DPIC Adds Eleven Cases to Innocence List, Bringing National Death-Row Exoneration Total to 185," Death Penalty Information Center, February 18, 2021, which notes that "the data now show that for every 8.3 people who have been put to death in the U.S. since executions resumed in the 1970s, one person who had been wrongfully convicted and sentenced to death has been exonerated." A 2014 study published by the National Academy of Sciences cited a false conviction rate of 4.1 percent for all defendants sentenced to death. Samuel R. Gross et al., "Rate of False Conviction of Criminal Defendants Who Are Sentenced to Death," 111 *PNAS* 7230–7235 (May 20, 2014), www.pnas.org/content/111/20/7230.

3. "Executed but Possibly Innocent," Death Penalty Information Center, accessed November 9, 2021, https://deathpenaltyinfo.org/policy-issues/innocence/executed-but-possibly-innocent.

4. There are many sources of information about this case, including Paul C. Giannelli, "Junk Science and the Execution of an Innocent Man," 7 *New York University Journal of Law and Liberty* 221 (2013); and David Grann, "Trial by Fire: Did Texas Execute an Innocent Man?," *New Yorker*, August 31, 2009.

5. The Innocence Project in New York City is currently working to prove the innocence of Ledell Lee, a man convicted of murdering his neighbor, sentenced to death, and ultimately executed in 2017. Nina Morrison—the stellar lawyer who played a key role in exonerating Felipe Rodriguez (Chapter 7)—managed to obtain DNA testing of the murder weapon, a bloody club allegedly used to bludgeon the victim. In 2021, those tests revealed the presence of genetic material belonging to an unknown male. Although Morrison acknowledged that the results were "incomplete and partial," this development has given hope to Lee's supporters that he might eventually be cleared. See Hannah Knowles, "Four Years After a Man's Execution, Lawyers Say DNA from the Murder Weapon Points to Someone Else," *Washington Post*, May 4, 2021.

6. Facts about this case come from Alley v. State, No. W2006-01179-CCA-R3-PD, 2006 WL 1703820 (Tenn.Crim.App. 2006);

Alley v. Tennessee, 548 U.S. 922 (U.S. 2006); Emily Bazelon, "Did Tennessee Execute an Innocent Man?," *New York Times*, February 10, 2021; Death Penalty Information Center, "Executed but Possibly Innocent"; "Petition for Post-Conviction Analysis," *In the Matter of Estate of Sedley Alley v. State of Tennessee*, Nos. 85-05085-85-293078, 85-05086, 85-05087, Criminal Court for Shelby County (TN), at Memphis, 13th Judicial District, April 30, 2019; and Adam Tamburin, "Family of Executed Tennessee Inmate Calls for DNA Tests in Renewed Hope to 'Find the Truth,'" *Memphis Commercial Appeal*, May 1, 2019.

7. Powers v. State, 343 S.W.3d 36 (Tenn. 2011).

8. See *Estate of Sedley Alley v. State of Tennessee*, Court of Criminal Appeals of Tennessee at Jackson, Appeal from the Criminal Court of Shelby County, Nos. 85-05085, 85-05086, 85-05087, May 7, 2021; and Yolanda Jones, "Appeals Court Denies DNA Testing in Sedley Alley Case," *Daily Memphian*, May 12, 2021, https://dailymemphian.com/article/21867/sedley-alley-dna-testing-tennessee-court-of-appeals.

INDEX

311

Daniel S. Medwed is University Distinguished Professor of Law and Criminal Justice at Northeastern University School of Law. A renowned innocence advocate, he is the author of *Prosecution Complex*. He lives in Cambridge, Massachusetts.